極東裁判と国際法

極東裁判と国際法
極東国際軍事裁判所における弁論

高柳賢三

書肆心水

序 言

「侵略戦争は個人責任を伴う犯罪である」というテイゼをわたくしは否定する。この否定はわたくしの学問的研究と熟慮の結果なのである。しかし、この立場は世人の誤解を予防するための若干のコメントを必要とする。

クライムという言葉を「罪悪」、「責任」という言葉を「道義的責任」と解して、右の提言が純道徳的志向をもつ提言であるとするなら、わたくしはこの提言に対し、全幅の賛意を表する。世界各国の政治家が侵略戦争は罪悪なりという道義的意識を強めこれを堅持し、各国民がかような政治家を支持しこれを監視することは、誠に望ましい道義的態度である。この場合には、侵略戦争と防衛戦争との限界が不明確である事実は大した問題ではない。むしろ侵略戦争がより広義に解せられるなら、ますます望ましい態度であるとわたくしは考える。「防衛戦争は道徳的である」という提言は、現代において世界輿論の一般的支持を得ている。しかし純道義的見地からこれを肯定しうるかどうか、わたくしとしてはすこぶる疑わしいのである。ガーンディは断乎としてこ

5

の提言を否定しつづけてその一生を了えた。かれは政治的闘争における真理の力を深く信じ、自衛のための武力の行使を否定しつづけてその一生を了えた。そして、インドは独立しえたのである。わたくしはキリストの聖訓を想起せしめるガーンディのこの態度が、現代世界の支持する道徳意識よりも、遥かに高次の道徳意識を表現するものと思うのである。そしてそれが又、世界平和の真の礎石たるべき唯一の道徳であることを信ずるのである。

道義は主体性を基礎とするが、法は相互主体性を基礎として成立する。道義は各主体の至上的意味での義務があるが、法は他の主体に一定の行態を強要しうる限界いかんにその本質がある。道義は現実の世界を超越した高い立場に立つことによって、その価値は高まるのである。しかし、法は現実の特定社会に妥当するような規範であるところにその価値がある。かくして例えば、正当防衛権に関する法原理についても、国内法に妥当である規範が、直ちに国際法において妥当であるとはいえない。それは国家とよばれる社会と国際社会とは、その性格がいちじるしく異なるがゆえである。国際法は主権国家から成る社会の現実に照らし、理性と経験にみちびかれつつ、過去数世紀にわたって、徐々に成立した法の体系である。それは国内法に対比すれば、はるかにか弱いアグレッシヴでない法の体系である。国際社会なるものの現実が、国際法のこうした在り方を決定したのである。

「侵略戦争は個人責任を伴う犯罪である」というテーゼも、やはり右の見地から考察せねばな

らないのであって、わたくしは道義的立場ではなく、この法的立場からこれを否定したのである。ガーンディのより高い道徳のアナロジーに基いて「防衛戦争も個人責任を伴う犯罪である」ということを国際法上主張するものがあるとしたら、わたくしはさらにつよく、この提言を否定するであろう。日本国新憲法は戦争そのものを抛棄した。これはまことにガーンディの道義思想に合致し、日本国民の新たな道義的決意を表明するものであって、主体性の表現としてわたくしはつよくこの立場を支持する。しかし、日本国民は、他国の為政家に対して、国際法上の提言として、この行態を強要することは許されない。

かくしてわたくしは、検察側の理論的挑戦に応じて、法理論として二つのことを主張した。第一は国際条約及び国際慣習法に照らして、「侵略戦争は個人責任を伴う犯罪である」という法的提言は国際法上存在しないということである。国際連合憲章もかかる提言を認めてはいないのである。もしこれが正しいとすれば、法に非ざるこの提言にもとづいて、個人を処罰することは、人類多年の政治的闘争によって確立した正義の初歩的原理たる事後法禁止の原理、ないし罪刑法定主義の侵犯となるから、裁判所はこれを避けねばならないということである。

第二は立法論的見地からみても、かかる提言は、国際法のよって立つ各国民の受諾をうくる可能性なき法的原理であるということである。ある特定の戦争が侵略戦争であるかどうかの決定に必要な公正な裁判機関について、戦勝国の政治家に対しても裁判管轄権をもち、その判決に服せ

7　序言

しめるごとき機関を設けることは、事実上不可能である。国際政治の複雑な現実にてらして、侵略戦争と防衛戦争とを分かつ基準を定めることは、過去二十年にわたり各国の学者、政治家によって多大の研究的努力がはらわれたにかかわらず、遂に失敗に帰したのである。なんらの基準なくして、又はある独断的基準によって、これを判定しうるものとするならば、戦敗国政治家がいつも侵略者であるとの判定をうける、危険な傾向を伴うこととなる。又政治家の行動を対象とする公正な刑事裁判は、各国政府からこれに関聯性ある、あらゆる国家機密的な文書や証言の提出が、前提要件となるのであるそのものの権威をきずつけることとなる。又政治家の行動を対象とする公正な刑事裁判は、各国政府からこれに関聯性ある、あらゆる国家機密的な文書や証言の提出が、前提要件となるのである。しかるに各国政府はかかる用意をもっていないのが現実である。国際的関聯をもつ政治家の国内的刑事裁判は、証拠の問題でゆきづまるゆえに、法律家はかかる裁判をきらったのである。国際裁判についても、かかる提言が国際法上の原理として真に成立したと仮定する場合、刑罰による威嚇が将来の侵略的政治家を防止する一般予防的効果を生むものとはいえないであろう。交戦国の政治家は自らの首を救うために、反って勝利のみに熱中して慣習と条約で成立した交戦法規を無視し、又敗戦の色濃厚な場合でも、国民をかつて戦争完遂に盲進せしめ、無用な犠牲を生ぜしめる逆効果を生ずるかも知れない。けだし戦に勝ちさえすれば、戦争犯罪者とされるおそれはないという心理に、為政者が動かされ易いからである。

尤も各国に対し優位に立つ世界国家が現実に成立すれば、事態はおのずから異なってくる。そして右の提言は世界国家のレジームが妥当する法的原理となることであろう。かかるレジームの出現は、同時に現在におけるような性格の国際法が姿を消すことを意味する。しかし現在及び近き将来については、われわれは国際法のレジームを前提として、この提言の法的価値を考察せねばならない。

わたくしは、一九四八年三月三日から三月四日にかけて、極東国際軍事裁判所で、検察側の冒頭陳述と最終陳述における戦争犯罪法理論を、全体として又個別的に反駁する形式で、以上のような私の思想を展開し、又その他の法律上の論点に対し意見を陳べることを許された。検察官と弁護人とが、原告としての国家と被告としての個人とが、刑事裁判において対等の地位にたち、公正なアンパイアとしての裁判所に対し、相互に自由に反対な意見を陳べうることは、英米刑事裁判の特色である。極東裁判は聯合国を原告とする軍事裁判ではあるが、右の英米的裁判方式に従って公判が行われたので、検察側も弁護側も平等の地位を与えられ、右のごとき法理論をわたくしは、大胆かつ率直に述べることが許され、多くの日本人と均しくわたくしも又、法廷にただよったフェア・プレイの精神に感銘をうけたのである。

弁護人として裁判所を補助するという、わたくしに課せられた任務を果すために、わたくしは先ず、共同謀議罪、事後法、宣戦、等この歴史的事件にふくまれた個々の問題について、いくつ

かの論文を起草し、それら論文を基礎として、検察側冒頭陳述の反駁を書きあげた。それが第一部である。しかるに検察側は、最終陳述において更に新しい法律論を提出したので、約二週間のうちに至急これに対する反駁を書きあげた。それが第二部である。かくして出来あがったファイナル・ドラフトは、簡潔且つ力づよくということを目標として起草されたのである。本書に収録された英文テキストがそれである。法廷における弁論では、論旨をきずつけない範囲で、若干省略した箇所があるが、ここには右のファイナル・ドラフトをそのまま収めた。日本文はその訳文であるが、この方には、公刊にあたって若干の修正を加えた。

わたくしのこの弁論は、第一次的には弁護人として、被告の弁護のためになされる主旨であったことは勿論である。しかしここに論議されたいくつかの国際法上の論点は、当面の判決いかんを越えて、永く法学界において論議されることであろう。このことを期待しつつ、わたくしは敗戦国民の一人ではあったが、何人をも恐れず、何人をもはばからず、ひとえに学的良心に導かれつつ、二箇年にわたって研究を重ね、この短い草稿の完成に力をそそいだのである。それは通俗的意味での「被告人弁護」を目標とするのではなく、国際法に関する世界的イッシュに対し向けられた、わたくしの拙い学問的アルバイトであった。有斐閣の好意によって、これを一冊の書として公刊するのも、主としてそのためである。（一九四八・一〇）

　　　　　　　　　著　者

目次

序言 5

序説 17

第一部

第一 降服文書と裁判所条例 25

第二 共同謀議 40

第三 侵略戦争 47

第四 国際法条約等を侵犯する戦争 81

第五 殺人の罪 85

第六 「通例の」戦争犯罪 90

第七 個人責任 93

第八 検察側の提唱する新国際法理論 110

第二部

一 「戦争犯罪人」 119

二 不戦条約と自衛権 123

三 共同謀議 126

四 殺人の罪 133

五 「通例の」戦争犯罪 136

六 被告人の責任 147

結　語 155

極東裁判と国際法　極東国際軍事裁判所における弁論

凡　例

一、本書は、高柳賢三著『極東裁判と国際法　極東国際軍事裁判所における弁論』（一九四八年、有斐閣刊行）の新組復刻版である。

一、本書では新字体漢字、新仮名遣いに変更して表記した。（但し「欠缺」を除く。）「廿」は旧字体ではないが便宜的に「二十」に置き換えて表記した。

一、送り仮名を現在一般の慣例により加減したところがある。

一、踊り字（繰り返し符号）は「々」を除いて使用せず、文字に置き換えて表記した。

一、読み仮名ルビを付加した。（　）で括ったルビは読み仮名ではなく意味を示すものである。「ママ」など校訂上の注記もルビで記した。

一、現在一般に漢字表記が避けられるものは仮名に置き換えて表記した。（例　独逸→ドイツ、海牙→ハーグ、蘇聯→ソ聯。）又、「しゅん厳」と「峻厳」は「峻厳」に統一した。その他、漢字表記と仮名表記の不統一が著しく目立つ場合（「平和に対する罪及び人道にたいする罪」の如き）のみ統一した。

一、元の本の片仮名語の表記は、例えば「モスコオ」のように長音符（音引き）を使わない例が大多数であるが、「モスコー」の表記も混在しており、また、「ハーヴァド・ロオ・レヴュウ」と「ハーヴァード・ロオ・スクール」のように一名詞において長音符の使用／不使用の不統一が見られる上に、同一語においても「ハーヴァド」、「ジャクスン」と「ジャクスン」のような不統一もみられる。本書では長音符を使用しうる場合は長音符を使用し、同一語の表記不統一を統一した。（「海牙」「ヘイグ」の不統一は「ハーグ」に、「寿府」「ジェネヴァ」の不統一は「ジュネーヴ」に統一した。）

一、元の本では多くの片仮名語（そのほとんどが固有名詞）が「　」で括られているが（前半においてはほとんどすべて）、この「　」は、強調でもなく、引用でもなく、古い時代の慣習の残滓と見るべきもので、現在ではむしろなくもがなのものであるから、この版では削除した。又、鍵括弧内の鍵括弧は『　』の使用で統一した。出典文献名を括る「　」の有無は原則としてそのままに表記した。又、出典文献等を示す丸括弧の直前に句点がある場合と直後にある場合の不統一は後者に統一した。

一、明らかな誤植と誤記（英文版に照らしてそう言える場合も含む）のうち一義的に訂正しうるものはそれと指摘することなく訂正した。（英文版も同様に訂正した。）

序説

裁判長並びに裁判官各位

法は共通の義務意識である。

刑法は、これを無視したら罰を受ける義務を伴う、共通の義務意識である。

政治家は、共通の国際法上の義務意識の下に、その比類なく重要な任務を行う。

しかし政治家はこれまで、国際法上の義務に違反したら軍法によって専断的に刑罰を課せられるという共通の義務意識の下に、その任務を行ってはいなかった。

かかる刑事責任意識の存在しないことが、明白な事実であるがゆえに、かくのごとき刑法は成立していないのである。かかる刑事責任意識が存在すべきであるかどうかは本件には関聯性がない。かくのごとき法なきにかかわらず、刑罰が課せられるとすれば、それは無法なる暴力行為に外ならない。スピクマン教授やウォルター・リップマン氏のように戦略的立脚点から世界の政治

外交を眺め、かかる観点のみから三国軍事同盟（スピクマンはそれを世界情勢の論理的締結だとした）の促進とか、「大東亜共栄圏」の樹立とかについて、共同謀議を行ったものが被告人のうちに仮りにあったとするならば、こうした行態はたしかにソ聯米国又は英国の感情を極度に刺戟する種類のものであるにちがいない。又世界政治に対するこうした行態は、戦争そのものの廃止を理念としつつ、軍備の撤廃を規定する日本国新憲法の明文及び精神とは氷炭相容れないものである。こうした政治的行態は心ある人々から見れば好ましからざるところであろう、しかしそれは言論及び結社の自由の範囲に属する事柄であって、国際法はこれを禁止し又はこれを犯罪とはしていないのである。又もしも日本政府の為した行為が、国際法上違法であって、日本があらかじめその判決に服することに同意した国際的機関によって、それが違法と宣言された場合、又は日本が敗戦した場合には、国民全体がその結果を甘受せねばならぬのである。かような場合において、日本の指導者がかれらの政治上の失策について、自国民に対して負う政治上の責任はまことに重且つ大である。しかしかれらの行為が国際法の法則に照らして犯罪を構成するかどうかは、これとは全く別個の問題である。もしそれが犯罪を構成するならば、同じような事態の下において、アメリカやイギリスやソ聯の指導者達も、国際法の定める刑罰をうけなければならない。しかしもしそれが国際法上犯罪を構成しないのなら、国際法そのものの名において、かれらは無罪の宣告をうく

べきである。又国際法の認めるなにらかの犯罪を被告人が犯したことが合理的疑いをのこさぬ程度に証明せられない以上、かれらは無罪であると推定されるべきである。

本条例の犯罪規定が単に実力行為にすぎぬのなら、すなわち降服文書の条項と一般に承認せられた国際法上の法則にかかわらず、聯合国が発した命令にすぎないのなら、弁護側が国際法に照らして本条例の規定を論議することは、たしかに無駄な努力である。しかし、首席検察官の劈頭陳述によると、検察側もこうした立場に立ってはいない。被告人の行為が、聯合国政府の政策に基いて一方的に決定せられた犯罪規定に該当するがゆえにではなく、それらの行為が国際法上犯罪を構成するがゆえに、「有罪」の宣言が与えらるべきであるというのが、検察側の主張である。

検察側は、かような立場から、その博識と犀利な論理を縦横に駆使しつつ、本条例の犯罪規定が現行国際法の法則を宣明したものであることを論証せんとしているのである。弁護側は、本条例の規定はこれを国際法に照らして解釈すべきであるとの検察側の見解に心から賛同する。しかしながら上述の犯罪規定が現行国際法を宣明したものであるとの見解には、絶対に承服できないのである。

ニュルンベルグ裁判においては、裁判所は条例の規定に関する検察側の解釈を一部排斥している。このことは弁護側の意を強うせしめるものである。弁護側の見解によれば、ドイツと日本とでは事実的状態、従って又法的事態が全くちがっている。本裁判では降服文書と条例の規定との

関係を決定する、より大なる任務が裁判所に課せられているのである。又ニュルンベルグ裁判所の条例とは異なり、本裁判所条例は国際法の真の法則と原理を確定するがための便宜的指標にすぎぬので、被告人等の有罪無罪は国際法の真の法則と原理によってのみ定まるのである。

かくしてわれらは、首席検察官が一九四六年六月四日の劈頭陳述（英文記録三八三ないし四七五頁、特に三九四ないし四三五頁）中に解明された本条例の犯罪規定に関する解釈をば、逐一的に且つ全体として反駁するために、主として国際法との関連において該規定を論述する。われらはなるべく首席検察官による主張展開の順序を追うこととし、本論を次の八項目に分ける。

一、降服文書と本裁判所条例
二、共同謀議
三、侵略戦争
四、条約等を侵犯する戦争
五、殺人の罪
六、「通例の」戦争犯罪
七、個人責任
八、検察側の提唱する新国際法理論

なお最終弁論において検察側の提出した、新しい議論に対しては、第二部において別にこれを

反駁するであろう。

第一部

第一　降服文書と裁判所条例

ニュルンベルグ裁判の判決は、その裁判所条例の規定について次の如くいう。

「本裁判所条例の制定は、ドイツ国が無条件降伏をなした諸国の至上立法権の行使に他ならない。これら諸国が、その占領地に対して立法を行う権利をもつことは、従来文明世界の認めるところであることは疑いの余地がない。」（ニュルンベルグ記録一六八一頁）。

ドイツ政府は、一九四五年五月連合国の征服によって、国際法において通常用いられる用語に従えば、デベラチオによって、消滅するに至った。従って連合国は、その完全な支配下にある地域に対して、主権を行使しうるのである。連合国は該地域においてその思うがままの統治を行いうる。いわばルイ十四世のような専制君主の如く振舞うこともできる。従って又、裁判所を設けて、自己の好まざる人物を、いわゆる事後の法律によって、処罰することもできる。けだし、かかる事後立法禁止の法則は、正義の原則であって、必ずしも連合国の主権を拘束するものではな

いからである（ニュルンベルグ記録一六八七一頁）。いな、さらにすすんで、全然裁判を行わず行政処分によって、これらの人達を処断することもできるかも知れない。少なくともかくのごとき主権の行使は、国際法の原則に牴触するものではないともいえるかも知れない。それ故「侵略戦争の計画、準備もしくは開始がロンドン協定以前において、個人的責任を伴う国際法上の犯罪であったか否かを考慮することは、必ずしも当裁判所にとって必要」ではなかったのである（ニュルンベルグ記録一六八七一頁）。従って、ニュルンベルグ判決における国際法上の論議は、英米法律家のいわゆる、オビタ・ディクタすなわち判決自体には必ずしもこれを必要としない附随的な論説である。

少なくともニュルンベルグ判決は、右のような立論をその論拠とするのである。われわれは、連合国の各政府と日本政府との法的関係は、連合国とドイツとの間のそれとは、まったく異なる基礎の上に立つのだという明白な事実について、まず裁判所の注意を促そうとする。

連合国政府の権限、及び連合国によって最高司令官として任命せられ、降服条項実施のため適当と認める一切の措置を執る権限を附与されたマッカーサー元帥の権限は、まことに広汎なものといえる。とはいえこれらの権限は、無制約的のものではない。マッカーサー元帥は、降服条項実施に適当且つ必要と認めらるる範囲において、至上権を附与されているにすぎない。それ故同元帥によって代表せらるる連合国の地位は、ルイ十四世のそれに似たものではなく、むしろ、ウィリアム及びメリーのような近代立憲君主のそれに類似するものである。

ドイツと日本との間に存する、かかる法的地位の根本的相違は、休戦に至ったそれぞれの経緯の差違に基くのである。日本はドイツと異なり、降服当時未だ連合軍のじゅうりんするところとなっていなかった。日本本土はまだ占領されてはいなかった。なおしばらくはつよい武力抵抗を行って、連合軍に若干の損害を与えうる立場にあった。かかる状況の下において、日本政府は連合国の和平申入れを受諾することとなったのである。そして受諾の条件はポツダム宣言の条項に示されている。降服文書自体も正式に明文を以てポツダム宣言の条項を援用している。すなわち「下名はここにポツダム宣言の条項を誠実に履行すること、並びに右宣言を実施する為連合国最高司令官の要求することあるべき一切の命令を発し、且つかかる一切の措置を執ることを天皇、日本政府及びその後継者の為に約す。」又「天皇及び日本政府の国家統治の権限は本降服条項を実施する為適当と認むる措置を執る連合国最高司令官の制限の下に置かるるものとす。」とあるのがこれである。

右の文書は「降服文書」という形式をとってはいるが、日本軍隊の無条件降服のみならず、その他締約当事国を拘束する若干の条項を定めた一つの国際協定の性質をもつものである。降服文書に基く連合国に対する日本国の義務が、無制限のものでなく、該文書の条項に限られているのであるならば、連合国各政府が、日本に対してなしうる要求には、一定の限度があるわけである。そういう場合とはちがい、ドイツの場合とはちがい、日本はこれらの制限の遵守を要求する権利を有する。そう

27 第1 降服文書と裁判所条例

だとすれば、連合国においてもまた遵守せざるべからざる、これに照応する義務が存することになる。何故ならおよそ法律関係は一方的たることをえないからである。そしてかかる相互的な権利及び義務の準拠は、降服文書の不可分的な一部をなすポツダム宣言の条項のうちに示されているのである。

東京湾頭の降服文書調印式における、聯合国最高司令官の高邁な次の言葉は、降服文書にあらわされた約束を、戦勝国も敗戦国も、厳格に遵守することの重要性を、強調するものではないか。「人類の大多数を代表するわれらは、不信、悪意ないし憎悪の心を以てここに会合しているのではない。いなむしろ戦勝者たると敗戦者たるとを問わず、ひとしくより高い道義的純潔の境地に、われらの精神を昂むべきである。ひとりそれのみが、われらすべての国民を挙げて、ここに負担せんとする約束の忠実なる遵守を無条件に誓諾して、われらの奉仕せんとする神聖な目的を達せしむるものである」。

極東国際軍事裁判所における今次の裁判の法的根拠は、降服文書中に援用せられたポツダム宣言中の「我等ノ俘虜ニ対シ残虐行為ヲナシタル者ヲ含ム一切ノ戦争犯罪人ニ対シテハ峻厳ナル裁判ガ行ワルベシ」という条項である。

(甲) 「戦争犯罪」

さて、本訴訟の現段階においては、裁判権の問題としてでなく、全く別の観点、即ち条例の規

第1部 28

定の解釈という点から、前掲章句中の「戦争犯罪」という辞句の解釈について、裁判所の考慮を促したい。

（一）「戦争犯罪」及び「戦争犯罪人」という言葉は、国際法においてすでに充分に確定している術語である。オッペンハイムによれば、戦争犯罪とは軍人その他の個人の行為にして、敵国が犯行者を捕えた場合、処罰することのできる敵対行為その他の行為をいうのである（ラウターパクト編（一九三五）のオッペンハイム著「国際法」第五版第二巻四五二―四五三頁）。この場合、「戦争犯罪」という言葉は道徳的意味においてではなく、技術的な法律上の意味に用いられている。それは、従来認められた交戦に関する特定の法規に違反する武装軍隊の構成員の行為、武装軍隊の構成員に非ざる個人が武器を執って行う一切の交戦行為、間諜、戦時叛逆及び掠奪を含むものである。戦争犯罪は戦時中、又特に戦場において犯される行為であって、通常は軍事裁判所において簡易手続によって処断される。

いわゆる「戦争犯罪」のうちにどういう種類の行為が含まれるかについては、学者の間に多少の意見の相違があるとしても、戦争勃発前になされた行為は、たとい戦争と歴史的関聯があるとしても、これに含まれないことは確かである。かくの如き法律専門語が外交文書中に用いられている場合には、他にこれと異なる趣旨であることが立証されないかぎり、法解釈に関する周知の準則に従って、その術語の意味に即してこれを解釈しなければならない。

（二）右の解釈が正当であることは、前掲章句の後に続く「我等の俘虜に対し残虐行為を為したる者を含む」なる辞句によって、さらに明らかにされる。俘虜の虐待は術語上の意味における「戦争犯罪」の一つの型態にすぎないからである。

ポツダム宣言にいわゆる「戦争犯罪」がかかる通常の一般に認められた意味に用いられたものであることは、該宣言が俘虜の虐待（おそらく非戦闘員による場合をも含めて）の如き戦争犯罪中の特定種類のものを包含せしめんとして、その点を表示することに意を用い、わざわざ右行為が戦争犯罪中に含まれる旨特記している事実によっても明らかである。もしもいわゆる「平和に対する罪」及び「人道に対する罪」をもこれに含ましめんとの趣旨なら、俘虜の虐待ではなく、そのことこそ、これを包含するむねが特記されたであろう。

（三）右の解釈の正しいことは、連合国政府及びその指導的政治家等が、枢軸各国に対して発したいわゆる「警告」なるものを、照合考察することによって、さらに明らかとなる（グリュック、「ニュルンベルグ裁判と侵略戦争」ハーヴァード・ロー・レヴュー第五十九巻、三九二、四一八、四一九頁、註七五参照）。

各国政府及びその指導者等が為した宣言及び演説を、それが如何なる機会になされたものであるかを考慮しつつ、注意深く吟味するならば、彼等が枢軸各国民が犯したと称する犯罪に言及している場合常に戦争中に為された行為、例えば占領地の一般国民に対する残虐行為とか、俘虜の虐待とかの行為に関聯するものであることが明らかとなるであろう。われわれの知っているかぎ

り、それら警告のうち一としていわゆる平和に対する罪に触れているものはない。一九四三年十一月のモスコー宣言で「その犯罪が一定の地域に限定せられざる重大戦争犯罪人」に言及した場合ですら、その前後の関係から判断すれば、それは単に、その発した命令が「一地域又は一戦場において遂行せられたに止まらず、数個の聯合国軍隊に対する軍事行動に関連をもつ」如き首脳部の人士を指すに止まり、そのいうところは明らかに前者すなわち戦争中に為された行為に関するのであって、後者すなわちいわゆる「平和に対する罪」に関するのではない。一九四五年八月八日のロンドン協定は、このモスコー宣言の拡張解釈にその基礎を置いているようであるが、かような解釈は同宣言の歴史的経緯からみればすこぶる不自然な解釈であるといえる。いずれにせよ、モスコー宣言はひとりドイツのみに対してなされたものであって、日本に対するものではなく、またその後に発せられたポツダム宣言の条項は、「戦争犯罪」なる字句の本来の意味を、モスコー宣言によって、一方的に変更するような解釈を正当づけることはできないのである。

この点はハーヴァード・ロー・スクールのシェルドン・グリュック教授の「ニュルンベルグ裁判と侵略戦争」と題する論文中の一節 (前掲三九七頁) によってさらによく証明せられる。教授はいう──

「従来公刊せられた諸種の資料のうち現在利用しうるものに基いて判断すれば、枢軸諸国が責を負うべき犯罪のうちに、侵略戦争の開始と『平和に対する罪』とを含ましめんとする考えは、

米国の政策に関する限り、重大戦争犯罪人訴追の米国代表首席検察官が、一九四五年六月七日大統領に対して為した報告書に由来する。ロバート・ジャクスン判事は右報告書中において、今や侵略戦争を為すことが違法にして且つ犯罪を構成するとの法的原則に基いて行動すべき機は熟した、と述べている。」

同じ頁に掲げられた註の中で、グリュック教授は次の如く告白する。

「筆者の著書たる『戦争犯罪、その訴追と処罰』（一九四四年）中では、筆者は未だ侵略戦争の開始遂行の行為を国際犯罪となしうるやに就いて、全然確信をもたなかった。筆者は主として一九二八年パリにおいて調印せられた戦争の抛棄に関する条約（ブリアン・ケロッグ条約）の厳格解釈に基いて、この問題に対し消極的結論を下したが、それは又実際的な政策の考慮によっても影響を受けた。

戦争の法規慣習に関する周知の原則及びハーグ条約、ジュネーヴ条約に照らして指導的なナチの罪人どもの責任が明白であったので、議論の余地のある理論を含み、且つ裁判手続に適せざる長期間の歴史的調査をも要しかねない侵略戦争の『罪』に対する起訴の如きは、徒らに不必要且つ危険な紛糾を招くだけであると考えたのである。しかしこの問題をさらに熟考した結果筆者は侵略戦争を国際犯罪と考える上において、パリ条約は、他の条約並びに決議と相俟って、国際法として認めるに充分なほど発展した慣習を証明するものと認めうるとの結論に達した」と。

第1部　32

アーネスト・ディ・ハウザーの「ニュルンベルグの舞台裏」（サタデー・イヴニング・ポスト誌海外版、一九四六年二月号所載）には、六週間にわたるロンドン交渉においてジャクスン判事の新奇な着想は聯合国諸代表の反対にあい、ロンドン協定に具体化せられた政策につき最後に意見の一致を見たのはようやく八月八日であったと書かれている。右の決定もニュルンベルグ裁判に関して為されたのである。聯合国政府が東京裁判についても同様の方針をとることに一致したのはそれよりさらに後のことに属すると推定しうるのである。「ポツダム宣言」は一九四五年七月二十六日公表された。米国の、グリュック教授は一九四四年において、侵略戦争を起した者どもを処罰せんとのかれの願望を「戦争犯罪」なる周知の言葉を拡張することによって為しうるかどうかにつき大いに悩んでいた。ジャクスン判事は、一九四五年において、かかる拡張が全く新奇なることを認めているのである。そして、右辞句を拡張した連合国の政策は長期にわたる商議の後、ようやく一九四五年八月八日に至って初めて決定せられたのである。しからば同年七月二十六日のポツダム宣言中の辞句をば、かかる拡張せられた意味に解釈することは不可能なことであるといわねばならない。

（四）そればかりではなくポツダムに集まった連合国の政治家等が日本の政治家及び軍人をしてその武器を捨てさせようとする賞讃に値すべき努力に当って、責任ある指導者なら犯すものはほとんどない戦時中の蛮行という周知の犯罪とは別に「戦争犯罪人」として厳重にこれら指導者を

処罰するようなことを、条件の一つであると主張することは、とりも直さず連合国政治家の政治的聡明に対する大きな侮辱である。当時の戦況に鑑み、かかる条件は必然的に日本の指導者を絶望的ならしめ、かれらを馳って最後迄戦いぬくようにさせる危険を伴うことを、これら政治家達は充分に見抜いていたにちがいない。それ故かれらが、「ポツダム宣言」中にこの種の字句を挿入したいと考えたとしても、かれらは慎重を期するため、これをさけたであろう。従って日本の指導的政治家及び軍人をして右の字句をいわゆる「平和に対する罪」を含むものと理解せしめることは、連合国の政治家達の意思ではなかったと結論して差支えない。それは又常識上当然すぎる程当然の結論である。

（五）　右のような考察にも拘らず裁判所においてなお疑問ありとし、戦争犯罪なる語は不明確で二様の意味にとられうるとせられるなら、われわれは「不明確な文書はこれを作成せる者に不利益に解釈すべし」という周知の解釈規則に裁判所の注意を促したい。この法格言が国際的性質の協定の解釈についても適用せられる法の一般原則であることは、常設国際司法裁判所の判決によって明らかにされている。ブラジル公債事件において、同裁判所は、文書の意義が不明なときは、提供者に不利に解釈するのが文書解釈の一般原則であると判示した（同裁判所刊行物第一輯第二〇、二一号、三四頁）。

さらにローザンヌ条約の解釈に関する勧告的意見は、条約の条項の字句が不明確な場合には、

許される解釈のうち当事者にもっとも少ない義務を負わせるような解釈を採用するのが正しい原則であると述べている（第二輯、第十二号、二五頁）。われわれは「一事項の表示は他の事項を排除す。」という右と均しく周知の解釈に関する規則に裁判所の注意を喚起したい。この格言もまた常設国際司法裁判所によって適用せられているのである（第一、第二輯、第四二号、一二一頁）。

（乙）事後法と裁判

「ポツダム宣言」は『峻厳なる裁判』が行わるべし」という。行わるべき裁判は、それがいかに峻厳であり、慈悲によって寛和されないものであるとしても、とにかく「裁判」でなければならない。

文明国においては、裁判は法による裁判を意味する。すなわちたとえ裁判官がいかに善良であり又聡明であっても、その裁判官の個人的な正邪の念によるのではなく、確立された法の規則及び原則によって裁判を行うべきことを意味する。

本裁判所が軍人のみでなく連合国国民中からえらばれた極めて著名な法律家をふくめて構成せられている事実は、連合国自身、又法に従って右の「裁判」を行わんとの意図をもつことを裏書きするものである。

特に刑事裁判において、裁判は確立した法規に則って行うべしとの準則の正当性は、多年にわたる政治的経験その他によって、既に試験済みである。英国におけるスター・チェンバーの歴史

は、時の権力者が、最も忌むべき似而非なる裁判によって、自己の嫌う政治的集団、もしくは政治家を抑圧、駆除ないし「清算」するために、刑事法の機構を利用する傾向あることを証明して余りあるものである。事後法禁止の法則はすべての文明国において刑事裁判の準則として承認せられている。そしてこの準則は、国際的又は国内的政治犯罪に関する事件においては、特に尊重せられなければならない。

英国議会はその無制約的権能にもかかわらず、一六八八年以降においては政治犯人を処罰するため事後立法を行ったことはない。又アメリカ合衆国憲法は、州法たると聯邦法たるとにかかわらず、ひとしく事後法を禁止している。そしてアメリカの立法史を通じて、政治犯に対する事後立法はきわめて稀であるようである。南北戦争かような事後立法が行われ、南部聯邦の援助者の処罰を定めた州法及び聯邦法に関連した二つの事件が合衆国最高裁判所に提起されたことがあるが、同裁判所は当時の興奮した民衆感情のただ中にあって、フィルド判事を通じ州法聯邦法ともに違憲であると判示し、その歴史に永遠の栄光をそえたのである（カミングズ対ミズーリ州、ウォレス判例集第四巻三三三頁（一八六六）、エキス・パーティ・ガーランド、ウォレス判例集第四巻、二七七頁（一八六六）。

一九四四年二月二四日アメリカ法学協会に対して提出された基本的人権に関する報告書第九条には、「何人といえども犯罪として訴追を受けたる行為がその行為の当時施行せられたる法律に違反せざるかぎり、有罪の宣言を受くることなく、又犯行当時科し得たる刑より重き刑を科せら

るることなし」とある（クインジー・ライト「戦争犯罪人」アメリカ国際法雑誌、第三十八巻、二五七頁、註三の引用による）。そしてこれとほぼおなじ内容の原則は、三十ヶ国の憲法に規定されているということである。「法律なければ刑罰なし」という原則は又憲法上の明示的保障の有無にかかわらず、大陸法系諸国における刑事司法の基本原則の一つをなしている。なるほどこの原則は、ナチドイツにおいて、裁判官に対し「健全なる国民感情」に従って事件を裁判する権限を付与した一九三五年六月二十八日の法律によって無残にも打ち破られた。即ち右法律は「法律により処罰しうるものとせられたる行為又は刑法の根本観念及び健全なる国民感情により処罰に値すると認めらるる行為はこれを罰す。行為に直接適用ある刑罰法規の存せざる場合に於ては、その根本概念が該行為にもっともよく該当する法律によりこれを罰す」と規定した。しかるに常設国際司法裁判所はその勧告的意見において、このヒットラー立法をダンチッヒに適用することは、同市の統治は法の支配によるべし（法治国）との要件に違反するものであると宣言した。周知のように、ドイツ人は国会放火の故を以て、該火災の当時における放火罪の刑は有期懲役刑にすぎなかったにかかわらず、ヴァン・デル・ルッベの斬首を許したのであったが、このことは、極東の島国人をふくむ全世界の法律家の良心に衝撃を与えたのである。首席検察官が援用せんとする「文明の要求に応じ、一般人の良心の明白な表現である原理」なるものは、法的訓練なき人には「刑法の基本概念と健全なる国民感情に照らし刑罰に値する」なるナチス的原理と同様に当然の原理であると考

えられるかもしれない。しかし刑事裁判におけるこのような曖昧な原理は、実際上はナチス的理論とひとしく圧制的な原理である。又シャム国の裁判所が一九四六年三月二十四日戦争犯罪人処罰に関する新しい法律は事後法であり、遡及的に適用することを得ないという理由でピブン元帥と今次戦争中日本と協力した十一人の主要「戦争犯罪人」を釈放したよしである。この報道が真実なら、それはまさにシャム国裁判所の栄誉でありその信頼を高むるゆえんである。事後処罰は裁判の仮面をかぶった私刑に他ならないという感情は、欧洲におけるいわゆる啓蒙期の所産ではなく、東西古今を通ずる普遍的な正義観念をあらわすものである。尤もそれは古今の暴君によってしばしばやぶられはした、今後文明諸国が、国際法上の義務に違背した個人を処罰する法典を制定することがあるとすれば、罪刑法定主義はその根本原理の一つとせられるであろう。またそうせられなければならない。

従ってわれわれは、共同謀議の罪、いわゆる平和に対する罪及び人道に対する罪（「戦争犯罪」の一部をなす場合はこれを別として）は未だ国際法の認めざるところであると主張する。かりにそれが戦時中に各国民を拘束する法となったと仮定しても、本件で問題となる行為がなされた当時の法ではなかったのである。いやしくも正義の問題が反省される場合には常に不正とされる事後法たること明白である。かくの如き事後法を被告人に対して適用することは、文明的裁判ではなく、又ポツダム宣言のいわゆる「裁判」でもない。

一方において戦争犯罪なる用語の自然な解釈にもとづき、他方において文明的な裁判の通念に照らして、われわれは本裁判所条例中の共同謀議、「平和に対する罪」及び「人道に対する罪」──それがいわゆる「戦争犯罪」中に包含せられざる限り──を規定する部分は本裁判所の適用すべき法でないと主張する。あたかも連邦議会法律中合衆国憲法に違反する部分、英国の委任勅令中議会制定法によって委任せられた範囲を蹂越する部分が無効である如く、本裁判所条例中、基本文書──即ち降服文書中にもその条項が挿入されているところのポツダム宣言──に違反する部分は無効であると宣言せられねばならぬ。当事者の一方が約諾した義務は、相手方において勝手にこれを加重しえないことは、遍く認められる法の一般原則である。

第二　共同謀議

首席検察官は、共同謀議を犯罪とする理論が、国際法上の一制度であると明言してはいない。

しかし首席検察官がこのことを前提とするものであることは、「本裁判所条例中の本項の規定は別に新しい法を創設したものではない」（英文記録三九六頁）と述べているに徴して明白である。右にいわゆる「法」とは「国際法」を指すものとすべきである。しかしこの場合については、侵略戦争の場合と異なって、首席検察官は多数国家の参加した会議において、共同謀議が国際法上の「犯罪」であることを認めた事例を一つも挙げておらない。又共同謀議を犯罪と定めた条約、宣言、ないし決議の如きをも挙げておらない。ただ単にマリノ対合衆国事件における合衆国聯邦控訴院の意見を引用するに止まる。そしてそれから次の如く結論する。

「本犯罪は大多数の文明国の熟知し且つ承認するところであり、その要領においては各国ともきわめて類似しておるので、本犯罪の一般概念を適切に言いあらわしたものとして、合衆国の上

これは誠に驚くべき議論である。比較法に志す法律家なら、すべてみな共同謀議を犯罪とする原則が、英国法制史独特の所産であることを熟知している（スティブン、英国刑事法史第三巻二〇二─二二七頁、ウィンフィルド、コンスピラシーと訴訟濫用の歴史（一九二一）、R・S・ライト、クリミナル・コンスピラシー、ハーヴァード・ロー・レヴュー第三十一の法（一八七三）、フランシス・B・セイヤー、クリミナル・コンスピラシー、ハーヴァード・ロー・レヴュー第三十五巻三九三─四二四頁）。それはおそらく他の法体系には存在しない刑法理論であるる、そして国際的に妥当するためには、全ての法体系を認めるところでなければならないに拘わらず、そうでないことは少なくとも確かである。

ハーヴァード・ロー・スクールのフランシス・B・セイヤー教授は、「共同謀議の理論は変則的、地方的な理論であると共に、そのもたらす結果もかんばしからぬものである。ローマ法はかような理論を知らず、又それは現代大陸諸国の法典中にも見当らない。大陸のの法律家でかような理論を聞知している者は稀である」と述べている（セイヤー前掲四二七頁）。議会政治や法の優位や刑事陪審や人身保護令状や信託などの場合とは異なって、大陸法系の法律家はアングロ・サクソン独特のこの制度を余り高く評価してはいない。特に「共同謀議者の全てが外部行為に参加する必要はない。その一人がかかる行為をなせば、それは全員の行為となる」（英文記録四〇四頁）という理論の如きは不当であり、著しく法的良心に反するものであることは明白である。

われわれは、右の如き理論は人類の部族時代に行われた集合的責任主義に逆戻りするものとの感を抱かざるをえない。しかもかかる理論を一切の平和に対する罪、戦争犯罪及び人道に対する罪にまで推し及ぼそうとするのであるから、益々以て不当である。なぜなら右の理論によれば、一度ある戦争が何等かの理由で侵略戦争又は国際法もしくは条約を侵犯する戦争と宣言せられれば、自国に対して戦時的奉仕をなした者は全て、他人が犯した殺人その他のおそるべき犯罪につき、たとえ何時、何処で、誰がかかる罪を犯したのであるか全然知らなくても、これについて責任を負わねばならぬこととなるからである。

英米の法律家自身大陸法系の法律家に対し、共同謀議の理論は、時の権力者の好まざる集団を処罰するに熱心な検察官や裁判官にとって、誠に便利な法律上の武器であると語っているのである。かれらは又、英国においてはこの理論がアダム・スミスの著書に描かれているように（アダム・スミス、諸国民の富に関する研究、第一巻第十章第二部二三一頁）、十八世紀において、又故パスフィルド卿の指摘するように（シドニー・ウェッブ、労働組合運動史第二版（一九二〇）七三頁）、十九世紀の前半期において、当時の支配階級に好ましからざりし社会的集団であった労働組合の組合員を処罰するため実効的に利用されたというであろう。さらに進んで、又英国国民の間においても進歩的な裁判官や法学者達は、この理論を英米普通法に光彩を添えるものとは考えていないとつけ加えるであろう。

ケンタッキー州対ドノウヒウ事件（ケンタッキー州判例集第二百五十巻三四三頁、サウス・ヴェスタン第二輯第六十三巻三頁）の反対意見中には、「その主たる危険は、それが将来において常に人々の夢想だにしなかった新しい犯罪をつくり出す基礎となることに存する」と述べられている。

ハーヴァード・ロー・スクールのセイヤー教授は本問題について綿密な研究をなした後次の如く述べる。

その輪廓きわめて曖昧、その根本性格すこぶる不明確なこの理論は、法に対しなんらの力も光輝も添えるものではない。それは紛れもなく猫の眼のように変る意見や生硬な思想の浮砂に人を捲込む理論である」（セイヤー、前掲三九五頁）。

「かかる原則の下においては、何人といえども他人と協力した場合、後日未知の裁判官の予断的な好悪や社会的偏見によって、自己の自由が左右されることとなりかねないのである。かくの如きは正に法による裁判と対蹠的なものである」（セイヤー、前掲四一三頁）。

「共同謀議の理論は、その用いられる全ての場合においてわが英米法の中の魔魂なることを実証したのである。私はこの理論が、過去の判例の間にひしめく残映にすぎなくなる時代の近からんことを祈るものである」（セイヤー、前掲四二四頁）。

かくも嫌悪すべき理論を国際社会に導入せんとの提議に対し、事後法的導入の方法は別とするも、英国の故キロウェンのラッセル卿や、米国の故オリヴァー・ウェンデル・ホームズ・ジュニ

ア判事の如き卓越した法律家は果して何と言うことであろう。またこれに関連してハドスン判事の次の言葉はすこぶる適切な警告である。かれは言う、

「国際裁判所の裁判官が、たまたま自己の熟知している特殊な国内法律体系の原理を国際法に導入しても差支ないと考えるが如きは、まことに危険なことといわなければならない……」（マンリ・O・ハドスン、「常設国際司法裁判所の適用する法」、ヘンリー・ビール及びサミュエル・ウィリストン記念ハーヴァード法学論集（一九三四）一三三、一三七頁）。

次に特に奇異なのは、首席検察官が「進行的共同謀議」と命名した共同謀議理論の応用形式である。

ドイツの第三帝国の場合と異なり、被告人等が「相互に意見の合致せる集団」を形成していたことを証明することは勿論不可能であり、首席検察官も又「被告人の間には意見の鋭い対立と烈しい争いが存したものの如くである」ことを認める（英文記録四七一頁）。しかもなお、首席検察官はまことに検察官らしく、「岩石のうちにも教訓を読みとる」態度で――国家の軍備や、国家利益の保護のための武力行使や、戦争という制度が未だ過去の遺物となっていない世界において――国民の国際的経歴にあらわれる一切の発展的事態の中に、共同謀議、いな擬制的共同謀議を発見しようとする。もしも首席検察官の理論が正しいものとするなら、英、仏、蘭各国の膨張の中にも、ロシア帝国の発展の中にも、さらに又アメリカの原始十三州から現在の偉大なアメリカ共和

国への漸次的発展の中にも、同じように進行的共同謀議を認め、それら諸国の主要な政治家及び将軍は、かれら自身の政治的信条が、帝国主義的であったと反帝国主義的であったとにかかわらず、共同謀議罪を犯したものと論断することもできるわけである。

ニュルンベルグの裁判所は、その基本法たる裁判所条例の下においては、狭義の戦争犯罪又は人道に対する罪を犯す共同謀議に参加した者を処罰する権限をもたないと裁定した（同裁判所記録一六八八四頁）。そればかりでなく同裁判所は、ナチ党もしくはナチ政府の活動に重要な関与をなしたことが、犯罪としての共同謀議の証拠となるものであると言いきることを躊躇し、「共同謀議が成立するためには、その違法な目的の輪廓が明らかになっていなければならず、又謀議成立の時が決定及び行為の時からあまり遠くてもいけない」と言っている（同裁判所記録一六八八二頁）。これは、無実の者を陥れるにあまり便利ではあるが、法律的良心に衝撃を与える最もいまわしい部分を、ある程度共同謀議の理論から排除したことになるのであるが、同判決は共同謀議の理論そのものはこれを排除しなかった。しかしニュルンベルグの裁判所においては、裁判所条例の規定は英国における議会制定法のごとく絶対に裁判所を拘束すると考えられていたのに対し、極東国際軍事裁判所においては、条例の規定はアメリカの議会制定法と同じく、より高次の法、即ちポツダム宣言中に厳粛に明定せられ降服文書に取入れられた条項に従わねばならぬのであることに留意せねばならない。

かくしてわれわれは、ニュルンベルグ判決において「平和に対する罪」に対し適用した如き緩和された形態においてもなお、共同謀議の理論は行為の当時国際法の制度ではなかったこと、いかなる国際法学者といえどもかかることを夢想だもしなかったのだと主張するものである。

第三 侵略戦争

（甲）侵略戦争は国際犯罪か

首席検察官は次に「侵略戦争」を論ずる。

先ず「侵略戦争は国際法上の犯罪であるか、起訴状の全期間を通じて、かかる犯罪であると考えられていたか」と設問し、これに対し首席検察官は然りと答える。そして「一つには、この問題に関して国際法が存在すること、二つには、それは国際法によって犯罪とされていること」の二点を証明せんとする（英文記録四〇五頁）。

首席検察官は先ず最初にカルドーゾ判事、ライト卿、サー・フレデリック・ポロック、英枢密院司法委員会、常設国際司法裁判所規程、米独混合仲裁委員会の裁決等の如き尊重に値すべき権威が、国際法の慣習による発展ということについて、披瀝した一般的見解を引用しているが、国際慣習の生成の問題についての以上の見解の大部分は、国際法学徒なら誰でも熟知している月並

47

な見解にすぎない。
そして首席検察官は次の如く結論する。

「以上によって、……全体の福祉に関する事項について多数の文明国によって一定の行動がとられれば、それによって国際法の原則が成立するに至ることが証明されたので、今や侵略戦争の問題は極めて多数の国家により考慮され、その結果違法とされたのであるから、それら国家の全員一致の評決は、国際法の一般原則たるの権威を荷うに至ったことを証明するであろう」と（英文記録四一五頁）。なるほど上述の諸大家の見解を援用することによって、首席検察官は、一の歴史的過程として多数文明国の一致した行動が国際法の原則を確立する傾向のあること、及び国際司法裁判所は国際法について一定の法源を認めており、その法源中には国際慣習も含まれていることを証明したものといえるであろう。しかし全体の福祉に開する事項についての多数文明国の一致した行動が、単にそれだけで、国際法の一般原則を樹立するといった法的原則は、なんら証明されておらず、又証明することをえないであろう。又首席検察官の採用した諸権威も、かくの如き法理を樹立せんとする趣旨でないことは勿論である。例えば有名なパリ宣言をとってみよう。

「商船私掠ハ今後之ヲ廃止ス」ということが、一八五六年のパリ会議において海法に関し採択された宣言の一部をなし、爾来北米合衆国、スペイン及びメキシコを除く全ての文明国が、右宣言の調印国となった。然らば多数文明国のなした一八五六年のこの宣言は、商船私掠の禁止を国際

法の原則にまで高めたのであるか。右宣言はすべての国際法学者によって、単に調印国相互間においてのみ拘束力をもち、右の三ヶ国による、もしくはこれに対して行われる商船私掠は適法であるとされたことは、周知の事実ではないか。

一八九八年合衆国政府は、今後商船私掠を行わずパリ宣言の規定を遵守する旨の意思を表明した。この事実は、かかる意思表示なきかぎり合衆国は商船私掠を差控える義務のなかったことを示すものではないか。又スペインが拿捕免許状を発する権利を固守したとき、それは正当な行為であって、なんら国際法の原則に反したものでないとされなかったか。

さらに又、一九二九年七月二十七日の俘虜の処遇に関するジュネーヴ条約は、多数の文明国によって調印せられた。例えば非調印国たるソヴィエト聯邦は、該条約の規定は、国際法の一般原則を具現しているものとして、自らもこれに拘束を受けると考えているのであるか。

然るに首席検察官は、前記命題を以て歴史的過程の問題としてでなく、法的原則として妥当することを前提とするもののごとくである。そしてかかる前提に基いて、多くの国際条約を援用し、これらの条約によって侵略戦争がすでに久しい以前から、国際法上の犯罪であったことを証明するうると主張する。しかしその援用する証拠は、この主張を証明するものでないことは明白である。（英文記録四一六頁）。首席検察官の考えている各規定中の「成ルベク」とか「事情ノ許ス限リ」とかの字句は、首席検察官の

（一）　首席検察官が第一に援用する条約は、第一次ハーグ条約である

49　第3　侵略戦争

主張とは反対に、調印国が未だ国際紛争を平和的手段によって解決すべき法的義務を負うだけの用意のなかったことを示している。「死活的利益」及び「国家の名誉」の問題をしばらく措くとしても、正当防衛の考慮は締約国の右の如き法的義務の受諾を許さなかったであろう。このことは例えば、本起訴状附属書Ａ第十節のオランダの右の如き主張たる「従ってオランダ政府は、最後に述べた攻撃を受くるや、直に自衛のため日本に対して宣戦した」を見ても明らかである。

（二）首席検察官の次に援用する条約は第三ハーグ条約である（英文記録四一六頁）。首席検察官は、右協定によって、開戦の宣言なき戦争は、国際法上の犯罪たる烙印を捺されたと主張する。しかしこれはもとより首席検察官の独断論にすぎない。

明瞭且つ事前の通告なくして戦争を開始すべからざることを認めた本条約は、主として戦争状態が何時に発生したかを明瞭ならしめるために、それが望ましいことに由来する一つの技術的規定である。右通告と戦争開始との間に二十四時間の期間を設くべしとのオランダの提案が本会議において否決された事実は、このことを物語るものである。従ってそれは、戦略上の目的のためのみなされる「奇襲」を禁止するとか、これに犯罪の烙印を捺すとかいう趣旨の規定ではない。背信ということは主として良心の問題であり、戦争は開戦宣言の有無に拘わらず背信行為でうるのである。洋の東西を問わず古代及び中世の社会においては、開戦の宣言は武士道と関聯するものであった。かかる武士道的観念は、今日でも一般人の感情のうちに生きており、又、周知

の如く、敵国を「不信」呼ばわりして、戦時宣伝に利用されている。グロチウスはその著「戦争と平和の権利」の中で、「諸国民が適法な戦争開始のために開戦の宣言を要するものとするに至った理由は、二、三の論者の主張するように、秘密裡に事を運んだり、巧妙な詭計を用いたりすることを禁ずるためではない。若干の国民は戦いの時と場所をも指定したと言われるが、かかる問題は法の問題ではなく、武士道の問題である。そうではなく、その理由は戦争が私人によって勝手に行われるのではなく、双方の国民もしくはその元首の意思によって行われるのであることを、明確ならしめるにあったのである。なぜなら開戦宣言は、匪賊同士の闘争や国王と臣下との間の闘争の場合には生じないような、特殊な効果が生ぜしめるからである」と述べている（第三巻第三章第七節）。

近代国際社会において宣戦が望ましいと考える主な理由は、もはや武士道ではなく——これは主観的良心の問題である——戦争状態のもたらすさまざまの効果を決定するための、法技術的な手段にすぎないのである。グロチウスの時代以来、かれの禁止にも拘わらず多数の大国が宣戦なくして戦闘を開始している。英国のモーリス名誉中佐は、一八八三年「宣戦を伴わざる戦争」（ロンドン、政府印刷局一八八三年）と題する労作を公刊して、一七〇〇年から一八七二年までの間に起った多くの戦争の開始を検討したが、一九〇四年四月、「十九世紀以後」誌のうちに次のように書いている。「数字的にいえば、私の比較的詳しく検討した期間を通じて、英国は三十回、フランスは

三十六回、ロシアは七回（但しトルコ及び支那を含む隣接アジア諸国に対する慣行的な無宣戦戦争は算入しない）、プロシアは七回、オーストリアは十二回、北米合衆国は少なくとも五回、戦争開始の宣言を伴わない戦争行為を行っている」と。

英国、フランス、ロシア、プロシア、オーストリア、北米合衆国の如き大国がかかる国際法の技術的勧告に従わなかったとの故を以て、戦争に関する背信と裏切行為の常習犯人であったと主張するのは、誠に奇怪千万なことといわざるをえない。

日本、アメリカ及びイギリスを含む各国政府の見解の如何に拘わらず、第三ハーグ条約が調印国に対して法的義務を負わしめたものであるかどうかは、学説上争いのあるところである。ローレンス、ウェストレイク及びベロットの如き英国の著名な国際法の諸権威は、右条約のフランス語の原文に照らして、調印国に対しなんらの法的義務を課したものでないと考えている。ウェストレイクは、右条約は本問題に関するそれ以前の法を大して変更したものではないと考えている。又古典的なピット・コベットの「主要国際法判例集」（ヒュー・エッチ・エル・ベロット編纂の一九二四年版）の第二巻第十八頁には次の如く述べられている。

「同時に調印国は、事前の宣戦なくしては絶対に戦争行為をなさざる旨を誓約したのではなく、単に、交戦国相互間においては、戦争行為を『事前且つ明瞭なる通告なくして開始すべきではない ought not to』ことを認めたにすぎない。その目的が開戦の宣言を発する権限を有する者との通

信が困難な場所か、又は相手方が不意打であるといって非難する理由の存せざること明白な状況の下において、敵対的な準備もしくは作動を排除するために、即時実力を行使する必要が生ずるような場合を、除外せんとするにあったことは明らかである」と。そしてベロットは慣習及び条約の課する制限にも拘わらず、戦争行為の開始は結局は主として戦術の問題にすぎないようであるといってその議論を結んでいる。

右に引用した一節は、他の学者の編纂にかかる同書の一九三七年版においても変更されてはいない。

しかしながら他方、第三ハーグ条約の調印国は法的義務を負担したのだと主張する論者もある。例えばオッペンハイムは、「ハーグ条約の結果、事前の開戦宣言なくして戦争行為を行うことが禁止されるに至ったことは疑いない」と言い、(オッペンハイム国際法第一巻第五版第九六節二四九頁)さらに国家が計画的に、事前の開戦宣言もしくは条件附最後通牒を発せずして敵対行為を開始したる場合は、国際法上の義務違反となる、との趣旨を述べている。しからばオッペンハイムのいわゆる「国際法上の義務違反」は「国際犯罪」と同義であるか。この点については著者自身、国際上の義務違反はいわゆる「国際法に反する犯罪」とも、又いわゆる「国際犯罪」ともこれを混同してはならないことを注意しているのである(オッペンハイム、第一巻第五版第百五十一節二七五頁)。

それ故かりにこの後の学説が正しく、この国際法の技術的な規則の違反が国際法上の義務違反となるものとしても、かかる違反行為は、オッペンハイムの見解を以てしても単なる契約違反、もしくはたかだか民事上の不法行為の性質をもつにとどまり、首席検察官の主張するごとく、「国際犯罪」の性質をもつものではない。

第三ハーグ条約の調印国が、右の技術的規定の違反に関与した政治家に刑事責任を負わしめ、いわんやこれを死刑に処することに、合意したものと考えたような国際法学者は絶無である。

（三）首席検察官はさらに進んで、「一九一九年日本を含む戦勝国は国際条約の侵犯が可罰的犯罪であることに意見一致した」と述べる（英文記録四一六頁）。

首席検察官はおそらくヴェルサイユ条約第二百二十八条ないし第二百三十条ではなく、第二百二十七条に言及しておるのであろう。なぜなら前者は、聯合国並びに締盟国の軍事裁判所が、戦時法規慣習を侵犯する行為（即ち「通例の」戦争犯罪）をなした者に対して行うべき裁判を取扱っているものだからである。第二百二十七条はホーヘンツォルレン家のウィリアム二世を「国際道徳並びに条約の神聖に対する最大の犯行につき」起訴すべきこと、及び特別に構成する裁判所によって、公正なる裁判を行うべきことを規定している。しかし右規定は、侵略戦争もしくは条約侵犯の戦争を「国際犯罪」ないしは、なにらかの法律上の犯行としておらず、単に道徳と信義に対する犯行としているにすぎないことを注意せねばならぬ。オランダ政府が「ドールンの郷

紳」の引渡しを拒否したのは全く適法な行為であった。なぜならかかる犯行は、犯罪人引渡条約に掲げられた犯罪のうちには含まれていなかったからである。購和会議におけるウィルソン大統領の法律顧問であったジェイムズ・ブラウン・スコットは、「オランダは明らかに政治的な犯行について、ドイツ皇帝を引渡すことを拒むことによって、世界に大きな寄与をなした」とすら考えたのであった（スコット「カイゼルの裁判」、ハウス並びセイムーア、パリ会議の真相（一九二一）所載二三一頁）。

十五人委員会のアメリカ及び日本代表委員が国家元首に対する裁判に反対したことは、ここに改めて述べる必要もないほど周く知られている事実である。但し右委員会がルクセンブルグ及びベルギー侵入の如く、条約上の義務違反を構成するところの「世界大戦を挑発した行為及びその開始に伴う行為」を以て、その責任者たる官憲及び個人に対し、「刑事上の責任を問う充分なる理由と認めることを拒否したことは、注目に値する。第二百二十七条の規定はかような背景に照らしてこれを理解しなければならない。

（四）次に首席検察官は、一九二四年のジュネーヴ議定書の前文及び一九二七年九月二十七日の第八次国際聯盟総会の宣言をとりあげる。これらの文書のうちに「侵略戦争は国際的罪悪であ
インタナショナル・クライム
る」という字句が存するのである。この字句は超国家的イデオロギーが支配した当時のジュネーヴの空気を反映したものである。しかしソヴィエット聯邦は当時「反共産主義的な」聯盟の外にあった。北米合衆国も又、欧洲政治に捲込まれることをおそれてこれに加盟していなかった。合

55　第3　侵略戦争

衆国における国際法の最高権威たるジョン・バセット・モーアは、ジュネーヴ的国際法及びこれに刺戟されたジュネーヴ議定書は、国家内における法と、主権国家から構成される社会を規整する国際制度との間に、緊密な類似性が存するものと考える安易な仮説から生れたものであって、それは健全な国際法を破壊する「狂的な理論」であるとしてこれを攻撃したのではなかったか。英国自身も未だ強制調停を認める用意がなかったこと及び本条約の実際上の作用如何が疑問であるという理由から、議定書の批准を拒否したのではなかったか。かくして右議定書は遂になんら法的効力を発生するに至らなかったのである。又聯盟総会は世界を拘束する権能をもつものではなかったのみならず、右条約の前文中における「国際的罪悪」という辞句は、丁度「歯楊子を使わないことは衛生上の罪悪である」とか、「アルバート記念碑は美学上の罪悪である」とかいう言葉と同じく、単に非難の意を強く表現するために用いられているのである。首席検察官自身、その劈頭陳述において、「許すべからざる罪悪」という言葉を使っているが（英文記録三九三頁）、これもおそらく右のような強調的意味に用いられたものであろう。同様の事は又、首席検察官の引用した（英文記録四一七頁）一九二八年二月十八日の第六次汎アメリカ会議の決議における、「侵略戦争は全人類に対する国際的罪悪を成す」との宣言についても言いうるのである。かくの如き非難は、政治的もしくは道徳的考慮に由来するものではあっても、法的意味は全然もたないのである。

（五）最後に首席検察官は、一九二八年のパリ条約に言及する。

ブリアン氏が特定の政治的目的のために提案した米仏相互条約案から発展したこの有名な多辺的条約は、周知の如くその真の意味如何について、政治的及び法的見地から、いろいろな論議を惹起した。

該条約の本文は、一般に国策の手段としての戦争を排し、一切の紛争を平和的手段によって解決することを約する、極めて簡単且つ抽象的な表現をとっている。

この条約を以て、伝統的な国際法の全ての規定を時代遅れなものとする如き新社会秩序が到来したものであるとし、或いは歴史上の新紀元を劃するものであるとし、或いは又人類の心理における革命であるとする一派の論者もあった。しかしこの条約に対し鋭い分析を行った懐疑派は、友好通商条約に規定されている、条約国相互間には「永久の平和」あるべしとか、「完全且つ不可侵の平和」あるべしとかいう、より断言的な宣言と同じように、該条約のうちに平和への意志の敬虔な表現以外の何ものをも認めなかったのである。

ブリアン氏の如き俊敏な欧洲の政治家は、該条約のうちに国際聯盟及び欧洲政界に参与するの用意を表白した合衆国のジェスチュアを看取したのである。現にブリアンの友人であるボンクールは、「ブリアンにとっては、右条約は何よりも先ず合衆国を国際聯盟にひきこむ手段であった」とはっきり言明しているのである（一九三二年四月十日附ニューヨーク・タイムス紙記事、ジョン・バセット・モーア「理性に訴う」フォリン・アフェアズ誌第十一巻四号（一九三三年六月）五五四頁より引用）。

該条約のテキストばかりでなく、列国の間に交された事前の交換文書を注意深く分析した多くの著名な国際法学者は、同条約は古典的な「正当なる戦争」なる言葉を「防衛戦争」なる語を以て置きかえる、単なる国際法用語の変更をもたらしたにすぎないという結論に達している。中には該条約は戦争を違法とするどころか、反ってこれとは逆に、防衛戦争の適法性を確認したものであるとする者もあったのである。

こうした周知の歴史的背景を念頭に置きつつ、われわれは、調印国特に日本国が負担した法的義務、日本が違反したと検察側の主張するこの法的義務の、正確な意味内容を分析しよう。国際条約を解釈するにあたっては、当事国の真意を捕捉せねばならぬことは、全ての国際法学者の認めるところである。又かかる真意は単に条約文自体にとどまらず、さらにその予備的資料をも参照して確定せねばならぬことも遍く承認されるところである。そして実際上も司法裁判所や仲裁裁判所や外交官等は、条約の解釈について大いに予備的資料を尊重している。

ラルストンはその権威的著作「国際裁判所の法と手続」の中で次の如くいう。

「条約の調印に至るまでの出来事は、該条約を締結した当事者の意思を説明するものとしてしばしば援用され、当事者の意思を決定する上に最大の重要性をもつ場合が多い」（同書第二十六節一八頁）。

一九二一年、一方合衆国と、他方英国及び仏国との間の仲裁条約案が米国上院に提出された際、

ルート氏は次のように条約解釈についての定則を明瞭に述べている。彼は言った。もしもこれら条約が批准された場合には、その正しい解釈を決定するにつき、いつでもそれ以前の了解の記録を参照しうる。国際交通に関する法は、法律及び契約の解釈に関する国内法よりもはるかに自由である。条約の解釈については、署名前又は署名の当時なされた宣言、及び両国の代表者の交換文書及び意見の表示を考慮すべきことは、過去及び現在において普く認められている。文書中にふくまれる規定の範囲及び効果……を決定するため、これら諸宣言に照らして条約本文が解釈されないような事態は、決して発生しえないのである（議会議事録第四十五巻二九三五頁（一九一二年））。

フィリップ・マーシャル・ブラウンは、アメリカ国際法雑誌一九二九年四月号所載の「戦争抛棄に関する一般条約の解釈」と題する周知の論文において、特にパリ条約に関聯して次の如く述べている。

「国際法の原則中、条約の解釈は当事者の意思に照らしてこれをなすべきであるとの原則ほどはっきりと確立したものはないようである。かかる意思は当然条約文自体のうちに表示されていると推定されるが、その他にも、調印もしくは批准の際に条約に附加される特別の留保が、又は批准に先立つ交渉の間になされる解釈、説明、了解、制限、条件等を援用することも可能である。それ故戦争拠棄に関する一般条約によって負担した義務の性質につき、将来なんらかの意見の相違が生じた場合には、当然交渉に関する公の交換文書のみならず、サー・オースティン・チェン

バレン、ブリアン、ケロッグ国務長官、ボラー上院議員のような政府代弁者の言明を参照せざるをえなくなると思われる。本条約に対するこれらの人々の解釈は、最も綿密な吟味と尊重に値するのである。合衆国の公約に関するかぎり、アメリカによる批准の条件となった該条約の「真の解釈」なるものを保障している上院外交委員会の報告書は、司法裁判所による場合であると、国際輿論による場合であるとを問わず、ひとしく考慮されねばならぬところである。……。条約の各調印国の意思を確定するため、又各調印国をして本条約に基くその公約を厳密に尊重且つ信頼することは、常識の点からいっても、倫理的見地からしても、将又法的観点からしても、なされねばならぬことと考えられる」（同誌三七九頁）。

またチャールズ・C・ハイド教授の次の言葉も銘記すべきである。

「さてこれから……国際及び国内のいずれたるを問わず、司法裁判所が、これと異なる当事者の意思を示す他の証拠が存するに拘わらず、合意を記載した文書のみが、当事者の義務の性質を決定するものとみなす如き解釈公式の影響を排除しようとした努力に特に注意を払わなければならない」（ハイド・国際法第二版（一九四五）第二巻第五百三十一節一四七二頁）。

さてわれわれは、右の如き一般に認められた解釈の準則に従って、当時の責任ある政治家のなした声明を顧みることとしよう。

(イ) アメリカ合衆国

ケロッグ国務長官は、一九二八年四月二十八日の演説において次の如く述べる。

「アメリカの作成した不戦条約案中には、自衛権を制限ないし毀損するが如き点は少しも存しない。自衛権はすべての独立国に固有のものであり、又あらゆる条約に内在している。各国家はいかなる場合においても、又条約の規定いかんにかかわらず、攻撃もしくは侵略から自国の領土を防衛する自由をもち、自衛のために戦争に訴うる必要があるかどうかは、その国のみがこれを決定し得るのである。正常な理由ある場合には、世界はむしろこれを賞讃し、これを非難しないであろう」。

次いでケロッグ国務長官は、右条約調印を勧告せられた各国政府にあてた一九二八年六月二十三日の覚書において、フランスの強調した六項目の重大な「考慮事項」に関連して条約に対する彼自身の「解釈」を明らかにした後、次の如く述べたのである。

「かかる事情の下に、余はここに貴政府の考慮をわずらわすため、上述した変更を含む戦争抛棄に関する多辺的相互条約の草案を伝達するの光栄を有するものである」。

合衆国においては、周知の如く、本条約のモンロー主義に及ぼす効果につき大きな懸念が抱かれたのであったが、ケロッグ氏は一九二八年十二月七日上院外交委員会に対して、モンロー主義の保障は、本条約が自衛行為を排除せず、且つ自衛行為であるか否かは合衆国のみがこれを判定

61　第3　侵略戦争

する権利をもつことのうちに含まれているから大丈夫だといった。氏はさらに、アメリカ政府は国家の防衛又は国家に危険を及ぼすおそれある事態を防止するため必要と信ずる処置をとる権利を有すると述べ、この法則は全ての国家にも均しく適用せられることを認めた。国務長官は又、アメリカ政府は自衛の問題の決定をいかなる裁判所に委ねることをも承認しないであろう、又他国政府もこの点については同様承認しないであろうと述べた。

ボラー上院議員は、一九二九年一月三日の上院における演説及び討論において、何が攻撃となるか又何が防衛の正当性を理由づけるかを自ら決定する権利を拋棄する国はないであろうと述べ、又合衆国は、他国の行動が合衆国自身に対する攻撃の性質を帯びないかぎり、これに関して自衛問題を決定することには関与しないであろうと明言した (議会議事録第二会期一二六頁及び一二七一頁)。

そしてモーア判事は「私は従来常に (ボラー) 上院議員が一般に『戦争追放』の擁護者として知られている以上に大きな役割を演じたものと臆測していた。氏が一九二八年における大統領選挙において勿論戦争の拋棄を補強せんがためではなく、合衆国をして既に完璧を期して保障された自衛権の行使をば可能ならしむるために、たえず有力な海軍の存置を要望したのを見たとき特にそうであった」というている (モーア、前掲五五三頁)。

（ロ）英　国

一九二八年五月十九日、英国政府はアメリカ政府に対して、国策の手段としての戦争を拋棄す

る部分を引用した後、一定の地域の福祉と統一とは英国政府の平和と安全にとって特別の、且つ死活的な利害をもつものであること、並びにかかる地域に対する攻撃に対してこれを守ることは自衛手段に他ならぬ故、右地域に対するいかなる干渉もこれを甘受しえざる旨を宣言した覚書を手交した。右覚書中かかる地域の何たるかは指定されておらず、将来いかなる地域を以てかかる地域とするかについて、完全な自由が留保されていることに注意すべきである。右の覚書はケロッグ国務長官の演説中に解説されている「自衛権」に関する英国政府の、より具体的な解明であった。オースティン・チェンバレンは将来の異議ないし論争に対して効果的な先手をうつために、七月十八日の覚書に次の如き明確な条件を附している。曰く、

「五月十九日附覚書中、一定の地域の福祉と統一に関する部分については、英国政府は、新条約が右の点に関する英国政府の行動の自由を、なんらそこなうものでないことの諒解のもとに、これを受諾するものである旨再言するに止める」。

なるほどソヴィエット政府及びペルシア政府は英国の留保を認めることを拒絶した。しかし将来英国政府がケロッグ・ブリアン条約違反の責を問われた場合に、かくも細心な注意をもって起草され、条約の本文と共に正式に国際連盟に寄託せられた自衛に関するその解釈を採用しないという如きことは、ありえないことと考えられていたのである。

(ハ) フランス

ブリアンは、七月十四日の覚書において、左の如く言明した。

「これに加えて、共和国政府はフランスの立場から述べた各種の所見を満足せしめるため、合衆国政府が新条約についてフランスの立場から与えた見解をここに了承することを欣快とする。……かかる事態の下において、又かかる条件の下に、共和国政府は合衆国に対して、今や本条約に調印する完全な意図を有する旨を通告しうることを欣快とする……」。

(ニ) 日 本

一九二八年七月二十日、東京において田中義一男爵から駐日アメリカ代理大使エドウィン・エル・ネヴィル氏に手交した覚書において、日本外務大臣はケロッグ氏が四月二十八日に為した前述の演説に言及して、「貴下は……四月二十八日の演説中において国務長官の為したる説明を詳細にわたり再説せられ候」といい、さらに左の如く述べる。

「帝国政府は、本年五月二十六日附マクヴェー閣下宛書翰中に陳述せる如く、去る四月提議せられたる条約原案に対する帝国政府の了解はアメリカ合衆国政府の了解と実質上同一なるを以て今般提議せられたる修正に衷心賛同し得ることを欣快とする旨貴下に通報するの光栄を有し候仍て帝国政府は右の了解の下に今般提示せられたる案文の儘（まま）本条約に署名方訓令を発するの用意有之候（これあり）

一九二九年六月十七日及び六月二十六日枢密院会議にケロッグ・ブリアン条約草案が提出された際、久保田、富井両顧問官から、自衛は領土の防衛のみに限定されるものであるかどうか、支那及び特に満蒙において実力行使が必要となったような場合に該条約がこうした実力行使に適用せられるか、さらに英国と同様この点を明瞭にしておくのがよくはないかとの趣旨の質問が為されたに対し、政府の回答は、自衛は領土の防衛にとどまらず領土外にも及ぶものであるというにあった。実力手段による満洲その他の地域における権益の保護は、本条約は自衛行為を排除するものではないことによって充分認められているというのであった。この点は戦争抛棄に関する一般条約批准に関する枢密院会議の審査報告書中に明記されている。それ故、自衛の性質について日本の外務大臣が枢密院会議において為した説明と実質的には同一であったのである。勿論各国政府は、真面目にとりあげるに足りない単なるジェスチュアとしてこれらの宣言や留保をなすものではない。むしろそれとは反対に、それらは締約せられた義務についての、各政府の諒解の卒直且つ真剣な公式声明である。あたかもそれが本条約第一条に書き入れられたと同様に、条約上の義務の固有且つ本質的な部分を構成するものである。

各国の指導的政治家の言明、特にアメリカ上院におけるケロッグ長官及びボラー上院議員の明瞭且つ疑いの余地を残さない、条約案の説明に照らして、パリ条約締結国の意思が、次の如きも

のであったことは明らかである。

(1) 本条約は自衛行為を排除しないこと
(2) 自衛は領土防衛に限られないこと
(3) 自衛は、各国が自国の国防又は国家に危険を及ぼす可能性ある如き事態を防止するため、その必要と信ずる処置をとる権利を包含すること
(4) 自衛措置をとる国が、それが自衛なりや否やの問題の唯一の判定権者であること
(5) 自衛の問題の決定は、いかなる裁判所にも委ねらるべきでないこと
(6) いかなる国家も、他国の行為が自国に対する攻撃とならざるかぎり、該行為に関する自衛問題の決定には関与すべからざること。

首席検察官は右条約の本文に「犯罪」という語が用いられていないことを認めるが（英文記録四一七頁）、右条約の本文のみならず、交換文書のどこにもこうした観念は見出し得ないのである。聯盟式「制裁」観念はアメリカ国務長官にとっては禁物であった。首席検察官はこの条約によって締約国は侵略戦争を「違法」としたのだと主張する（英文記録四一七頁）。「侵略戦争」という響きの好い言葉は、後に明らかにされるように、曖昧で捕捉し難く且つ定義し得ざる言葉である。しかし仮に一歩譲って交戦国自身の非自衛戦争と認めた戦争は、本条約によって違法であるとしよう。首席検察官は次いでそれが国際「犯罪」だと言明するのである。首席検察官の論理はわれわ

れの到底理解し得ないところである。条約当事国が、交戦者自身の自衛行為と認めた戦争を違法なりとすることに合意したとの事実は、かかる条約の違反を当然犯罪としたものではない。それは契約違反もしくは民事上の不法行為ではあっても、決して犯罪ではない。あることを違法とする約束は、当然にそれが犯罪を構成すると何故いえるのか。

当事者の意思を探究することを第一次的原理とする契約解釈の根本原則に裁判所は特に注意を払っていただきたい。本件において引用せられたすべての契約的文書の当事者の意思は、それらの契約の条項違反が、個人に対して恣意的に決定される刑事責任を伴うものというにあったと考えることが果してできるのであるか。もしも当事者が真にかかる意思を有したのであったとしたら、必ずその旨を明示したであろう。政治家に刑罰を科するというような全然新奇な事態にふさわしい、段階的刑罰と手続とを定めたであろう。

なるほど、第一次世界大戦以後、一派の国際法学者が、侵略国に対する共同制裁の遂行ということに、世界平和への道を見出さんとしたのは事実である。この派の人達は、中立に関する規則を厳守し、これによって武力闘争と無秩序の局地化をはかることに平和への道を見出さんとした。前者は現行の中立に関する諸法則を修正することによって、正統学派の見解にはげしく挑戦した。聯盟規約に規定せられた制裁を実施し、且つケロッグ・ブリアン条約を補強せんと努力した。そして一九三四年九月ブダペストにおける国際法学会の会合において、このような試みがなされ

のであった。右会合ではパリ条約違反の法的効果についての討論の後、周知の「ブダペスト解釈条項」が作成せられた（国際法学会、第三十八回会議報告書六六頁）。

さらに一九三六年以降、一群のアメリカの法学者によって、右と全然同じではないが、これと同様な試みがなされ、彼等の研究の結果は、アメリカ国際法学会がハーヴァード国際法研究の一部として、一九三九年十月に「侵略の場合における国家の権利義務に関する条約案」となって公にされた（アメリカ国際法雑誌第三十三巻第四号追録）。

ブダペスト解釈条項は、その解釈の当否については激しい争いがある（例えば一九三五年二月二〇日のイギリス国会におけるブダペスト条項討議、上院議事録第九十五巻第五輯一〇〇七段以下）。又かかる解釈はパリ条約の締約国を拘束するものでないことは勿論である。しかしともかくそれは現行法を明らかにせんとする趣旨であった。これに反して一九三九年の右条約案は、将来の法に関するものである（前掲八二八頁）。それは「現行法ではなく、将来いかなる法の発展が可能であるかを示唆せんとする」学究的な試みである（前掲八二六頁）。右の条約案には又次のようなことわり書きがついている。

「侵略の場合における国家の権利義務に関する条約案を考察するにあたって、該案の全体的構成、その基礎理論及びその多くの個々的規定並びに原則に関して、根本的な見解の相違が生じた。それにも拘わらず本研究会が本条約案を提示する所以のものは、本問題に関する本研究会の討論が、この問題を更に解明するために全世界の学者によって継続されることを希望するからに他な

らず、ここに公にする条約案が、顧問委員の一致した意見を反映するものであるとの意味は、全然もっていないのである」（前掲八二七頁）。

右条約案の内容に賛成すると否とに拘わらず、フィリップ・シー・ジェサップ教授その他の顧問委員諸氏が「政治的論争や感情の紛糾を伴うこの問題」の研究を冷静に、「一時的な外交上の趨勢や、熱狂的支持や偏見に動かされることなく」遂行したことに対しては、大いに敬意を表すべきである。

ブダペスト解釈条項も右条約案も、パリ条約の侵犯もしくは「侵略」が国際犯罪を構成するとは言っていないことを、特に注意すべきである。右条約等の起草者は、一定の心理的色彩を帯びるに至った「侵略」なる言葉を用いたことについて、弁明をすら行っているのである。それは又、右条約案の目的は、一国が武力を行使せざる法的義務に違反して武力に訴え、しかも当該違反国のあらかじめ承諾を与えた手続によって、かかる違反あることが正式に決定せられた場合における、国家相互間の法的関係を規定するにあると述べている。「共同安全保障」の制度に対する賛否の意見を表現したり、聯盟規約やパリ条約の如き特定の条約を「補強」したり、「正当な」戦争、「不当な」戦争の問題に立入ったりすることは、その意図するところではないとするのである（前掲八二五頁）。

さらに又、ブダペスト解釈条項及び右条約案の作成に関与した共同制裁支持に傾く法学者達す

ら、パリ条約を侵犯する戦争又は侵略戦争の法的結果を考察するにあたって、かかる戦争の責任者たる個人の処罰というが如き見解は、毫も表明しなかったことを注意すべきである。この事実は現代的思想如何の問題について、実際上決定的な意義をもつものである。そこでは個人の刑事責任の問題は全く排除せられているのである。いなそれに関する論議すら行われなかったのである。

以上述べたところによって、首席検察官の挙示した証拠によっては、侵略戦争が文明諸国によって承認された慣習によって国際的犯罪となったとの主張は、なんら証明されていないこと明白である。

首席検察官は、自らの結論が国際法学説の承認を受くるものなることの証拠として、ライト卿の「戦争犯罪と国際法」についての論説を引用している（英文記録四一八―四一九頁）。ライト卿はたしかに著名な法律家であり、卿の見解に対しては大いに敬意を払わなければならぬ、しかし卿は世界の立法者ではない。卿は本論文においては、裁判官としてではなく、弁護人として自国の政府の主張を支持する目的で明らかに一方的な議論を展開しているのである。こうした役割を演ずることは無論不当なことではない。しかし卿の強い独断論は国際法に精通した法律家の一致した意見を代表するものではない。国内裁判所たるとも国際裁判所たるとを問わず、この問題に関する国際慣習の在否を判断するについては、国際法学者の一致した意見ある場合にのみこれに依拠

第1部 70

しうべく、各国政府の政策やその公然たる支持者の見解に依存することは許されないのである。「一羽の燕で夏を卜する」ことができないように、卿の独断論によって国際法を卜することはできないのである。

仮にライト卿の立論が一九四八年における全ての現代の国際法学者の承認するものであるとしても（そんなことは絶対にないのであるが）、そして又国際法が今次大戦中において急速に且つわれわれをまごつかせるほどに変化したのだと仮定しても（われわれは全くそれを知らなかったが）、かかる新奇な法規を当法廷の被告人に対して適用することは、明らかに遡及的適用であって、それは不当である。

首席検察官は、侵略戦争が国際犯罪であるとの立論を証明するために、明らかにそれだけでは不充分な各国際条約そのものよりは、むしろ国際慣習をその論拠としているようである。

しかし一定の行為が、国際法上義務又は権利であるとの信念の下にかかる行為をなす明白且つ継続的な習慣が生じた場合にのみ、国際法学者は国際慣習ありとしていることを注意しなければならない（オッペンハイム、国際法第二巻二四頁）。常設国際司法裁判所規程第三十八条は「法トシテ認メラレタル一般慣行ノ証トシテノ国際慣習」を国際法の法源として認めている。右の用語はあまり洗練されておらず、批判の余地を存するものであるが、しかし全ての国を拘束する国際慣習が存在することを証明するためには、法的信念のみならず一般の慣行が立証されなければならぬこ

71　第3　侵略戦争

とは極めて明白である。

国際会議や条約の前文においてなされた漠然たる、そしてしばしば単に修辞的な宣言のみでは不充分である。われわれはすべからく心素（主観的要件）のみならず、体素（客観的要件）即ち各国の一般的な慣行に着目せねばならぬ。然るに各国の実際上の慣行は、侵略戦争が責任ある国家もしくは国家の中の責任ある個人の刑事責任を伴うものであるとの命題を否定するものである。イタリヤのエチオピア侵入は国際聯盟によって侵略戦争とみなされたが、聯盟の科した制裁は経済断交にすぎなかった。ムッソリーニ及びその内閣は勿論のこと、イタリヤに刑罰を科することを提案した者は一人もいなかった。一九三九年のソヴィエットロシアのフィンランド侵入に対してとられた唯一の手段は、単なる除名処分であって侵略戦争の烙印を捺されたが、これに対して侵略戦争の指導的な政治家軍人を処罰することを考えた者は一人もなかったのである。そしてソヴィエット聯邦又はその指導的な政治家軍人を処罰することを考えた者は一人もなかったのである。

最後に、本裁判においては、日本国家の有罪無罪ではなく、個々の被告人の有罪無罪が争点であることを強調しなければならぬ。この両者は全然別個の問題である。首席検察官は、侵略戦争の張本人個人を処罰するための条約が締結せられたことも、又かかる国際慣習が確定されたことも立証していない。これは検察側主張にとって致命的であるとわれわれは考えるのである。

（乙）法的概念としての侵略戦争

第1部 72

侵略戦争は国際犯罪であるとの首席検察官の命題の今一つの重大な難点は、「侵略」とか「侵略者」とかいう辞句が漠然として定義しえないことである。

先ず最初に首席検察官の引用に係るウェブスター辞典の「最初の攻撃」という単純素朴な辞書的定義をとりあげてみよう（英文記録四一九頁）。侵略者というのは最初に発砲した者の謂である。ブリアン曰く、「大砲の一発はまさに大砲の一発だ」そして「それは聞えるししばしばその痕を残す。」まさにその通りである。しかしこれは単に物理的な標準にすぎない。それはなんら道徳的もしくは法的な意味内容を有たないのである。従ってこの定義に従えば、更に「正当な侵略」「不当の侵略」の区別をする必要が生ずるであろう。モーア判事は「国家は戦争を始める場合には、常に外部行為を排除するために戦争を始めると称するが、かかる行為のために戦争をしようとする傾向を強めるであろう。他に援助してくれる武力があるという確信は、必然的に戦争をしようとする傾向を強めるであろう。しかのみならず、侵略を理由付けるため、往々巧みに相手の外部行為を挑撥することのあることは顕著な事実である」と述べている（モーア前掲五六八頁）。ウェブスター辞典が上述の定義として「挑撥せられざる攻撃」を掲げるのはおそらくかかる理由に基くのであろう。

しかし近代国家にして、なんら挑撥によらないで、戦争を始めるような国があるか。日本外の高官のある者は、例えば一九四一年十二月八日の日本の戦闘開始は右の定義に該当するだろうか。休戦前すでにそこには重大な挑撥があり、このことを否定することは歴史の歪曲であると云った。

モーア判事は語を継いでいう、

「……最初に実力行動に出ることが、安全の為の唯一の手段たる場合もある。この原則の重要性は各国もしくは国家的集団があくまで軍事力の優越を維持せんと努める場合ますます増加する。そしてポルトガルは仏、西両国の混合軍隊が一七六二年自国の国境を俳徊していた際、右の原則に基いて行動した」（前掲五六八頁）。

次に同じく首席検察官の引用した別な定義に考察を加えてみよう。

「侵略者とは既に紛争を平和的解決に委ねることに合意したるにかかわらず、かかる誓約に違反して戦争に訴うる国をいう」（英文記録四一九頁）。

これは明らかに不完全な定義である。何故なら仲裁条約が存しない場合においても、侵略戦争の可能性はいくらでもあろうし、又それは仲裁手続に委ねることに合意した国家が、後日自衛のための軍事行動の必要を認むる可能性や、さらに紛争は存せず単に重大な脅威のみ存する場合を無視しているからである。右の定義の下にメキシコ及び南米諸国及び支那においてかつてしばしば行われたように不統一国家において秩序を維持するために軍隊を上陸せしむることは正常といえるかどうか（ハーバート・アーサー・スミス、大ブリテンと国際法、国際法上の問題に関する英国政府の見解を示す公文書集、第一巻（一九三二第二節（不統一国家）一八－三〇頁）。米墨両国共平和的折衝を試みることなく、又平和的折衝が失敗した場合に、仲裁手続を先ず試みないで実力に訴えてはならぬ旨を、明文を

以て規定した一八四八年の米墨条約にかかわらず、一九一四年米軍は突然ヴェラ・クルズを撃ってこれを占領したが、この場合合衆国は侵略国であるかどうか。又英国が一九二五年、国際聯盟規約所定の解決方法をとらずに支那へ軍隊を派遣したことは、侵略行為であるかどうか（この点に関する英国政府の法的弁明についてはスミス前掲二五─二九頁に引用せられたサー・オースティン・チェンバレンの一九二七年二月八日附聯盟事務総長宛覚書参照）。

われわれは首席検察官の引用していない長短さまざまな幾つもの定義づけの試みについてここに詳しく論ずる必要はない。最も長いソ聯政府の詳細をきわめた定義は、明晰であるよりも辞書的であるとして批判された。又最も短い「自国外における軍隊の存在」というフランスの提案はフラー少将をしてこの提案を考案した人は「気狂いか又は『ユーモリスト』にちがいない」といわしめたのである。それらはみな定義しえざるものを定義せんとして失敗したのである。オースティン・チェンバレン卿は、「それ故余はかかる侵略者の定義づけの企てに対し依然として反対するものである。けだしかかる定義は無実を陥れるわなとなり、罪ある者に対しては道標となるから」といった。又ケロッグ国務長官はケロッグ・ブリアン条約が討議された際、不戦条約の範囲を侵略戦争に限定せんとの仏国の提案に対して、一つはまさに右の理由によって、これに反対したのではなかったか（ケロッグ、「合衆国の戦争防止政策」アメリカ国際法雑誌第二十二巻、第二号二五九頁）。

前記「侵略の場合における国家の権利義務に関する条約案」の起草者は「侵略」を単に形式的

に定義するに止めているのは賢明である。草案は次の如く規定する。

「(本条約ニイワユル)

(ハ)『侵略』トハ一国ガ行フ武力行使ニシテ該国ガ受諾スル義務アル方法ニヨリ義務違反ヲ構成スルト決定セラレタルモノヲイウ」

右の条約案は単に将来の法のみを問題としているものである。パリ条約においては締約国は広汎な自衛権を留保し、しかも自衛権に属するかいなかはこれを行使する国のみがこれを判断すべきものとした。締約国は当時他の一国もしくは数国又は国際的機関をして、武力行使が「国策ノ手段トシテ」為されたか自衛権の行使であるかを決定せしめる意志はなかったのである。かかる法の状態を改善せんとするのが、右の条約案の目的の一つであった。国際聯合憲章によれば、安全保障理事会は侵略の問題を決定する権限を与えられた。しかし安全保障理事会において、その決定に全員一致を必要とするとの原則に関し、侵略の問題に関する決定が専ら特定の国家に対する政治的列関係の如何によって左右されるつよい傾向のあることを示すものである。それは又あらゆる戦争を世界戦争化せんとする、世界平和に関する刑事的構想に、本質的な限界あることを物語るものである。

第1部 76

それはともかくとして、国際連合憲章の規定は何が侵略であるかについて何ら精確な知識をわれわれに与えていないのである。

モーア判事は言う。

「侵略者の問題を最初の一瞥で決定しようとすることが、正義を無視したものでないかぎり、事実の公平な調査にたよらねばならぬ。従ってわれわれの目的が不浄なものでないことは経験によって決定的に証明された。しかしそれには時日を要する。国際聯盟総会は日支事変について一九三一年九月二十一日管轄権を取得し、リットン委員会の報告書は、一九三二年九月四日支那の北平で調印せられ、総会は一九三三年一月十七日自己の任命した委員会の報告書を採択した。この手続が実際に費した期間は十七ヶ月に及び、しかもなお最後の結論は未だ得られなかったのである」（モーア前掲、五六八、五六九頁）。

又リットン報告書自身、その最後の章において、次の如く述べている。

「前章を読んだ者にとっては、本紛争の包含する問題は、しばしばいわれるように、簡単でないことが明らかであろう。

いな問題は著しく錯雑して居り、全事実とその歴史背景について精しい知識を有（も）つ者のみが、これら問題について、はっきりした見解を述べる資格を有するのである。

本件は一国が事前に国際聯盟規約所定の和解手続を尽すことなく、他国に宣戦したというごと

77　第3　侵略戦争

き事案ではなく、又一国の国境が隣国の軍隊によって侵されたというような簡単な事件でもない。けだし満洲には、世界中の他の如何なる地にも見出しえないような特徴が多々存するからである」。

又二十世紀前半期の国際組織の実情の下にあっては、全ての良心的な政治家は、必要な自衛行為と認める行為をなす国家の権限の範囲に関して、重大な問題に直面せざるを得なかったのであることを注意しなければならない。

アメリカ、イギリス、フランス、日本の政治家達が、ケロッグ・ブリアン条約に調印するにあたって広汎な留保をなしたのは、かような理由に基くのではなかったか。ヒットラーの行った戦争は、或いは他から攻撃される差迫った危険があると考えていない人達によって開始せられたのであったかも知れない。従って、その侵略性の問題は、ニュルンベルグ裁判所に対して余り困難な問題を提示しなかったのかもしれない。しかし、本裁判の記録は、ドイツの場合と日本の場合とが、他のいろいろの点と共に、この点についても全く異なっており、日本の行った戦争が「侵略的」性質のものであるか、「防衛的」性質のものであるかを、しかく速断することは、一般大衆の偏見に盲従するものであるとか、故意に歴史を歪曲するものであるとの非難は、受けないとしても、少なくとも「独断論」のそしりを免れないことを明白に示してはいないか。いわゆる侵略戦争かどうかは、畢竟見解の問題である。見解の問題について意見を異にするからといって、人

第1部 78

を殺人者とすることは、言葉を以て人を殺すものである。政治家がもっともデリケイトな政治的決定をなすにあたって、犯した過誤の故に、かれらに対して犯罪人とか極悪人とかの悪名を被せることは、著しく正義に反するものといわねばならぬ。

衡平——および自然法——は民事裁判においてはともかく、少なくとも国内的政治と密接な関聯をもつ性質の刑事裁判については、正に「魔物」である。われわれが侵略を定義することをやめ、問題を個々の事件毎に、特定の戦争が侵略的であるか防衛的であるかを裁判所の決定に一任するとすれば、かかる裁判所の判決は、拠るべき何等の基準がないため、必然的に時代の政治的偏見に支配される傾向を伴うであろう。なぜなら「侵略者」という言葉は、「アメリカ帝国主義」とか「赤色帝国主義」とかいう言葉と均しく、国際政治において、全世界から相手方を仲間はずれにさせるために用いられる讒謗の言葉だからである。

以上の考察に鑑み、われわれは首席検察官の説論は、それが現行法でないばかりでなく、又これを法とすべきでないと主張したいのである。首席検察官の提言は事情に通ぜず且つ思慮なき人達を惹きつける力を外見上もっている。しかしわれわれがこれに熟慮を加えるとき、それは実際上不正を招来せざるを得ない法原理である。その適用の結果は、不正が征服せられたという印象ではなく、むしろ「被征服者は不正であることが浮世のおきてだ」といったブルワーの言葉が依然として正しいのだという印象を一般人に与えることとなる。かかる原理を適用することは、将

来の戦勝侵略者が、その被害者の犠牲において利益を収めるための最も危険な先例となるであろう。われわれはかかる法理は、国際法の神聖なる境域から追放せらるべき似而非なる法的原則であると主張したいのである。

第四　国際法条約等を侵犯する戦争

次に首席検察官は、国際法、条約、協定及び保障を侵犯する戦争の計画、準備、開始もしくは遂行に関する「平和に対する罪」なるものを論ずる。そして「この点について、法は充分に確立しておって数世代にわたって実施されている」というのである（英文記録四二〇頁）。

かつてケロッグ条約成立の当時、アメリカ国務長官が自衛行為の制限は無数の先例によって明瞭に確立していると述べたのに対して、国際法学徒は、これ等の無数の先例が何であるか分れば誠に興味深いことであると言ったが、かれらの好奇心は遂にみたされなかった。同様に、いわゆる「平和に対する罪」中この部分は「充分に確立しておって数世代にわたって実施されている」との言葉に接して、国際法学徒はいずれも目をこすって、自らの驚くべき無知を嘆くことであろう。

国際法及び条約が遵守せらるべきことは、被告人をも含めて、いやしくも分別ある者の少しも

疑わないところである。首席検察官は、「これら被告人は、これら（即ち条約の規定）が全く無意味な言葉にすぎぬと主張するであろうか」と問われる（英文記録四二二頁）。しかし国家は国際法や条約を無視してもかまわないと考えるほど、被告人が低劣な道徳の持主であるとするのは著しく不当である。なるほど国家は特定の場合に、国際法及び条約について、解釈上意見を異にすることもある。又時には一国が他国に対して法違反もしくは約束違反を云為することもある。しかしこれは公正な裁判所が決すべく、又かかる裁判所によって始めて判定しうべき事項である。一般国際法の規定もしくは条約の条項の違反があった場合に、何人もそれが違法であることを疑う者はない。しかしある国家の行為を違法であると宣言することと、かかる行為を発起した個人たる指導者を有罪とし、これに極刑を科することとの間には、大きな懸離がある。全ての文明国は契約違反もしくは民事上の不法行為をことごとく犯罪とはしない。前者に対しては賠償が、後者に対しては処罰が、通常の救済方法である。

首席検察官は一例として第三ハーグ条約を引用する（英文記録四二一頁）。われわれは先に述べたことを再びここで繰返そうとはしない。仮に百歩を譲って右条約の違反が、あらゆる場合に違法であるとしても、それは責任者たる個人の犯罪を構成するものではない。

条約を侵犯する「平和に対する罪」の如きは国際法に未知のことである。かかる主張はさきにも述べたように、ヴェルサイユ会議において採用しがたきものとして排斥されたのである。

法はむしろ首席検察官の主張とは反対の方向に確立している。被告人は首席検察官の主張するように（英文記録四二頁）、自己の行為が「犯罪」であることを勿論「知って」はいなかった。なぜなら、何人も被告人が国際法上犯罪人ではないことを「知っていた」からである。

上記「侵略の場合における国家の権利義務に関する条約案」には、本文に対する註釈中に、次の如き章句のあることを注意すべきである。

(1) 合衆国は一九〇七年の第三ハーグ条約の締約国であるが、同条約第一条は、理由を附した開戦宣言の形式又は条件附開戦宣言を含む最後通牒の形式を有する明瞭且つ事前の通告なくして、戦争を開始すべからざることを規定している。合衆国が最後通牒もしくは開戦宣言なくして戦争を開始しても、それは本条約にいわゆる「侵略」を行ったことにはならない。

(2) 日本は一九二二年の華府（ワシントン）九箇国条約の締約国であるが、同条約第一条は、締約国が「支那の主権、独立並びに領土及び行政の保全を尊重」することを規定している。日本が正常の理由なくして支那の領土を征服しこれを併合しても、それは本条約にいわゆる「侵略」を行ったことにはならない。

右の説明は、「侵略」に対して、自己があらかじめ承諾した手続によって侵略国たる決定を与えられた国家に不利益な、特定の法的効果を付与せんとする将来の法を提案した条約案の起草者等も、単に第三ハーグ条約とか、九箇国条約の如き条約に違反したというだけでは、その戦争を右

の意味の「侵略」に該当するものとは認めなかったことを意味する。それは又、制裁派に属する法学者すら、首席検察官の主張するような広汎な原則を確立した法と認めてはおらず、又その提案する将来の体制の下において、右の如き条約違反の責任者たる個人に直ちに刑罰を科することを提案してもいないことを意味する。

第五 殺人の罪

次にわれわれは、被告人が殺人罪を犯したものであるとする、すこぶる奇異な訴追事由に関する首席検察官の釈明に遭遇する。

首席検察官は日本の刑法典を引用して、法律上正常の理由なくして故意に人を殺害することは、文明国においては殺人の罪を構成すると論ずる（英文記録四二五頁）。この議論を承認するについては重大な制限を必要とする。即ち不法なる殺人は、英米においても必ずしも死刑に該当する謀殺罪「マーダー」ではなく、それは単に故殺罪「マンスロータ」として、一ヶ月の拘禁刑又は罰金刑を科するを以て足りるとされている場合もあることである。そして又ある国では殺人罪又は死刑は科せられていないことである。首席検察官は語を次いでいう。「本件においては、死亡はことごとく交戦の結果として生じたものであり、戦争が違法な戦争であったから、本来の違法な行為から、自然に且つ通常生ずる結果も又違法性を帯びる。この法理は日本の法律においても認

められている」。

われわれは首席検察官の論法に承服することをえない。首席検察官は先に「違法な」という曖昧な形容詞を用いる。そこでは「国際法上違法」という意味で用いられる。次に同じ言葉を、「国内法上違法なる行為の結果を一切伴う違法」の意味をももたらして用いるのである。しかし国際法学徒は誰でも、国際法の原理はそうでないことを知っている。戦争が国際法もしくは条約に違反して開始されたとしても、国際法はそうでないことを知っている。戦争状態は発生して、交戦国のいずれの側も戦争法規の保護を受ける権利を取得するということが、国際法学者の一致した見解である。

ローレンス教授は、なんらの挑撥をも受けず、又事前の外交交渉をも行わずして攻撃を加えるという極端な場合を引いて次のように説いている。

「完全な平和裡にあって予め自己の要求を知らしめず、又外交手段で満足をうる努力もしないで他国を攻撃することは、国際的匪賊行為に他ならない。又おそらくそれはこうした取扱いを受けるであろう。」

しかしかれは附加える。

「しかしかかる憎むべき手段によって開かれた事態は、それにもかかわらず戦争であって、双方とも戦争法規に従ってその軍事行動を行うことが期待される」（ローレンス、国際法原理、第七版（一九二五年）パーシー・ウィンフィルド校訂、三三三頁）。

なるほど海賊は全人類に対する犯罪人として処罰される。しかし海賊はいかなる政府からも授権を受けずして行動するものである。政府の授権に基いて行動する正規の軍隊の一員や、戦争開始につき政治的責任を有する者を、単に戦争が違法な方法で開始せられたというだけの理由で殺人犯人として取扱うというが如きはすこぶる奇異な教説である。

しかし国内法ですら通常これらの者を、政治犯人として取扱うのであって、通常の「兇漢」もしくは「殺人犯人」としては取扱わず、国際法も又これを犯罪人引渡しから除外している。

完全に組織された社会である国家内部において、内乱を計画、準備、開始した者は、違法な行為を犯すものであることは明白である。国内法は当然これらの者を大逆罪の犯人として取扱う。

首席検察官はさらに第四ハーグ条約の各規定を引用する（英文記録四二五—四二七頁）。

そのうち同条約第二十三条はいう。

「特別ノ条約ヲ以テ定メタル禁止ノ外特ニ禁止スルモノ左ノ如シ。

（ロ）敵国又ハ敵軍ニ属スル者ヲ背信ノ行為ヲ以テ殺傷スルコト」

首席検察官は右の規定から次のような結論を引き出すのである。

「従って、日本と平和関係にあった他国に対するかかる攻撃中に人を殺害した行為は殺人罪となるに至ったのである」（英文記録四二七頁）。

しかし先にかかげたウェストレイクやベロットの如き著名な権威の意見に鑑みても、重大な挑撥を受け、長期にわたる外交交渉の努力を重ねた末、一国が他国に対して突然戦略的攻撃を加えた場合に、しかも相手方において事態が極めて緊迫し、戦闘の開始を予期し、且つこれに備えていたような場合に、かかる攻撃が第三ハーグ条約によって違法とされ、且つ又「最も悪質な背信行為」とよばれうるかはすこぶる疑問である。しかし首席検察官の結論は右の規定から直に演繹されえない。何故なら「背信の行為を以て殺傷する」との辞句は明らかに、「既に行われつつある戦争中」にという意味である。然らざれば右にかかげた法文中の「敵国又は敵軍」なるものは存し得ないであろう。第三ハーグ条約の規定する、宣戦を伴わない戦闘開始に関する行為のごときは、もとより首席検察官の引用する右規定にふくまれるものではない。

「兎の手品」の比喩は今日の流行であるようだ。イギリス国会において、国内輸送機関の国有に関する政府の計劃を批判するにあたって、レディング卿は、政府は比較的短い期間に「国有という帽子の中から社会主義の兎を」とり出す事にすこぶる堪能であることを示したといった。又全印議会においてアチャリア・クリバラニ氏は、イギリス側の提案した憲法草案を批判して、ヒンドスタン語でイギリス人は都合の好いときに、いつでも帽子の中から兎や卵をとり出すといった。私もこの世界的流行を真似て、検察側の議論を特徴づける精巧に編み上げられた詭弁の網を

一気に解消せしむる為、兎の手品にたとえる事を許されたい。手品師は通常の帽子を借りてきて、これを、テーブルの上に置く。そしてこれに向って何やら呪文を唱える。さて帽子をとりあげる。するとテーブルには小さな兎が、うようよ走りまわっている。帽子の中にもともと兎がいたのではない。手品師が兎をその中に入れたまでである。

検察側の議論はまさにこれと同様である。検察側は普通の帽子、即ち国家国民を拘束する国際法という綺麗なそして上品な周知のシルクハットを持ってきて、これをテーブルの上に載せる。そしてこれに向って呪文を唱える。その呪文の中から「違法」とか「犯罪的」とか「殺人」とかいう言葉が次第に大きく響いてくる。そして帽子をとりあげると、たちまち裁判所の中には、国内法のここかしこから借りて来た新生の国際法理論が現れて、観衆を驚かせる。どこからそれらをもってきたかは重要ではない。もともとそれらの理論が、シルクハットの中になかったことだけは確かである。検察側に於てそれらを、シルクハットの中に入れたのである。

89　第5 殺人の罪

第六 「通例の」戦争犯罪

「通例の」戦争犯罪及び「通例の」戦争犯罪の一部をなすかぎりにおいての「人道に対する罪」については、国際法の確定法規に従って有罪が立証された場合に、正当に構成された裁判所においてこれを処罰しえ、又処罰さるべきであることはわれわれもこれを認める。

由来戦争は非人道的なものである。人間がこれに与えた一切の理由づけや弁解を除去して「汝殺すなかれ」というキリストの示された最高道徳から判断すれば、戦争は防衛的であると侵略的であるとにかかわらず、必然的に殺人行為を伴う制度と認むべきである。戦争に伴う血なまぐさい軍事行動が、これに関与する者を残忍たらしめ、そのため敵国の戦闘員のみならず、一般市民に対しても、特に彼等に敵対行動の嫌疑ある場合には、惨虐行為が加えられる傾向のあることは、戦史の汎く示すところである。これら惨虐行為は戦争に必然的に随伴する誠に悲しむべき現象である。しかし、罪ある者に対し刑罰を科すべきことは、国際法の命ずるところであり、且つ又

かかる犯罪の遂行者に対して峻厳な裁判が為さるべきことは、日本政府が、その名誉にかけて履行を誓約した降服文書の条項によって疑いない。戦争の法規慣例に違反して惨虐行為を現実に犯し又はこれを命令した者を、正当に構成された裁判所において処罰することは然るべきことである。但しヴェルサイユ会議に於ける十五人委員会においてアメリカ代表委員は「消極的犯罪」、すなわち「通例の」戦争犯罪においては他人の死亡を防止しなかったことに対する責任の理論を全面的に否定して居ること、又英国法においては他人の死亡を防止しなかったことにつき過失あってもそれは死刑に該当しない故殺（マンスロータ）にすぎない点について裁判所の注意を促して置きたいのである。

おそらく首席検察官は、ドイツの場合と日本の場合とが同じであるとの安易な仮定に基いて、様々の戦場において違反者達が犯したかもしれない全ての交戦法規違反の行為について、被告人等からの命令があったものと想像しているのであろう。しかしかかる「上からの命令」はこれを証明することができない。そこで首席検察官は、その「上からの命令」なる訴追事由につき「推定」を、しかも「推定」のみを根拠としているのである。けだしその結論にいう。

「これらの殺人行為は、以上述べたる如き極めて広範囲な地域において極めて長期間にわたり、又極めて相類似せる型に則って行われ、且つ幾つもの抗議が中立国によって確実に伝達せられた後においても、多数の犯行が繰返された点からみて、われわれは上からの、すなわち被告席にある被告人の積極的命令のみが、かかる犯行を可能ならしめたものと推定せざるを得ない」（英文記

録四二九頁)。

しかし被告人が、いかなる段階の地位において、命令を発したかが明らかにされねばならない。段階の如何を問わず、もしくは一定段階以上の者はすべて、有罪なりとの無差別的推定を為すこととは、正義の本質に背馳し、全世界の良心の反撥を招くことであろう。

検察側の主張する惨虐行為その他の違反行為が、かりに同一の行為類型をとっているとしても、それは当然にかかる推定を理由づけるものではない。かかる型は国民性もしくは民族性の反映であるにすぎぬのかもしれない。犯罪は芸術上の作品とひとしく、種族の慣習を反映する一定の特徴を示すのである。又、地理的、経済的及び軍事的条件が相互に類似していることも、ある程度かかる検察側の主張する惨虐行為その他の違法行為の「類型性」を説明することもあろう。本件のごとき重大事件においては、上からの命令なる推定、並びに何人からそれを発したかの点は、合理的疑問の余地を残さぬ程度に立証せられなければならない。

惨虐行為に関する証人の証言をきいてみると、これらの行為が同一の類型をとっておらず、むしろ証人の国籍に応じて、さまざまな型を示しているとの印象が強い。かかる事実は「上からの命令」を否定するのみならず、全然別個の事実を物語るものである。

第七　個人責任

首席検察官はさらに進んで、被告人の個人責任について論ずる。首席検察官は、国際法もしくは国際条約を侵犯する戦争の計劃、準備、開始、遂行が個人責任を伴うとのテーゼを理由づけるために、かのサボタージュ事件であるエクス・パーティ・クイリン事件に対する合衆国最高裁判所の判決を引用する（英文記録四三一頁以下）。しかしエクス・パーティ・クイリン事件は、合衆国議会がその制定する法律において、戦争法規違反の全ての犯罪を細目にわたって不動の形式に法文化することの代りに、裁判所の承認し適用しうる範囲で軍事裁判所の適用すべき普通法の体系を採用することが可能であるかどうかに関する事件なのである。これは、違憲でないかぎり、その欲するような形式によって立法を行いうる聯邦議会の法律の解釈の問題であるにすぎない。聯邦議会の意志に対して最高裁判所が下した解釈は、他国民を拘束することにはならないのである。さらに又従来の慣習によって、軍事裁判により個人を処罰してきたような、既に充分確立した

交戦に関する普通法を、援用の方法によって採用することと、国際法及び条約を侵犯する戦争の計画、準備、開始、遂行は当該国家の責任のみでなく、当該国家のために行動した個人の刑事責任を伴うものであるという、全く革命的な理論を採用することとの間には、大きな隔りがある。かかる刑事責任は、国際法学者及び国際慣習によってはっきりと否定されており、又いずれの国の責任ある政治家でも、国際条約を商議する際、右の如き原則に考え及んだ者は絶対にないのである。もしも右の如き解釈が商議の際提案されたとしたら、それらの条約は成立に至らなかったことであろう。例えばケロッグ条約の当事国は、これに違反して戦争をなした場合、かれらが殺人罪を犯したことになるという意思を有したと考えることができるのであるか。国際聯合憲章のうちにもかくの如き理論を見出すことはできない。もしもかかる趣旨の規定が置かれたとしたら、同憲章自体が採択さるるに至らなかったことであろう。

次に個人責任に関する国際法の原則を一瞥しよう。裁判所も熟知されるように、現代の独立国家から成る社会を規律する、すこぶる柔軟且つ非侵略的な法体系である。現代の国際法は当然に我々の知っている国際団体が世界政府にまで発展することともなれば、消滅し、世界法がこれに代ることとなるであろう。ルネッサンス以降のヨーロッパ社会の現実を母胎として生れたかような国際法の本質的性格は、その後数世紀にわたる発展と、他の大陸への地域的拡大にもかかわらず、今日においても依然として変ってはいない。それ故国際法を強行す

るものは世界政府ではなく、各自の領土に対して実効的統制を行い、自己の主権に服する全ての者の行為、及び自己自身の行為に対して責任を負う能力を有する、組織ある国家なのである。国際的責任に関する原理は、この極めて特殊な法体系における右のような根本的事実を充分に認識して、初めて真の姿においてこれを把握しうるのである。

義務と責任は国家及び国民に対してのみ課せられるものであり、個人に対しては課せられないというのが、国際法の一般原則である。国際的義務の違反は、違反国家の団体責任を生ぜしめる。戦争や報復の如き国際法の制裁は、国際法違反の行為を行った個人に対してではなく、該国家の構成員全体に科せられることと同様に、刑事及び民事上の制裁の対象は、あたかもニューヨーク州のある市民が犯した叛逆行為に対する処罰が、正義の要求として同州の人民全体に対してのみ科せられ、無辜の市民に及ぶことはないと同様に、刑事及び民事上の制裁の対象は、罪ある当該市民に対してのみ科せられ、無辜の市民に及ぶことはないであろう。しかし今日の国際社会を支配する法体制における責任の法理は、かくの如きものではないのである。

尤も、戦時及び平時における国際交通の実際的経験から、個人責任の課せられる若干の例外（それらが真に例外とみるべきか否かは別として）が認められるようになった。最も古い例外は海賊行為の場合である。近代国際法の成立以前から存在する国際慣習によって海賊は法の保護を受けない者、「人類全体の敵」とみなされた。国際法上海賊はその母国の保護を受ける権利を失い、

95　第 7　個人責任

全ての国は自由にこれを捕えて処罰することができる。この例外的規則によって、その海賊の属する国は、これを保護するために、公海自由の原則を援用することができず、他方他の国が海賊行為を働いた人又は船の所属する国に対して、封鎖破りと戦時禁制品の運搬である。国際法は封鎖破り及び禁制品運搬者に対して、積荷の没収という形で、特別の制裁を認めており、捕獲国の捕獲審判所によってこれを強制しうることになっている。第三の例外は、交戦法規の違反、即ちいわゆる「戦争犯罪」であり、この場合には一国の正規の軍隊に属しない個人に対して、その国の軍事裁判所は略式手続によってこれを処罰しうるのである。

国家は自己の行為、換言すれば個人が政府の命令に従い又はその承認をえてなした国家行為に対し団体責任を負う。ある行為が国家行為であるというのは、問題の行為がその国家に帰属せしめられ、実際にこれを為した個人に帰属せしめられないことを意味する。かような行為によって害を受けた国家は、右の国家に対してのみ国際不法行為上の責を問うことができ、行為者個人の責任を問うことは、充分に確立した国際法の原則である。有名なマクレオド事件においては、一八三七年にカロライン号を捕獲するため、合衆国に派遣せられたイギリス軍隊に所属していたマクレオドが、一八四〇年にニューヨーク州において捕えられ、アメリカ市民を殺害した廉によって起訴された。国務長官ウェブスター

氏は、一八四一年三月十五日附で法務長官クリッテンデン氏に対して次のような書面を送った。

「現在余の謂わんと欲するところは次のことに尽きる。即ち『カロライン』号攻撃は国家の行為であるから、もし合衆国政府が右の行為並びに自己の義務に関して下す判断により適切と考える場合には、報復又は戦争に訴えることを正当づけるものである。しかしこの場合提起される問題は、公的な政治的な問題、即ち独立国相互間の問題であって、これに関係した個人を逮捕し、恰も国内法違反に対すると同様に、通常裁判所の審判に付することは許されないのである。当政府が主張しているように、カロライン号攻撃が国家の行為として不当であるとすれば、これに対する法的救済は国際法の規定によって認められた救済にこれを求むべきである」(モーア、国際法先例集第二巻第百七十九節)。

「国際法の漸進的法典化に関する専門家委員会」が、一九二七年三月ないし四月の第三会期において採択した報告書は、次のように述べている。

「裁判所が外国政府の主権行為に関して裁判権を行使しないという法則は、被告人が……たとえ訴訟当時には官吏たるの資格を保持していなくても……かかる資格においてなした行為……又は主権国家から与えられた権限に基いてなした行為……について個人として訴追せられる場合にも適用せらるべきである。」(国際聯盟公表、法律部、一九二七年、米国国際法雑誌一九二八年第二十二巻補遺一二五頁)

97　第7　個人責任

カルル・ストルップ編纂の国際法外交辞典（一九二五年）第二巻二頁にも次のように述べられている。

「国家はその全ての国家機関に対して責任を負うが、右機関は、国家機関としての資格において行動するかぎり、自らは責任を負わない」。

しかしこの国際法の根本法則にも、周知の例外が若干存在する。例えば間諜や戦時叛逆は明らかにこれに該当するものであって、この場合にはたとえ敵国政府の命令に基く行為であっても「戦争犯罪」としてこれを処罰するのである。しかしかような個人無責任の一般的法則に対する例外は、慣習又は合意に基く国際法の特別の法則によって明白に立証されなければならないのである。

国家の行為又は私的行為に対する個人責任は国際条約によってこれを規定することができる。奴隷売買、海底電線切断、遠海海豹捕獲の如きがそれである。個人無責任の一般原則に対するような例外を樹立せんとした（結局流産に終ったが）比較的最近の試みは、一九二二年二月六日ワシントンにおいて締結せられた潜水艦使用に関する条約である。同条約第三条は、「商船の攻撃、捕獲、もしくは破壊に関する本条約の規則を侵犯したる国家公務員は、上官の命令に基きたるといなとを問わず戦争法規を侵犯したるものとみなし、海賊行為の場合と同じく裁判処罰を受くべく、その現存する地域を管轄する国家の軍事又は非軍事官憲の裁判に付することを得」と規

定した。

各国が国際法の基本原則に対する右のような例外を認めることを非常に渋り、国際協定によってかような例外を定めるにあたっては、極めて細心の注意を払っていることから判断して、第三ハーグ条約もケロッグ・ブリアン条約も、首席検察官の主張するごとく、国家の行為に対する個人責任をとり入れることによって、右の一般原則に対する例外を認めんとするものでなかったとは、極めて明白であるといわねばならぬ。締約国の真の意思がかような例外を認めんとするにあったのであれば、条約中にそれを明示したはずである。

上述せる如き国際責任の制度は、現代の国際社会の現実に基礎づけられたものであり、それは、国際社会の現実にてらして実際上正義に合致する機能を営みうる唯一の制度である。国内法から得た概念にとらわれた頭で、又世界国家が現在の事実であるとか、直ぐにもこれを樹立しうるとかいうような不当な仮定の上に立って、この責任制度を批判する如きは誠に愚かである。国内法にも精通し、且つ人類の福祉に対する真摯な胞負を抱いた人たちが、現在の制度を樹立したのである。この制度の下に「国家の行為」ということが大きく浮かび出ているとすれば、それは主権国家を完全に認めることによって、平和と秩序が維持せられている国際社会の現実の反映に他ならず、世界各国は未だかような国際社会に代るべき世界国家の主権と世界法の支配に対する用意を有するものとは認められないのである。国家の官吏が他日異国の裁判官によって「戦争犯罪

人」と宣言せられることを免れるために、自国政府の命令が果して国際法、条約、協定、保障に違反しないかどうかを、一々自ら決定しなければならぬ如き状態の下において、国家の政治的経済的ないし軍事的任務が遂行されうると考える如きは、国際社会の現実に対して盲目なるものである。

他日戦勝国によって侵略戦争ないしは国際協定を侵犯する戦争と宣言されるおそれのある戦争の共同謀議、準備、開始及び遂行を、その国の政治家及び軍人の個人責任を伴う犯罪であるとする如き条約が提案された場合に、少なくとも右の事実は、多くの国をして容易に調印を肯ぜしめない有力な理由の一つとなるであろう。いずれにせよ、国際協定によって特にかかる刑事責任の存在を明白に規定せざる限り、国際法上個人責任を伴う平和に対する罪なるものが存在しないことは明らかである。

ケロッグ・ブリアン条約やハーグ及びジュネーヴ条約のような条約は、政治家に対して刑罰を課する趣旨であったと考えることを得ない他の一つの理由がある。それは国際関係は相互的に極めて密接に結びつけられているために、関係当事国と他の国家との関係に重大な危険をもたらさずには、裁判所における真の事態は明らかにしえないことである。又独立主権国家から証拠を得ることは必ずしも出来ることではなく、又全然不能なこともしばしばある。何故ならこれらの国家は、その国家に迷惑を及ぼすような秘密な事項を公表することを好まず、これが提出

を拒否するからである。右のような考慮は、国内の刑事訴追に於ける弁護側の妨害となることは極めて稀なのである。

右のような事態は、一国の政治を行う政治家と、政治とは何ら関係のない一般人との責任について重要な差異を来たすのである。国際法及び国際条約の署名国が、この重要なる事実を了解して居ったことは明白である。世界を動乱に導くような証拠を提出せしむることとなしには、政治家に対する公平な裁判は出来ないのである。それは政治家に対する非民主的な優遇ではない。又それは旧式な法人格擬制を国家に適用する結果ではない。政治家の行動は右のような非常なる危険なしには弁護ができないという真理の正しき認識にそれはもとづくのである。各国が危険に曝されることを欲しないが故に、政治家の行動は裁判所に於て適当に弁護しえないのである。それが外国関係に依存する弾劾事件とか、ビルス・オブ・アテインダーとかビルス・オブ・ペインズ・エンド・ペナルティズが、一致して嫌われ排斥された理由の一つである。被告は外国の官庁から証拠を得ることの不可能なことと、外国との関係を攪乱することの危険によって、手をしばられることとなるのである。パナマ収賄事件、ドレイファス事件、カイヨー事件等は、国際政治的要素が間接に関係して居る場合に、真の公平な裁判が困難であると云う真理の、極めて稀薄な反映にすぎない。政治家免責の原理は、単純な伝統ではない。それは必要に基くものである。国際法たると国内法たるとを問わず、凡そ法は立法によって発達すると共に、判例によっても

発達するとする点については、われわれは心から首席検察官の意見に賛同するものである。しかし、裁判判例による法の発展は、ある法体系の根本精神と、その根本原理の枠の中で行われるものであり、又行わるべきである。われわれが欧米における法の歴史を一瞥するならば、裁判所がその適用する法を発展せしむるに当って、いかに注意深く且つ控え目であったかが分かるであろう。裁判所の仕事は、恰も大自然の運行と同じく、徐々に人目につかない程度に行われてきたのである。決して突然に又乱暴に行われたのではない。かるが故にかれらの業蹟は恒久性をもつのである。裁判所は確定した法を施行するために存在する。現行法を適用すべきである。そしてもしも裁判所が法を変革しようと試みるなら、それは正に立法府の権能を僭奪するものである。

なるほど裁判所が往々法の仮面の下に、実質的に立法する場合もある。しかしかかる司法的立法は、試験的に且つ細心な注意を払って、ある場合にはこれを包摂し、他の場合にはこれを排除するやり方で、徐々に行われるのであって、その執行する特定の法体系中の基本原則を覆すというような方法で、それは行われるのではない。ホームズ判事は、南太平洋会社対ジェンセン事件（合衆国最高裁判所判例集一九一七年、二四四巻二〇五頁二二一頁）において次の如く述べる。

「私は裁判官が立法することを認めるに躊躇するものではない。しかし裁判官は法の間隙を埋めるために立法しうるにすぎない。その機能は大塊から粒子への微細化作用に限定されている。

第1部　102

コンモン・ローの裁判官は、自分はコンダレイションの理論は無意味な歴史的遺物にすぎないと考えるから、自分の法廷ではこれを認めないと言うことはできない。又限定管轄権を持つ海事裁判官も同様に、自分は主人と雇人に関するコンモン・ローの法則は立派な法則だと考えるから、本裁判所においてもそっくりこれをとり入れたいと思う、ということは許されない」。

往々国際法に新しい犯罪を導入しようとする現在の試みと、中世イギリス法における新犯罪の導入とが類推的に論ぜられる。しかしかかる類推は皮相的で、これに基く理由づけは明らかに誤謬である。中世のイギリス刑法は、社会生活のうちに浸潤していた唯一つの信仰——即ちローマ教会の——によって緊密に統一せられた小さな社会を規律するためのものであった。これに反して、国際法の規律対象たる社会は、さまざまの文化と相異なる社会観、政治観をもつ多数の主権国家から成る全世界的社会である。中世のイギリスにおいては、裁判官は多くカトリックの僧侶であり、刑事問題に属するかれらの判断は、中世的正義観念を反映するものであった。然るに当法廷における著名な裁判官各位は、異なった宗教、社会、政治観念と、異なった法伝統をもつ諸国家を代表している。中世のイギリスにおいて王座裁判所がとり入れた新しい犯罪は、いずれもキリスト教の道徳律によって極悪の烙印を押されたものであり、又そのとり入れ方も既存の、裁判所によって運用されていた法体系を、漸次的に拡張する方法によるものであった。従って裁判所がこれを犯罪として取扱い、適当な罰を科しても、それは何人に対しても驚愕や不満を与える

103　第7　個人責任

ものではなかった。全然新奇な犯罪を認めたといって非難する声は聞かれなかった。被告人自身すら、全然新奇な事項について審判せられ断罪せられるものであるとの不平を述べる者はなかった。かれらは爾余の人々と同様、自己が犯罪者であると感じていたのである。然るに本裁判において新しく犯罪とせられるものは、その当否につき意見の分れうる政治的行為であり、検察側の提議する原理は確立せる原理に全然相反し、従来の概念及び慣行からはまことに驚くべきものがある。そして全世界の学者達は、かような手続に、これを承認しがたいものであり、それは人をその意見の故に処罰し、政治的経綸の問題を、法の一方的な宣言によって決定せんとする試みに他ならぬと宣言しているのである。これらの大法律家の宣言の当否は、ここに問題ではない。少なくともかような宣言がなされていて、これを無視しえないことは事実である。これによって一派の論者の主張する類推論は、完全に解消せざるをえないのである。

革命的な法の変更は、全関係者をして改正提案に対する賛否の論議を尽さしめて、初めて妥当に行いうるのである。かくの如き法の変更は、これを正常とする証拠も又これを非とする証拠も著しく制限され、結局当事者の弁護人においてたまたま利用しうる施設と知識とに依存するところ大ならざるをえない裁判所の、到底よくするところではないのである。もしも国際法になんらかの根本的変更が必要であるならば、国際聯合のような国際団体が、世界立法府にまで発展するとすれば、こうした団体がこれを行うに適した機関である。それはたしかに、国際司法裁判所や、

第1部　104

又は国内的もしくは国際的軍事裁判所の仕事ではないのである。

首席検察官は、破壊技術の発達の程度に照らして、世界は末梢的な法律論を待ってはいられないという（英文記録四六一頁）。しかし法は末梢事ではない。幾世紀にわたって経験を重ね理性の吟味を経て築きあげられた国際法の規則と原理は、しかく無雑作に「法的瑣末事」として捨て去るべきではない。おそらく首席検察官は、この点において、大戦争の後自らが歴史における中枢的な位置を占めているとの自負心をいだく世代を特徴づける、あの新秩序への熱情に捉われているのであろう。しかしわれわれは、「新秩序」とか「非常時」とかいう観念が、時の権力者が適当な法の手続を無視するための周知の手段であることに留意しなければならない。もし首席検察官の主張する如く、人類の惨禍を未然に防ぐために、世界各国間の交通を規律する新しい原理を樹立しなければならぬという意識が、真に各国民の間に遍く存するものとすれば、かような目的のための方法として既に確立している多辺的条約締結の方法によって、容易にこれを実現することができるであろう。われわれはこの際、一六四一年ティグビー卿がストラフォドのビル・オブ・アテインダーに際してなした有名な金言について、裁判所の記憶を喚起しておくことは不適当ではあるまい。

「ビル・オブ・アテインダーによる議会の権限には、人間の生死を左右する二重の権力が含まれている。その一つは司法権であり他の一つは立法権である。前者の規矩は何が法的に正義であ

るかであり、後者の準拠は分別と政策の見地から見て、何が全体の利益と生存に適しているかである。しかし判決においては両者を混同してはならない。われわれは適法性の欠缺をば良心の問題によって補充してはならない、又政策的な考慮からすれば妥当を欠くことを、法的正義の口実を以て弥縫してはならない」。

或いは既にこれらの政府高官に個人責任を負わしめる原則を、国際法に導入すべき「時機に立至」っているのかもしれない。しかし征服者の一方的見解であるかの如き外観を呈するやり方で、かかる原則を国際法に導入することは、その真価について世人の疑惑と不信を招かずにはおかないので、絶対にこれを避けなければならない。かかるやり方によって反ってこの原則の確立そのものが、何世紀も遅れることになるであろう。

首席検察官は、裁判所に対して国際法の体系に根本的変革を加うべきことを要請した後、再び例の共同謀議罪の理論を恰もそれが既に国際法の一制度をなすものとして援用し、裁判所条例の犯罪規定についてその論議を結ぶのである。かくして首席検察官は極めて妥当な個別刑事責任の原理を無視して、「日本政府において有力な地位を占めてこれを動かしその地位により違法な戦争を共謀し且つ計画、準備、開始、遂行したこれらの人は、かかる行為の結果生じた全ての犯罪行為の一つ一つにつき責任を有する」と言明する（英文記録四三三Ｂ至四三四頁）。首席検察官は又、若干の法域において認められている、犯罪の計画に関与した者は全てみな、その遂行中共謀者が

犯罪を犯した場合、自らかかる犯罪の事実を知ると否とにかかわらず、又かかる行為を禁じたと否とにかかわらず、これらの犯罪の全部につき、又各々他者の行為について責任を負うという、別個の国内刑法の理論と同種のこの法理についても又、数人の者が違法な計画の実行に当った場合、共同謀議罪の法理を引用し、これによってその立論を強めようとする（英文記録四三四頁）。

これがいかに些細なものであっても、かかる計画の遂行中その一人が犯した犯罪が自己の与えた注意に反して行われたにせよ、該犯罪の事実を知らず、又たとえ自らは右犯罪の大小如何にかかわらず、罪の一部をなすものでないとして排斥されんことを我々は裁判所に対して要請する。この理論によれば、例えば猟に出かけた一団の人々が、違法に猟を行う際、そのうちの一人が、これを妨害した番人を故意に殺害した場合に、他者は全てかかる行為を現実に知らなくとも、又これを知ったならばこれを防止するために万全を尽したであろう場合でも、殺人の罪を犯したものとするのである。純歴史的な理由に基いたかくの如き特殊且つ不当な理論が、世界の全ての国民によって法として受けとられることは、常識に対する冒瀆である。

首席検察官は唯一つの点、即ち公の地位は被告人を保護せずとの理論を除いては、本裁判所条例中に規定された法は、条例起草の当時でなく、被告人の行為当時の国際法の規則と原則であったと主張する。この立論によれば、事後立法の問題は本件では問題にならず、被告人を処罰する

107　第 7 個人責任

ことは不当ではないというのである（英文記録四七四頁）。

この事後法の問題についても又、我々は全面的に首席検察官の主張を争いこの点についての裁判所の判断を仰ぎたい。ここに具体的な例を挙げて例証しよう。仮に本裁判所の被告人の一人が米国に送られ、米国大統領が単独又は他国と共同して創設した軍事裁判所によって、共同謀議ないし侵略戦争の罪を問われたとしよう。そして禁錮刑の言渡しを受け、聯邦裁判所判事に対してヘイビアス・コーパス令状を求めたとしよう。この場合首席検察官は、被告人の聯邦憲法第一節第九条の事後法禁止の規定に反して拘禁せられているとの理由で、釈放を受ける権利はないと真面目に主張されるのであるか。カルダー対ブル事件におけるチェイス判事の古典的な解釈によれば、右の場合は明らかに前記の条項に該当するものではないか。右の解釈による事後法は次の如くである。「第一法制定前にされた行為で、行為の当時無罪であった行為を犯罪とし、かかる行為を処罰する法律。第二犯罪を重くし行為の当時より重大なものとする法律。第三刑罰を変更し、行為の当時犯罪に対して法の定めた刑罰よりも重い罰を科する法律。第四犯人を処罰するため、行為の当時必要とした証言を減少又は変更する法律。証拠規則を変更して犯罪を行った当時必要とした証言を減少又は変更する法律」。

事後処罰禁止の法則は、アメリカ法独特の技術的規則ではない。華府（ワシントン）においても東京においても、火は燃え水は流れる。それと均しく、右法則に基く法則である。それは自然的、普遍的正義に基く法則である。華府（ワシントン）においても東京においても、火は燃え水は流れる。それと均しく、右法則の侵犯は、洋の東西を問わず均しく不正且つ圧制的であると感ぜられるのである。我々はここに

繰返して、「通例の」戦争犯罪の場合を除き、本裁判所条例の犯罪規定は明白に且つ全部事後の法であり、従ってポツダム宣言における「峻厳なる裁判」ではなく、法による裁判の正反対であるヒットラー式の漠然とした「一般感情」による裁判として、排斥せられていることを主張するものである。

第八　検察側の提唱する新国際法理論

首席検察官は、侵略戦争及び国際法並びに条約を侵犯する戦争は、国際犯罪であって、かかる犯罪に対しては、当該国家のために行動した個人に対して、通常の凶漢の受くべき屈辱的処罰を科しうるものであるとする。この新奇な、そして首席検察官によればきわめて有益な、国際法の原則をば歴史的新判決によって創造することを裁判所に対して、つよく要請する（英文記録三八九頁）。

国際法に至大の影響を及ぼすべきかくのごとき提言を受け入れる前に、われわれはそれを単なる空想的なそして無思慮な道徳感情の表現としてではなく、又国家的ないし世界国家的背景の下にではなく、主権国家から構成された複雑な国際社会の背景の下において、現実に作用する法原理としてこれを吟味せねばならぬ。

戦争によってかきたてられた一般民衆の感情が未だ沈静せず、かつ革命的な昂奮につつまれた

時期にあって、ある国際的団体が全員一致でかようなな提案を採用することは可能なことである。しかし大国たると小国たるとを問わず全ての国家が、それが実際的意味合いを充分認識してこれを承認しうるような条約の形に、この提案が、技術的に構成されうるかは大いに疑問であるとせねばならない。

戦時にあって「侵略者」という言葉は交戦国の双方が独善的に又世界輿論の同情をひくがために、相手方に対してあびせかける形容詞であることは、かくれもない事実である。そして交戦国の一方が敗れた場合、果して戦勝国自ら自国が侵略者たることを容認して、その責任者たる政治家及び軍人を処罰するであろうか。人間性に根本的な変革がもたらされないかぎり、侵略者、又は国際法及び条約の侵犯者であると宣告されるのは、常に戦敗国である。戦敗国は遠い昔から、領土の喪失と賠償の支払いによって処罰されている。そして戦敗国の政治家や軍人は、威信の失墜、社会的生命の喪失、また愛する祖国が廃墟となるのを目撃する苦痛によって充分に罰を受けるのである。これらの罰に加えてさらに、戦争の終了を特徴づけた旧怨の永久的な忘却、赦免、宥恕という高い精神からはるかに後退することを意味するものである。そしてそれはかえって、平和的国際交通に対して攪乱的要素を導入することとなるであろう。もしも各国民が別々の個体として存続するとするなら、かれらは他国民から、その額の上に捺された犯罪の烙印を永久に想記させられることを喜ばないであろう。他

111　第8　検察側の提唱する新国際法理論

国民も完全無欠ではなく、利害干係や偏見から超然としていたとは考えないからである。戦争は全部これを違法としいやしくも戦争の準備を為した者は、戦争が自衛的であると侵略的であるとを問わず、国際法及び国内法によって処罰さるべきものとすることは、ケロッグ・ブリアン条約のごとき制限的そして曖昧な約束よりも正常且つ合理的であり、又世界平和を促進するゆえんでもあろう。しかし違法となるべき「戦争」なる名詞にて「侵略的」とか「国際法もしくは条約に違反する」とかの形容詞をつけ加えることは、抽象的にはすこぶる合理的にみえるが、実際的には「無辜に対しては罠、罪ある者に対しては道標」として作用する重大な危険をそのうちに蔵するものである。

われわれは又、かかる根本的変革が国際法及び国内法に対して重大な影響を与えるものであることを認識しなければならぬ。一九三七年二月二十日に東京大学でなされた「法の将来」と題する講演において、ロスコー・パウンド教授は、規範体系の中における一つの変化は、他の多くの点にも影響を及ぼし、これによって経済秩序の安定を大いに傷つけることがあることを指摘して、熱心ではあるが軽卒な法律改革論者に対し重大な警戒をなしたのである。教授は、仕事を行う場所についての被傭者の既得権を主張する「坐り込みストライキ」についての新奇な理論が場所の所有者がもはやそこで働く者の抑制と選択とができなくなるために、従来一般的安定を維持してきた傭主の刑事的民事的責任に関する多年固定した二つのコンモン・ロー上の原則の基礎を動揺

第1部　112

せしむることになることを指摘したのである。アメリカ法学界のこの重鎮は、国内法における比較的小さな変化によって生ずる影響に言及したにとどまった。しかし、戦争を計劃し、準備し、開始し、遂行した者を含む、戦争の張本人の刑事責任を認め、且つこれに加えて英米の共同謀議の法理の応用によってさらにこれを拡大する如き変革が、国際的分野にとり入れられるなら、それは国際法の他の部分に重大な影響を及ぼすばかりでなく、国内法に対しても予期しえざる影響をもたらすであろう。なぜならそれは国際法の多くの原理がよって立つ土台そのものを動揺せしむる変革であり、政治上経済上軍事上の国務遂行に対して、紛糾と混乱をもたらすからである。

文明諸国が数世紀にわたって辛苦を重ねつつ発展せしめた国際法の基本原理を、一時的な行政府の政策的要請によって変更するのは誠に危険な企てである。イギリスの枢密院司法委員会が、指導的判決であるザモーラ事件において「枢密院における王、いな凡そ行政府が、わが国における裁判所の適用すべき法を定め、又はこれを変更する権限をもつというような観念は、わが国憲法の原理と調和しない」と王に進言したことは、きわめて賢明且つ達識な態度ではなかったか（「ロー・リポーツ」一九一六年上告部第二巻七七頁）。ドイツのカール・シュミット一派の学者が、ドイツ第三帝国の政治的要請に合致するような新新国際法を創造せんとしたことは周知の事実である。かかる企図は法を政治に従属せしめんとするものであって、光輝ある法曹の伝統にふさわしからずとして一般に蔑視されたのである。かかる企図は、その動機は如何に善良であっても、戦争中の憎悪

113　第8　検察側の提唱する新国際法理論

と偏見の減退せざる今日に於ては、特に避けねばならないのである。各世代は次の世代に対する深甚な責任感を以て、そして感情的偽善の影響の下に正義を装って誤った行動に出ることのないように、その行動に対し充分反省することを要するといわれた。我々は我々の子孫の為にここにしばらく歩を停めて、「地獄への道は善意で補装される」という有名なドクタ・ジョンソンの鍼言、又、「この世におけるいみじくも表現した逆説に、深く思いをいたすべきではないか。

首席検察官は「復讐及び返報という卑しい下劣な目的」を力強く否定する（英文記録三八七頁）。しかし、第一次世界大戦の歴史を研究した者は、いわゆるドイツ式シュレックリヒカイトによって聯合国の間に惹起された一般的憤怒の念が、戦争の張本人処罰を要求する囂々たる声を捲き起し、聯合国の指導的政治家も、少なくとも一時は、かくの如き民衆感情を満足せしめざるを得なかったことを想起することが許されるであろう。第二次大戦に於ても、かくの如き民衆の感情を知ると知らざるとを問わず、同じような歴史は繰返されているのではないか。そして検察官諸賢は、この点に関し民衆の感情に唱和して行動しつつある各連合国政府の政策を実行するために、最善を尽していらるるのではないか。

首席検察官はかくの如き原理の確立が将来の侵略者を抑制するために必要であると主張する。しかしそれはまことに望ましいかような目的達成のために少しも必要ではないのである。なぜな

ら、敗戦を予想しながら、侵略戦争を始めるような政治家はないであろうし、又、自国が戦に敗れないかぎり処罰を受けるおそれがないからである。一九七〇年もしフランスが勝ったら軍事裁判所によって審理処罰されるかも知れないという恐怖によって、ビスマルクは戦争を止めたであろうか。又激昂する国民に対し、その指導者達の処罰という国際的威嚇を加えることは、恰も沸騰せる鍋に蓋をかぶせると均しい。正義を求める強い国民感情の存するかぎり、決してこれは平和を保障するゆえんではない。正しいそして平和的な変化をもたらすに適当な機構が設けられないかぎり、不平不満によって紛争は必然的に醸成される。又敗戦の危険はそれ自体戦慄すべきものがあり、それがもっとも有力な抑制となる。処罰は勝った場合には何らの抑制とはならない。なぜならかかる刑罰を甘受することなく、かえってこれを相手方に科するからである。いな指導者の個人的犯罪を認めるかかる原理は、反って将来の戦争をますます惨酷且つ非人道的なものたらしめるもっとも悲しむべき結果をもたらすであろう。なぜなら、交戦国の指導的な政治家や軍人は、単にその同胞の生命のみならず、己の首を救うために、手段を選ばずに迅速な勝利をうることに専心するであろう。そしてかような戦争においては、ハーグ又はジュネーヴ条約によってみとめられた交戦に関する法規慣習は、いずれの交戦国からも「法的瑣末事」として無視されることとなるであろう。軍事的必要、クリーグス・レーゾンの理論が支配的となるであろう。世界平和への途はこれとは別の方向、即ち人類の経済的社会的改善への国際的協力、及び国

115　第8　検察側の提唱する新国際法理論

際紛争の起った場合において、友好と正義の精神に基いて紛争当事者を和解せしむることにある。

第二部

以上は検察側の冒頭陳述中の法律論に対する反駁である、検察側は最終弁論で新たな法律論を提出した。又は別の法律論を補充した。我々は次の順序でこれに答えようと思う。

一、「戦争犯罪人」
二、不戦条約と自衛権
三、共同謀議
四、殺人の罪
五、「通例の」戦争犯罪
六、被告人の責任

一 「戦争犯罪人」

降服文書中におりこまれたポツダム宣言中の戦争犯罪人と云うのは、諸種の点から論じて、通常の戦争犯罪人と解すべきことは、既に述べた通りである。

（一） B—二節（記録、三九、〇〇一頁）に於て検察側は木戸日記を引用して、日本政府は該字句が「戦争勃発責任者」を意味することを認識して居たと云っている。日本語の「戦争責任者」と云う言葉は、休戦前には「戦争勃発責任者」のみならず、「戦時中に於ける責任者」をも意味したのである。そして木戸被告は後者の意味でこれを使用していた様である。天皇の御意思として表示さ

れている記事も、戦争責任者を後者の意味と解釈しても、そこに何等矛盾はない。即ち天皇の信任されていた将軍や提督に累が及びうることがあるからである。

戦争法規違反者の裁判を日本政府に委すと云う提案の周知の先例は、第一次世界大戦後ドイツ政府のなした要求であって、これは日本政治家も熟知していたところである。右の歴史的事例に於て裁判をうくべき者は、戦争勃発責任者ではなく、戦時中の戦争犯罪人であったのである。裁判所よりの質問に対する東郷被告の答も、後の解釈が正しいことを示すのである（記録三六、一三一頁）。そしてとにかく右条件の提案に関する木戸日記の記事は伝聞に過ぎないのである。

仮に百歩を譲って戦争責任者は「戦争勃発責任者」を意味するとしても、日本当局者が、通例の戦争責任者以外にも自らこれを及ぼす可能性を論議してはならない理由はない。本件の如き重要な事件に於ては、伝聞によって記述された些細なそして不明確な言葉は、被告人に有利に解釈さるべきは当然である。

（二）検察側は「当時幾分でも疑いがあったなら、質問を発することに依ってこれを明らかにすることが出来たはずである」という。これに対しては、右に説いた如く、第十項の字句の自然的意味は極めて明瞭であって、この点に関し疑いを抱かしめる余地はなかったのである点を指摘する。

（三）検察側は又言う「弁護側が本裁判所条例又は起訴状の各項目を攻撃せんとするならば――かかる攻撃がこの訴訟段階において許されるとしても――解釈上ポツダム宣言の字句

戦争勃発責任者を含み得ないということを立証する必要がある。」しかし弁護側は既に、戦争犯罪の自然的且つ一般に理解された意味と七月二十六日のポツダム宣言発表に伴う事情とに鑑み、ポツダム宣言に使用された字句は二様の意味を持ち得ないことを充分に立証したのである。然らばこの自然的且つ一般に理解された意味が、ポツダム宣言に使用された字句の意味でないというなら、このことは検察側において立証すべきである。しかし検察側の提出した唯一の証拠は次の二つである。（一）カイロ宣言。これは論点の解明について何等価値なきものである。（二）木戸日記の漠然たる記事。

聯合国政府を代表する検察側は、ポツダムにあった聯合国政治家が右字句の使用により何を意味したかを明確にするために、それら政治家の宣誓供述書を提出することは、極めて容易であったはずである。

斯る証拠は勿論それだけで決定的というわけではないが、検察側にとって有力なる証拠として役立ち得たであろう。検察側として特に容易に取り得たこうした措置を採られなかったとは、検察側の主張に深い疑問を投げかけるものである。

しかのみならず、本件の如き歴史的事件に於て、この重大なる論点を訴訟技術的な挙証責任の規則に委する如きは、軽率且つ不当である。この論点は、真理と正義の見地から、必要ある場合には裁判所の職権によっても明確にすべきであることを主張する。

（四）検察側がやっている様に、ドイツの戦争犯罪被告人に関する八月八日ロンドン協定及び裁判所条例についての議論をそのまま本件に適用することは出来ない。なぜなら、日本が条件付降服の条件を受諾したときには、ドイツの場合とは異なった取扱いを受けることを必然的に予期していたからである。又第七頁（記録三九、〇一四頁）の議論も右の議論と同様価値なきものである。なぜなら、侵略戦争とハーグ条約違反との非道性の軽重に関するニュルンベルグ法廷の意見いかんは、ここではなんら問題ではなく、問題の点は本件の被告が「戦争犯罪人」なる辞句をどう解釈する権利をもつかであるからである。戦争犯罪というのは戦場における軍隊の行動と戦時中に起った同様の行為に関する戦時法規の犯罪的違反をいうのであると被告人は理解したのであり、今迄で一般に了解されていたこうした解釈を拡大することは、圧制的であるというのが弁護側の主張である。

（五）B—七節（記録三九、〇一五頁）に於てドイツ皇帝は専制君主であったと言われている。これは勿論誤っている。ドイツ帝国憲法が聯邦憲法であったことだけによっても、そうでないことが明らかである。しかしドイツ各邦の君主又は国務大臣は起訴されなかった。B八節（記録三九、〇一七頁）において未遂に終ったドイツ皇帝訴追（この訴追が失敗に終ったのは主としてそれが良心に違反する種類のものであったからである）は「権利を確立した」と言う驚くべき主張は、勿論排斥さるべきである。

（六）戦争勃発責任者と通常の戦争犯罪人とを同一に取扱うことB―九節B（記録三九、〇一七頁）は早計であり且つ無根拠である。後者に対する取扱いは長年に亘って確立し、その罰則もきまっている。更にその処理は復仇に依って制約されている。然るに前者には復仇による制約がない。

T・A・ウォーカ博士はその「国際法学」にこういっている。十六世紀の宗教戦争の際交戦法規を全面的に廃止して見た。ところが復仇が断然増加して困った。そこで「古来の習慣を憧憬」することとなり、戦争法規が復活した。然るに交戦国が侵略者を処罰せんとする場合には、これに対し自らの感情以外何等制約がないのである。この点だけを考慮しても、検察側がなんら差別なきものとしている二者の間には、劃然たる区別のあることが分かるのである。

（七）B十五項（記録、三九〇二五頁）に於て、検察側は被告人が真面目に信じたところには相当な根拠がなければならないということを免責の根本的要件の一つに数えている。それは一般刑法理論として行き過ぎである。この議論で行くと真面目であっても馬鹿な又は思い過ぎた錯覚の為に死刑に該当する罪に問われることになる。これでは「不合理」であったというだけで、人を犯罪人とすることになる。

二　不戦条約と自衛権

不戦条約と国家の自衛権に関しては、すでに十分云い尽して居る。しかしながら検察側から新

しい議論が提出されたので、それに対しここに答えて置く必要がある。

（一）検察側はＢ―一〇節及び一二節（記録三九、〇一九―二二頁）において許さるべき自衛権は領土侵入に対するもののみであると云う。これはケロッグ国務長官が上院外交委員会で明確に説明して居る点、上院外交委員長ボラー氏が上院でなした演述、更にオースティン・チェンバレン卿がケロッグ・ブリアン条約受諾に際しなした声明のうちに暗黙にふくまれるところと全く相反するものである。これらの諸言明は既に引用したところである。ここで一九三二年五月二日に締結された仏ソ相互援助条約に言及した日本軍の防衛に及ぶものであることは、パナマ海峡地帯駐屯のアメリカ軍隊の防衛に及ぶものと均しく極めて明白である。自衛権は支那満洲に駐屯しておこう。これは両国のうちいずれかが他の欧洲諸国より挑戦なき侵略を受けたときは、或る条件のもとに、他の一国は直にその援助をなすことを規定した条約であるが、この場合の「侵略」はフランス又はソ聯の国土を侵された場合に限ることを特に規定している。これは明らかに、侵略行為に対する自衛権発動が、一般には領土侵略に対する防衛に限らないことを証明しているものである。

（二）Ｂ―一四節（記録三九、〇二五頁）には、自衛なりやいなやは裁判所の決定すべき事項であるとする。これは米国の最高政治家が繰返して、声明したところと全然相反する主張である。これら政治家はなにが自国の自衛権の発動であるかは各国が自ら決定しうべきであり、米国もそ

の他の国々もいかなる裁判所にもこれを附託することには応諾しないと述べているのである。そして国家の自衛行為に対し輿論は或いはこれを喝采し或いは非難するであろうといって居る。彼等のいわんとしたのはその言明通りである。自衛行為の国際法上の唯一の制裁は一般の非難を受ける可能性である。彼等の言わんとしたのはこれ以外には及ばず、又及ぶものとすべきでない。中米に於けるモンロー主義擁護の為めアメリカは戦争する権利ありと主張したジェイムズ・ブレインが、もし敵にとらえられた場合、アメリカの指導者は裁判にかけられて生命の危険に曝されると聞いたら、果して何と思うことであろう。

著者の理論上の立場からの主張であるかも知れないオッペンハイムのごときある学者の個人的意見又は自国政府の行動に対して抑制を加えるためになした提言であるかも知れない日本法律家の意見書などは、条約の解釈の第一原則は各締約国の真意を確かめるにあること、そしてこうした真意は単に条約の辞句のみでなく、それに関聯ある外交文書、その締約の際又は以前に指導的政治家のなした声明等に照らして探究せねばならぬという国際法の確定原則を変更するものではない。又この国際法上の根本原則が変更したことを示すような証拠はなんら提出されて居ない。

国際法は確かに各国民の合意により進歩成長して行く。しかしながら条約は締約国全部の同意なくしてその内容を拡大したり変更したりすることは出来ないのである。このことはパリ宣

2 不戦条約と自衛権

言や一九二九年のジュネーヴ条約や不戦条約のような国際法の一般規定に関して締結された多辺的条約の場合でも、又二国家間の条約の場合でも同様である。

(三) B―一四節、(記録三九、〇二五頁)に於ける検察側の主張は、自衛権の発動は相当予想しうる武力的領土侵入の場合のみで、武力包囲とかいわんや経済包囲の場合には及ばないと主張する。これは正にケロッグ国務長官が上院外交委員会でなした声明に背反する主張である。この点については、他の弁護人よりさらに詳論することになっている。更に我々は既に引用した上院外交委員長が、各国は何が自国に対する攻撃であるかを決定する権利をもつと言明した点につき、再び裁判官各位の注意を促すものである。

三　共同謀議

(一)「共同謀議」と云う言葉がすこぶる曖昧であるという事実は、国内法を類推して国際法上の犯罪を創造せんとすることがいかに危険であるかの極めて顕著な例証として役立つことを、裁判所は了解せられることであろう。英米法に依れば共同謀議は一つの軽罪に対する特殊な罪名で、非合法的行為を合同して企んだ場合を云うのである。そして首席検察官はその冒頭陳述に於てこれに関する聯邦裁判所の判例を引用して英米法にその根拠を求めたのである。これは所謂ミスデミーナであって、英法では最長期二ヶ年の刑に処せられる罪である。この意味で、こ

れは英米法独特の罪であろうとわれわれは云うたのである。

しかし通俗的には、この言葉は最も極悪な犯罪、即ち暴力を用いて政府を倒壊することを目的とする共同計画の意味で用いられる。即ち端的にいえば本裁判の被告人達はこの罪名の下に到底有罪となり得ないことは、誰にでも分かる程明々白々のこととなるからである。被告人等が倒壊せんとした叛逆罪の対象たる世界国家なるものは存在しないからである。

斯くして検察側は特殊な軽罪たる共同謀議罪を以て、国内法中最も重大なる罪を問い極刑を求めて居ることとなるのである。これは軽罪たる共同謀議罪の類推ではなく、実は叛逆罪陰謀の類推なのである。然るに被告人は叛逆罪に問われて居ないのである。

（二）刑事訴訟の伝統は検察側は常に最も明瞭且つ簡明な方法で立証を行いコジツケ的論法を絶対に排除することにある。従って検察側は叛逆罪が国際的に適用されねばならぬと想像し希望するだけでなく、それが適用さるべきある理由を示さなければならない。弁護側は適用なきことは明々白々であると確信するのではあるが、ここに積極的に国際社会と国家との本質的差異によって、その適用が排除さるべきことを論証する。

（三）叛逆罪の場合には、これに関与する者は充分に確立した社会の組織員である。そしてその社会は生活のあらゆる部面でたえず彼等に面接する。彼等のなす行為、そのとる食物について

127　3　共同謀議

も、これにたよるのである。それが彼等の属する国家である。叛逆罪は、国家を結び付けている組織を破壊して、暴力によって彼等の好む組織をもってこれに代えんとする企図である。従ってこれに対する危惧の念に刺戟されて、ある国、又は恐らく多くの国に於て、かかる計画を極悪非道の犯罪とするだけでなく、これに対する強い恐怖心から、計画に少しでも関与した者、この計画を知らなかった者をも均しく責任あり、有罪であるとしたことは、さほどあやしむに足りないのである。こうした場合、罪の軽重を問わず又計画が実行されたかどうかも問題とし
ない。従って総てが叛逆罪であり、総てみな有罪であるとする。

しかし本件では右の場合とは全然その趣を異にする。世界国家は存在しないのである。他国の便益を全然顧慮しないで、その輸出品に対し関税を課する国や、将来他国に対して使用される可能性のある軍備を具える国をこれを抑制し又はこれを処罰する世界政府は存在しない。全世界の教育家が若人の心のうちに世界社会の感念を育成することは誠に結構なことである。しかし世界社会の感念は今なお弱いのである。われわれはこの事実を悲しむかも知れない。しかしそれが事実である前提の下に運営されている。そして世界政治は今でも主権国家から成る国際社会という前提の下に運営されている。そして国際法の規範は、こうした現実を前提として成立するものとせねばならぬのである。

国際戦争は誠に恐るべき害悪であり、しかもその害悪は増大している。何人もこれを嫌い、

第2部　128

これを恐れる。戦争をしないように国家間に条約が締結された。何人もかかる条約に価値を置き、条約が遵守されることを希望する。

しかし他国に対する戦争——所謂「侵略戦争」の場合ですら——の共謀者と母国に対する叛逆者とを同列に置くことはできない。叛逆者は社会の全機構を破壊しその中枢神経に触れるものである。戦争の計劃者は国際社会——それは現実には獅子と小羊との共存する社会である——に対する敬虔な希望をうらぎっているだけである。われわれがこうした敬虔な希望を嘲笑する意図のないことは勿論である。われわれのここに指摘せんとするのは、一方戦争の準備を行うことと、他方叛逆罪の陰謀をなすこととを同列に置くべきでないということである。叛逆罪の陰謀に伴う惨虐な刑罰を独立国の政治家軍人の行為に対し、新奇且つ驚くべき方法で、適用することを正当化するような類似性はその間にないと云うことだけである。

（四）共同謀議の名のもとに叛逆罪を国際法のうちに導入せんとすることは、忠誠の誓いに基いた封建的のイギリス法の惨忍な規則、即ち少しでも叛逆罪に関与した者に対し最大の罪を無差別的に帰せしめる法理を国際法に導入せんとする試みである。しかしこれは簡素を特色とする国際法によって排斥せらるべきであることは明白である。国際法が個人の罪を認める場合があるとすれば、それは個人の行動に依って個人の罪を計らねばならない。

（五）検察側の最終弁論において始めて提出された共同謀議論に関しては、われわれは次の諸点

を付け加えて置く。

共同謀議が「起訴及び責任立証の形式」であるとの議論は論拠すこぶる薄弱である。手続の仮装のもとに国際犯罪たることの立証されてないような死刑該当の罪に対し、これを起訴し、これに対して責任を負わせんとすることはまことに驚くべきことである。

弁護側の見るところによれば、比較刑法によって共同謀議が国際犯罪たることを立証せんとした検察側の試みは、完全なる失敗である。検察側は共同謀議罪は文明国によって承認された法の一般原則として国際法の規則であることを立証する目的で、諸国の刑法典を引用する。そして法の一般原則は国際刑法の淵源をなすものであるとする。検察側のこの提言は、英米法における四つの事項を注意深く識別することによって容易に論駁することができる。

（イ）叛逆罪の陰謀。これは実は叛逆罪なのである。犯罪中最も重い叛逆罪においては、この罪に少しでも関与した何人をも逃さず又これに対して極刑が科せられるかも知れない。しかし国家とその基本的制度の安定が、総ての国家によって侵犯者に対する極刑によって保証されていると云う事実は、本件に於いて何ものをも立証することにはならない。けだし叛逆罪の陰謀を含む叛逆罪成立の基底となるべき、世界国家が存在しないことは明白であるからである。

（ロ）共同謀議罪。これはある違法な行為（ある場合良俗に反する行為）をなす共同計劃をそ

の本質とする。これが既に述べたように、裁判官、法学者の猛烈な非難の対象となっている犯罪である。共同謀議罪に関する英米のような広汎な理論は、われわれの知る限り、ローマ法系に於いては認められていない。ローマ法系の諸国中、ある国では重罪の陰謀を罰し他の国ではこれを罰していないことは検察側もこれを容認する。従ってこの場合には、「文明国の認むる法の一般原則」は存在しない。

（八）刑事代位責任。もしも数人が共同の不法計画をなす場合には、この計画の遂行中行わるる犯罪、に対して、計画されたる犯罪に対してのみならず、行われたる犯罪に対して責任を負う（その行為が計画されたる犯罪より重い罪であると否とに拘らず）と云う珍奇な原則は、刑事代位責任の原則と名づけ得るであろう。この原則は歴史的理由に基いて成立する英米法独特のものである。検察側は多数刑法学者から非難をうけている日本大審院の共犯に関する判例を引用するが、これも検察側の主張するような英米法の共同謀議罪程広汎ではない。それはとにかく、英米法の刑事代位責任の原則が普遍的であることは検察側によって少しも立証されていない。しかのみならず、この原則は明白にわれわれの正義心に背反するものである。とにかくそれが「文明国の承認する法の一般原則」と看做し得ないことは明らかである。

（二）民事代位責任の原則。これによれば使用者はその使用人又は代理人（機関）の職務執行中なした民事違法行為に対し責任を負う。この近代的英米の無過失責任の原則が、現在（一

九四八年）各国の民事立法に採用された程度を述べることはわれわれとして困難である。大多数の立法例は多分古典的な過失責任主義を今なお固守していることであろう。この原則は英国及び米国に於てさえも、刑法には適用しない。唯極めて微罪の場合に於てのみ、使用者はその部下の犯罪に対して刑罰を科せられる。この原則は閣員の刑事責任を支持するために検察側によって援用されて居るようであるから（K、一七節以下）ここに触れておいたのである。

（六）　検察側が「法の一般原則」に頼らざるを得ないと云う事実そのものが、その主張は国際法上何等の根拠なきものであることを明瞭にする。けだし右の国際法の法源は実定国際法が見出されない場合にのみ援用する趣旨であるからである。それはフーヴァ判事の有名な言葉「不明瞭の袋小路」に対して備える趣旨、即ち裁判所が適用すべき法がないと云う理由で裁判を拒否することを防止する趣旨である。それは国際法によって国家間の紛争を処理するために或る場合有用な法源であろう。そしてそれが一九二〇年常設国際司法裁判所の条例起草者の目的であった。それは国際刑法に於ては援用しえない法源であり、又援用してはならない法源である。これが援用は明白に文明国の通則たる罪刑法定主義の原理の侵犯である。

検察側はヒットラー立法の下における如く、その主張は類推のみに基くのであることを明言する。しかし国内法における叛逆罪の陰謀の類推は世界国家が現実の存在となるまでは、常にあやまった類推であることを銘記せねばならない。

四 殺人の罪

正当な理由なくして故意に人を殺した者を各国が殺人罪として取扱うから、殺人罪は国際犯罪を構成すると云う検察側の議論B—二一節（記録三九、〇三〇頁）が正しいとすれば、場所と人とにかかわらず、又検察側の所謂「国際的性格」（その意味は不明であるが）の有無にかかわらず、世界のいかなる場所でも、それは犯罪であることになる。しかしこれによって英国並びに米国によって終始支持され又有名なロータス事件においてフランスも又強硬に主張した「犯罪は地域的なり」という提言は、全然消失して了うことになる。これは到底認容しえないところであると弁護側は主張する。

更に殺人罪に対する免責事由は各国の法制上その軌を一にしていない。死刑を廃止した国家は裁判所の死刑執行の命令をもって免責事由とはせぬであろう。侮辱をうけた夫が間男を殺した場合、ある国では広い範囲の免責を認めるが他の国ではそれを認めない。如何にしてこうした雑多な法の状態をそのまま国際法規範として国際的に執行し得るのであろうか。それによってわれわれは自家撞着と変態的事態に堪えぬこととなるであろう。

A国ではXを殺人犯人となし、B国ではXを死刑に処するのは殺人と考えるかも知れぬ。極刑を課する国際法上の殺人罪なるものは、どうしても世界国家と世界法の存在を前提としてのみ成

立するのである。しかし斯かる世界国家は存在していない。又世界法は戦時における間に合せとして一般に行われて居る戦争法規違反者の処罰等少数の場合以外には存在していない。「殺人」はペルシャとフランスではそれぞれ異なった取扱いを受けるのである。普遍的な要素だけを取り出して国際法上の殺人罪を構成せんとすることは、事実にもとづかずして抽象を以てこれに代えることになる。しからば、先ず抽象的国際的殺人罪を作って、各国国内法の内容をこれに附着せんとする検察側の試みはどうか。

殺人罪の免責事由は各国まちまちである。検察側が殺人罪はいかなる場所でも同じであると言いうるためには、すべての国家で侵略戦争の遂行は免責事由とならないということを立証することを要する。各国裁判所はこれを免責事由とすべきではないことを立証してみても何等役に立たない。具体的に各国裁判所がこれを免責事由と認しない限り、世界中何処でも侵略戦争は死刑に該当する犯罪として取扱われて居るなどと推定することは許されない。そしてその証拠は少しも提出されていない。検察側の主張を支持するためには全世界が彼等の見解と同様であることを立証することを必要とする。スイス国又はペルシャ国の裁判所が無思慮に戦争を始めたと云う理由で、総理大臣を殺人罪として処罰するかどうか。

（二）Ｂ―二一節（記録三九、〇三〇頁）において殺人罪は国際法の一部であると云うのは単なる憶測に過ぎない。

諸権威、特に一九二〇年の国際裁判所条例を起草した著名な法学者による国際法の広汎な法源の理論は、単に国家を拘束する国際法の法源に関するのである。その法源は（一）国際条約（二）国際慣習（三）文明国家間で認められた法の一般原則（四）判例（五）国際法学者の教説（六）正義、衡平法、信義誠実これである。

個人行為に関する原則が国際法の一部なりとする提言をこれら起草者が説いて居ると主張している者があると知ったら、右の分類の起草者は恐らく驚倒することであろう。「文明国家が認むる法の一般原則」が掲げられたのは、国家の行為に適用される意味で類推的に加えたのである。これ以外の意味はありえないのである。

（三）国際法上に殺人罪が存在し――しかもそれは国際的性格をもたねばならぬと云う説明なき不明確な条件を附して――世界各国の裁判所が（それぞれ自らの原則に基きということらしいが）処理しうるという主張は、全然不当である。はげしく論争された管轄権の問題は、ここでは不問に附せられている。もしこの犯罪が「国際法上の犯罪」であるなら、何故各国裁判所がこれを取扱いえないのであるか。検察側の論旨の全体が憶測と架空の総合である。国内法しかも蒸溜された国内法が、国際法内に大量に移入されたと知ったら、故フィルモア卿はその一九二〇年の同僚と共に仰天するにちがいない。

（四）戦争が殺人罪を阻却するには、それが合法的でなければならぬと云うことは支持しえない

4　殺人の罪

提言である。けだし検察側の議論は、正常なる理由がなければ殺人は死刑に該当する罪として各国によって取扱われるという絶対的同意に依拠しているがゆえである。なんとなれば、国家にとって不法だとの意味において戦争行為が不法であるなら、殺人罪に対する免責事由とはならないことにすべての国家が一致していることは、少しも立証されていないし、そうした蓋然性すら存在しないのである。そして検察側の論議の基底は斯かるあやしい提言に対し各国が完全に同意しているということにあるのである。

(五) Ｂ—二五節（記録三九、〇三〇頁）において検察側は戦時中と戦争開始前に行われた不法行為との間に何等差異なしとする。これは問題の論点を全然逸している。論点は行為の違法性の軽重ではなく、単にハーグ条約の適用範囲いかんにあるのである。戦争遂行を規律するための条約は、戦争の遂行に何等関係なき行為にも及ぶものとすることはできないのである。

五　「通例の」戦争犯罪

通例の戦争犯罪は「俘虜サンメーション」（Ｊ—一—六一節）中に論ぜられている。これに関する法の問題は「被告の責任」（Ｋ）で取りあつかい「俘虜サンメーション」では単に事実の要約に止めるという趣旨である。しかし右の要約中には、法に関する一定の推定を前提としているので、ここにはかかる推定の若干の面について批評を加えることに止める。

(一) ジュネーヴ条約の準用に関する所謂日本の約束（J—四六節）

検察側はそこに日本を拘束する国際的合意があったものと推定している。弁護側の見解によれば、これは誤りである。米国及び英国が一九四二年に云ったことは、自分達はジュネーヴ条約に従うつもりだから、日本もこれに従うことを要望するというのである。右両国のなしたその他の宣言もやはり同種のものであって、やはり同じように理解せられねばならないのである。それはただ現在の態度に関するステートメントであって、法的拘束力をもつ約因のないものではない。それらは日本の行動を条件としたものではなく、全然独立、自発的であって約因のないものである。日本がこれを了承してもそれによって米国及び英国を拘束することにはならないのである。そこにはアグリーメントとかプロミス（J—一六〇B節）とかはないのであって、日本の声明も両国の意向を了承し同様の意志を表明したのにすぎないのである。この意志表示は前の意志の対価としてなされたのでなく、随意に行ったのである。従ってこのカウンタ・プロポーザルを「約束」であるというのは不正確である。これをなしたことが日本にとって有益であったとか、又「準用」の意味いかん、かの点は全然関聯性のない問題である。あたかも旅行者が他の旅行者に対して「自分は明日歌舞伎座に行くつもりだが君はどうか」と云い、これに対し「そう自分もやはりそのつもりでいる。」と答えた場合、そこには、道徳的にも法律的にも「合意」とか「引受け」とかは全然ないのである。右の例が法の範囲外だというなら、他の例をとろう。

株式所取引員が他の株式所取引員に対して「自分は今週銅を出来値次第で買いに出るつもりだが君はどうか」と云い、これに対し「左様自分もそのつもりだ」と答えた場合、この二人のいずれもその思うがままにふるまいうるのであって、銅を買おうが買うまいが全然その自由であるる。

（二）ジュネーヴ及びハーグ条約（括弧による挿入位置は原文のママ 一六〇B―一六一節）

検察側は「とにかく一九二九年ジュネーヴ俘虜条約は一九〇七年ハーグ条約のうちにすでに内在していたところを明示的に規定したものにすぎない」と云う。しかし、一九二九年の条約は単に現行法を成文化しただけでなく俘虜の状態を改善するためにこれを修正したのであることは明らかである。

ハーグ条約前文の一般的宣言は予見すべからざる場合の処理について、軍指令官の不当な行為につき国家に賠償責任あることを示さんとしたのであって、それ以上のことをそれから引出すことは許されない。それは国家がこれらの場合を予見して、軍指令官に命令を発することを国家に期待してはいないのである。

前文の宣言は右の条約が網羅的でなく、予期すべからざる事件が起った場合に、適用すべき法について軍指令官の判断が終局的だと国家が主張することは許されないということをいっているにすぎないのである。

第2部 138

凡そ条約の前文なるものは、いかなることをも制定することはできないのである。そしてこの前文は、その次の本文の条項が網羅的でないことを宣言したのである。一九〇七年ハーグ条約の主たる目的は国家の責任を確保するにあったのである。伝統によってみとめられ少数の場合にだけ認められる個人の責任については、ほとんど注意がはらわれなかったのである。いわんや政府高官の責任などは全然考えていなかったのである。前文における問題は、将校のグループと他のグループ——軍指揮官と内閣の何れに責任を帰せしめるかといったような問題ではなく、国家責任を確保するという問題であったのである。かるが故に、署名国は軍指揮官の専断的な判断にかくれて責任を免れることをえないものと宣言したのである。かかる宣言と共に以下本文で違反国は賠償責任を支払うべきことを規定し、大臣の責任などには少しもふれていないのである。それをゆがめて、政府高官に個人責任があるというような解釈がなされるとすれば、それは将来の政治家に対し、英国のチャンサリ・バリスターや米国のランド・タイトル・スペシアリストが払うような細心の注意を以て起草しないと、国際条約は危険極まるものであるとの警戒となるであろう。しかし、従来国際条約は同様な思想的背景をもつ友人の間の協約であって、寛宏な精神で起草されたのであることを忘れてはならない。

最後に検察側はハーグ条約中のガヴァメントと云う字句の使用から条約遵守についての閣員その他の個人責任を引き出している。

ハーグ条約に於けるガヴァメントというのは色々の資格でその時々統治をいとなんでいる個人をいうのではない。この言葉はステイトのシーノニムとして用いられる。最近の慣行によれば条約はガヴァメント間に締結されるという風に書かれている。しかし何人も大臣の職務を行っている個人、いわんやその下僚が、条約の当事者であるなどとは考えないのである。英国におけるドイツ俘虜はアトリ氏やモリスン氏やミス・ウィルキンスンによって個人的に管理されているとは誰も考えない。それは国家を意味するのである。何人もサー・スタフォド・クリプスやジョセフ・ウェスウッドや、ジョウィス卿が俘虜扶養の費用を支払う義務あることなどとは考えない。しかしハーグ条約第七条には俘虜をその権力内にもつに至ったガヴァメントは俘虜の扶養のための費用を支払う義務があるものとしているのである。

検察側の議論はガヴァメントの二つの意味即ち（1）「統治を行っている人」と（2）「国家主権の権化」との間の混乱にもとづいた誤魔かしであること一目瞭然たるものがある。条約の条項違反に対して責任があるのは国家なのである。ハーグ条約のいかなる個所をみても、大臣その他の文官が交戦行為を監督し抑制する義務があることとか、又交戦規則違反の罪を分かつ責任があるとかのことを示唆するものは絶無なのである。ハーグ条約はかかる義務と責任とを課することによって、全統治機能を軍法の下に置くことも勿論可能であった。しかしそのしないだけの聡明さをもっていたのである。そして条約制定者が、そうしたことをしないだけの聡明さをもっていたのである。そして条約制定者は、

第2部 140

明示的にさけたことを、驚くべき解釈を使用して試みないことが賢明であること勿論である。

（三）「共通の型」。検察側を支配している思想は「一般的断定には欺瞞が隠されている」というラテン語の格言によって特徴づけることができる。それは「共同計劃」又は「中央官憲から発した命令」の証拠としての「共通の型」の理論に特に顕著に現われている。

検察側は「日本人の行った犯罪は日本及び日本人の占領した『多くの場所』において、その性質についても又手口についても同一であった事実は、犯罪が各々の犯行者の思いつきで行われたのではなく『共同計劃』の一部として行われたというほとんど不可避的な推論に導くものである。又それら犯罪はその目的のための特別訓練又は『少なくもある』中央官憲から発した命令の結果であることをつよく証明するものである」という。

これでは重大な刑事的訴追の基礎とするには、余りにも漠然としている。けだし検察側は所謂「型」なるものが到るところで劃一的に存在するとさえも云っていない。ある場合にはそうでないことを自認するのである。それは「その目的の為の特別訓練」及び「少なくもある中央官憲から発した命令」の推定を打破していることになるのである。それだけでなく、検察側のいわゆる「型」を熟視するならば、逆にそれはその犯罪なるものが突発的なものであること、且つ「共通の計劃」もまた「ある中央官憲からの命令」なるものも、全然存在しないことを立証することとなっているのである。

(1) 逃亡せざる宣誓又は約束（J三一ないし三九節）。これ等各節の叙述は真に強制のあった事件を示さんとすることを目的としている。そしてシンガポール（三件）香港（二件）ボルネオ、ジャバ、善通寺及び台湾以外の場所に関して、なんら事件が掲げられていない点は重要である。インド、ビルマ及び比島に関しては何もいっていない、従ってこの型は大きなギャップを示している。又事実上所謂強制行為のやり方について共通なるものはない、あるときは監禁、あるときは殴打、あるときは脅迫、あるときは熱攻、あるときはそれらの結合である。どこにはたして共通の型があるのか。勿論そこには宣誓の要求という共通の特徴はある。しかしこれは厳格な監視を免れるがための公正な対価として、許さるべく且つ正常な処置である。又これらの事件はみな一九四二年の最初の九ヶ月に起っている。このことは反って不法な強制をやる公的政策のなかったことの有力な証拠ではないのか。もしこれらの残酷な処置がなされたとすれば、それは各地の下級将校の偶発的行為であったのである。

(2) 殺戮（J一四一―一四四節）

(イ) 色々な方法で行われたとされている所謂殺戮について「型」を発見することは困難である。検察側もそこに型を発見することができないのである。それをある動機で結びつけることを躊躇しているからである。やっかいをさける為であるとか、住民に恐怖心を起させるためだとかのあて推量はしている。しかしそこに型があるとは主張していない。そこ

第2部 142

に述べられた事件が仮に証明されたとしても、それは一九四二年の三ヶ月間に一定数の殺戮事件が起ったということだけである。たとえかかる事件が起ったとしても、それは「ある中央官憲から発した命令によった」というよりも、むしろそれとは逆に、直ちに抑止されたことを示すものである。

(ロ)（J—一四五節）。この節に叙述されている殺戮事件は仮にそれがあったとしても、ほとんど総て一九四三年にボルネオで行われたものであって地方的な叛乱の抑圧の際に起ったものである。武力による叛乱鎮定は仲々なまやさしい方法でできるものではない。暴力、いわゆる「戦争叛逆者」を前にしての軍事的処刑は、あらかじめ裁判の方法を必要とする場合には該当しないのである。

(ハ)（J—一四六、七、八節）の叙述は何等の「型」を示してはおらない。それが仮りに証明されたとしても、それは敵の侵入が近づいた際、時として俘虜が殺されたと云うことを示すのに過ぎない。検察側は、俘虜による幇助の供与を防止する為であったろうとその動機について推量するが、それは検察側が自認する如く、一つの推量に過ぎない。かかる場合における俘虜の「推量」によって「型」を証明することは出来ないのだ。次に検察側の殺戮は、時としては適当且つ許さるべき軍事的予防手段であるかもしれないのだ。検察側は侵入を「予見的」事件を取扱うといいながら、直ちに「空襲後起った」殺戮事件

（タラワ）を引用しているのは矛盾である。とにかく、この「予見的」型の事件の発生は極めて少数しか主張されておらない。それらの事件から何等の「型」を見出すことは出来ないのである。俘虜による脅迫の話や、書記による密令の話などは「強い傍証」ではなくして、それは極めて薄弱な証拠に過ぎないのである。もしも「中央」「最高」の日本の政策なるものが存在したのであったならば、それは少数の場所においてではなく、常に如何なる場所に於ても適用されたことであろう。

とにかく、仮想された「最高の政策」を「日本の」とし、表示することは不十分であってこれについて、如何なる日本人が責任があるのかを特記することが必要である。

日本軍隊のとる原則は、俘虜に対する義務は日本将兵の生命の保持に優先せずというにあったことは有りうべきことである。又、個々の場合に於て、指揮官がこの原則を不当に拡大したこともあり得べきことである。しかしそれは、それら指揮官がそうした命令を受けたことを意味するものではない。そして右の原則そのものは、ハーグ条約及び未批准の一九二九年のジュネーヴ条約に反するものではないのである。

憲兵隊の使用した拷問に関して、（J―一五六節）は次の如くいう。「その劃一性に照らしそれらは偶然に発生したはずはない。それは共通の訓練の結果であったに相違ない。しかしもかかる共通の訓練が与えられたとするならば、それは政府の政策事項であった

に違いない」。

右の「共通訓練」の推論は常識上ありえないことである。又拷問ということは或る職業にともなう共通の職業心理に起因するかも知れないからである。更に進んでなされた右の訓練は「政府の政策事項」であったという推論は、訓練は「軍事訓練」を意味することになるので、これ又誤った推論である。軍事訓練の詳細を監視することは政府の任務ではないからである。

（四）検察側がこの最終弁論を通じて広汎且つ不分化の「日本政府」という字句を使用したことは、検察側の責任理論に照応するのであるかもしれない。「日本政府」というのは「閣員のみならず、陸海軍将校、大使及び高級官吏を包含した広い意味で」使用されてると云う。且つ日本政府という言葉はこのサンメーションを通じて観察すると、この簡単らしく見える定義に更に「又はそれらの或るもの又は全部」という言葉をそっと附け加えたかの如くに使用されていることを発見する。こうした特記なくして概括的字句を用いて刑事責任の存在を主張することが、きわめて不当であることは明白である。こうした技術は国内裁判所に対する刑事裁判に於ては許容されないところであろう。例えば、或る戦争犯罪その他の事項が「日本政府」に知られて居ったという場合には、実際は少数の者しか知らなかったに拘らず、以上の定義に包含せられる者全部が知っておったという誤った推論に導きやすいのである。

又一定の政策が「政府の」政策であると云う場合には、実は単に海軍の軍略的政策にすぎないので、他の閣僚や、大使や、高級官吏は何等それに関係しなかった場合でも、彼等すべてがそれに対して責任があるかの如く響くのである。

通常の戦争犯罪に関する訴追についても、推定に基いて被告人に極刑を課すべきではなく、もし仮りに被告に罪ありとすれば、それは個人的犯罪の立証に基かねばならない。我々は、賢明なる裁判所が本サンメメーションに充満する「推定」によって誤られないことを要望するものである。

(5) (J—六節) において次の如くいわれている。

「他方本部門では検察側において証拠を提出しなかった俘虜収容所員の他の場所に関する弁護側の証拠を無視している。これは裁判長の弁護側に向けた言葉『チャージがなされた事項に対して答弁しなさい。チャージがなされて居ない場合、そこに欠点がなかったことを立証しようと試みてはいけない』によったのである。」

検察側が弁護側のそうした証拠を無視することは明白に不公正であるが、これは検察側の推測を基礎とする責任理論と関聯するものであろう。弁護側はよい状態の証拠を提出してはならない、悪い状態のチャージに対応せねばならないというのが裁判長の見解であるとするなら、このことはそれら特定の場所における将校に対するチャージに対しては尤もである。より高級

の将校に関してはその管理下の他の場所において、状態がよかったことの立証は、関聯性あること明白である。それは非難をうけた場所においても状態は良かったとの推論に導くからである。監督の欠点があったとされる被告の場合には、そのチャージに対してかれの監督が一般的に効果的であったことの立証は、関聯性があるものとせねばならない。反カトリック暴動に関与したことで起訴された場合、被告が法王の侍従長であったことの立証は関聯性があるのである。

六　被告人の責任

(1) 叛逆罪の誤った類推

「何人も諸犯罪の発生した原因である日本の侵略政策について幾分でも責任があったのでなければ、平和に対する罪、通常の戦争犯罪、又は人道に対する罪について起訴しなかった。」という（K—三節）。

これは戦争の蓋然性又はそれら犯罪の発生することを予見又は予期していなかった場合でもなおそうである！

これが起訴状全部にしみ渉っている誤った全理論の秘密を開くためのマスター・キーである。

そしてこれは国内法に対する叛逆罪の陰謀の設計図によって示唆された観念である。

147

検察側はいつも「推定」をこうしたアナロジーの根拠とする。しかし生命をかけて裁判を受けている被告は、こうした安易な方法で有罪とされるべきではない。しかもなお検察側も曖昧を免れえないのである。政策の形成に少しでも関与した者は、その政策から派生したあらゆる結果に対し責任を負うという十六世紀的な奔放振りを発揮しつつ、なお且つ更に進んで、一定の個人が政策形成に少しも関与していないのに、政策関与があったかの如く責任を負わすのである。「事態の黙認」はこれが形成と「均しい」というのである。

(2) 検察側の理論は外交使節に関する全理論を壊滅せしめる（K—四節）。この点については他の弁護人から詳論の予定であるから省略する。

(3) 終局的権能を与えられた者の責任（K—六節）。

この節は諸種の誤った推定の下に立っている。

第一は内閣と枢密院と内大臣はそれぞれの権限内で政策の形成について最高の責任を附与されているものとする。しかし枢密院は政策決定の義務はなく、単にこれを批評する義務をもつものだけである。内大臣の場合にはイニシアティヴはさらに少ない。

第二に終局的権能を与えられている者は部下の権力濫用に対して責を負うという我々のつよく抗議する原則の存在を推定している。英米法においてすら、ある人が使用人や代理人又は機関の行為に対して刑事責任を負うのは、微罪の場合だけである。バーテンが時間外にビールを売った

場合、旅館の主人が罰金を課せられるの類である。英国やスコットランドでは、この原則適用はこの程度であると我々は理解する。検察側もその主張についてなんら確信をもっていないらしい。けだしある箇所では、ある場合に「特にそう」であるといっている。ある提言は正しいか正しくないか何れかでなければならぬ。時としては「特にそうである」というのは、単純な真理としてそれが受け入れえないものであることを承認することとなるのである。第三に同僚や部下の決定を黙認することは自らその権能を行使したのに「均しいものと見做しうる」と述べる。ポリス・コートやジュージュ・ドゥ・ペイの慣行以外に根拠となることのない代位刑事責任を死刑罪について推定するなどいうことは、心あるものにとって、堪ゆべからざるところである。

(4) 上官の責任（K—八節）。

本節もおなじ刑事代位責任の理論の推定によって議論を進めている。事態によっては上官の匡正的干渉が必要であり、事態を充分に知り、且つ匡正の機会をもちながらこれを怠った場合国内法上責任を負うことのあるべきはこれを否定しない、しかし国際的責任については我々は勿論全面的にこれを否定する。

(5) 部下の責任（K—一三節）。

本節は下僚の責任を取扱っているが、下僚はその主張する政策又は行動が間違いであることを

明らかにするに足る充分な情報を必ずしももっていないという事実を考慮に入れていないのである。しかもなお、検察側はかかる官吏は非難の対象となった行為に全然関与しないか、又はこれに反対し又はこれに反対の進言をしなければ刑事責任を負うものとするのである。

(6) 閣員の責任（K―一四節）

本節もすこぶる大胆な推定をあえてする。

閣員はその同僚の主管する事項については、その同僚の方が自分よりも熟知しているものとして、少なくとも辞職するという程度まで自己の意見をつよく主張する能力はないと思うこともあろう。閣員は必ずしも外交関係や外交政策について、その職務上エキスパートである必要はない。或いはある提案について疑いをいだいて、閣議で決を求めることもできる。しかし同僚殊に主管大臣の方が自分よりも事柄を良くわきまえているものと推定しても少しも差支ないのである。検察側が閣員は「悪いということについて完全な認識をもち」、「そう信じている」とするのは著しく不当である。かれはそれが悪いなどとは考えていない。かれは内閣の同僚からそれは悪いことでない、君は心配しすぎているといわれ、それを承認したとしても、少しも不当ではない。現地を視察した取締役の報告にもとづいて、君は間違っているといった場合、陸軍大臣と外務大臣とが、そのよりすぐれた知識にもとづいて、侵略戦争について責任があるとすることはできない。農林大臣はニューギアーナにある財産について誤った報告書を出すことに他の取締役が同意を与

第2部　150

えたとしても、かれを犯罪人とすることができないのと同様である。或いは云うであろう。「侵略戦争」は明々白々たる事柄で容易にこれを認識しうるから、誰でもこれを拒絶せねばならぬと。いな。それとは逆に、それは国家の性質とか、物的地役の存在とその防衛とか、国家の利権に対する脅威とか、又すこぶるつきの難問である自衛権の存否とかに依ってきまるのであって、決定はすこぶる困難である。農林大臣は政策の皮相的面に動かされ、閣議で決を求めることもできよう。しかれは問題はきわめて難しく、自己は間違っているだろうと想像しても少しも差支ないのであろう。かれは自己の主張に対するうぬぼれの念にかけられて、早急に辞職する必要は勿論ないのである。しかるに検察側はこのことを要求する。

勿論閣員が辞職を断行せねばならぬような場合もあるであろう。しかし本件の場合はそうした場合には該当しない。それは複雑且つ不確定な自衛権の問題であって、自衛権の定義については、いかなる国家も満足な理論を与ええない種類の問題であるからである。

（7） 統帥部と内閣（K―一八節）。

この節で検察側は統帥部の外交政策に及ぼす絶大の圧力を強調するにかかわらず、この圧力を制御しえない内閣に責任があるとする。内閣は辞職して国を政府なきままの状態に委すべきであったのか、又財政的支出を拒否して国を軍隊なき状態に置くべきであったのか。内閣が軍の意見に従ったからといって、それは必ずしも非難さるべきではなく、又内閣又は閣員がその関与しえ

151　6　被告人の責任

ざるすべての計画について、責任を負わさるべきでないことはきわめて明白である。検察側もまた（K―二九節）「ある行為に対する責任は行為をなす力と義務に伴う」といっている。そして検察側によれば、内閣は統帥部を抑制する力はなかったのではなかったか。

(8) 枢密院（K―一九節）。

枢密院は米国の上院とか英国の貴族院とは異なって、ただ一定の重要な事項について意見を開陳するだけである。しかるにいわゆる「侵略政策」の形成に関与しえない枢密院を一定の事項についてのその行動が「侵略政策」の「形成に導いた」という理由で、処罰すべしというのである。こうした責任の負わせ方は、そのきわまるところを知らないであろう。すべての共産主義的著者は「共産主義政策の形成に導いた」ともいえるであろう。

(9) 内大臣（K―二二節）。

内大臣に関し「ある行為に対する責任はその行為をなす力と義務とから流出するという通常の推定がある」というのはやはり早計な推定である。

ここにいういわゆる「推定」の意味はA（日本皇帝又は日本の一般公衆）に対し民事刑事の責任を追及されずに、自由に進言をなす義務を行使する者はB（訴追者たる聯合国）に対して刑事責任を負うという意味に外ならない。各国において自由な進言をなす義務あるものは、自由にではなく、その及ぼすべき影響の制約の下に進言をなす義務があるというなら、それは「通常の推

定」は「通常」どころか、不当なそして圧制的な推定なのである。さらに進んでは公衆を啓発することをその任務とする新聞記者は、その自由な言論に対し刑事責任を負わねばならぬと主張することになる。これではフリー・プレスはその自由な姿を消すこととなるであろう。

内大臣は刑事責任の顧慮なく、絶対自由に進言しうるのである。即ち内大臣は英米法にいわゆるアブソリュト・プリヴィリッジを享有する。そして検察側は英米において法律顧問の享有するこの特権を、何等の理由なしに否定し去ろうとするものである。

本節で検察側は、その主張の基底をば全部くつがえして了うような自認をしている。元来検察側は被告の行為は法違反であると主張しているのである。しかるに内大臣が日本法上責任ある場合には、その責任は法によって課せられるが、法によって責任が課せられなければ「事実上の責任」があると検察側は明白に云っている。かくして「事実上の責任」と「法によって課せられた責任」とを同一視するのである。云いかえれば、被告に義務と責任ありの検察側の主張は実は法にもとづくものではないことを露呈しているのである。

一葉落ちて天下の秋を知る。検察側は不用意にも自らの主張する責任と法的責任とを鋭く対立せしむることによって、自らの主張の基礎が空疎であることを曝露したのである。

本節は内大臣による総理大臣の推薦は、日本慣習法の一部をなしているとの推定をしているが、これは誤りであることの極めて明白な推定である。何人がかかる推薦をなす慣習はあった。

153　6　被告人の責任

それも英米における「憲法上の約束」と均しく慣習法ではない。かかる推薦が内大臣によってなされるということは、憲法上の約束でさえなく、木戸侯爵がそうした意見を求められた最初の人であったのであろう。

結　語

裁判長並びに裁判官各位。極東国際軍事裁判所は、技術的には「軍事」裁判所とよばれている。しかしそれは、敵国の報復のおそれを除いては、その放恣的傾向を抑制する何ものもない武力闘争の事態の下に、略式手続によって戦争犯罪を処理する、法的な訓練も経験も、将又法的な公正や忍耐をも欠いている、お粗末な間に合せの軍事裁判所ではない。本裁判所は、敵対行動がすでに遥か以前に終了し、それが復活するおそれのいささかもない、きわめて平和的な雰囲気のうちに裁判を行っている。それ故全世界の人々は、本裁判所が熟達した法律家から成る裁判所の機能を有つと共に、世界政治一般特に極東政治の実際に精通した政治家、外交官、軍人、歴史家から成る特別陪審の資格を具えていることを期待する。被告人は通常の兇漢ではなく、高級の政治家軍人であって、その世界観政治観はそれぞれ異なっても、総べてその知見に応じて、極東政治の荒波の中に国政を動かして来た人達である。しかもその極東政治は過去一世紀における東洋と西

155

洋列強との政治的交渉に由来する歴史的所産であった。極東に於ける安定勢力としての日本は既に過去のものとなった。そして極東における平和と秩序とを確保する責任は、他の指導的国民が担うこととなった。こうした事態の下において、被告人の面接した困難がいかなるものであったかの真相は、正しく評価されることとなったであろう。極東諸国民、いな全人類の視線は、すべて本裁判所の歴史的な判決に注がれている。

本裁判の開始以前に、わが法曹界では、いわゆる裁判所条例なるものは裁判所に対し敵国の指導者を処罰する権限を与え且つこれを命ずるために、現行国際法の法則にお構いなく、包括的用語を以て規定せられた専断的な裁判指針にすぎぬとか、いわゆる裁判所なるものは、司法的機関ではなく、刑罰をふり当てる行政的機関にすぎぬとか、条例に表現された聯合国政府の政策と牴触する場合には、国際法は当然無視されるであろうから、今更むきになって国際法の議論をしてもはじまらないといったような意見がしばしばささやかれたのであった。

しかし一九四六年五月三日、本裁判の開廷に当って裁判長が述べられた「本日ここに会合するに先立ち、各裁判官は、法に従って恐れることなく、偏頗の心をもつことなく、裁判を行う旨の合同誓約に署名した」、「われわれの大きな任務に対して、われわれは事実についても法についても虚心坦懐にこれを考慮する」、「検察側は合理的な疑いの存せぬ程度に有罪を証明すべき立証責任を負う」との言葉（英文記録二一—二三頁）によって、右のような迷想はほとんど解消したのであ

る。法に優越する何者をも認めない英米の法伝統を知る者にとっては、裁判長のこれらの言葉の意味は明々白々であった。懐疑主義者はたしかにこれには面喰ったが、しかしなお「法に従って」とは「国際法に従って」という意味に用いられたのではなく、「条例に規定せられた法に従って」という意味にすぎないのだと言い張った。しかしさらに首席検察官がその劈頭陳述において、被告人達は国際法に関する行政府の決定によってではなく、現行の国際法そのものによって断罪せらるべきであり、本条例はかかる現行国際法を宣明せんとするものに過ぎないゆえんを明白にされた。これによってこの疑いは完全に解消した。

首席検察官自ら、コンモン・ローに育まれた著名な法律家である。私人に対する政府の特権を何ら認むることなく、行政府の法解釈も公正な裁判所によって排斥されることを認めるという英米司法裁判の特徴をなすフェア・プレイの精神を体得しておられるのである。そして政府の代表者も判決に於て自らの主張が全部排斥された場合にも、欣然としてこれに服するのである。かるが故に弁護人側は、裁判所が被告人の有罪無罪を決定するに当って、単なる条例の規定を何らかの法解釈によらず、（これによれば「戦争犯罪人」としての責任追求（ママ）を免れうる日本人はほとんどないことになる）被告人をも含めて万人周知の確定した国際法に依って裁判されるべきものと考えたのである。かくして弁護側は検察側の挑戦に応じて、現行国際法の法則によれば、被告人は釈放せらるべきであることを証明せんと努力したのである。

かくして、検察側及び弁護人側の双方の共通信念によれば、本裁判所は、被告人のみならず、全世界の政府が畏敬すべき国際法の尊厳を象徴すべきである。バーラマーキが二百年前（一七四七年）にいったように、国際法は諸国民又はこれを支配する主権者が服従すべき、それ自体において拘束力をもつ法である（バーラマーキ、自然法の原理、第二部第六章第六部）。本裁判は、一方検察官諸賢によってきわめて有能に代表されている戦勝国政府の政策と、他方敗れたりとはいえなお自尊心を失わない国家の政治家及び軍人たる被告人の自由と生命――いなより適切には国際面における基本的人権を争点としている。かかる基本的人権の擁護のためにこそ、本裁判のアメリカ弁護人諸氏は来朝されたのである。

われわれはこの歴史に先例のない刑事裁判において、その劃期的判決をなすにあたり、確定した国際法のみに基くべきことを裁判所に対して強く要請する。法の認めない犯罪に対して事後法に基づき厳刑を科するがごとき、正義にもとる処置は、必ずや来るべき世代の人々の心情のうちに遺痕を残し、東西の友好関係と世界平和とにとって欠くべからざる恒久の和睦を阻害する原因を作ることとなるであろう。賢明にして学識ある裁判所は万々御承知のことであろう。

来るべき世代の人々が――いな人類全体が――、この劃期的判決を広い歴史的視野からふり返って眺めるとき、三世紀にわたる期間において、西洋の政治家や将軍がその行った東洋地域の侵略について処罰をうけたことが一回もなかったことを想起して、かれらは、東洋の一国の

第2部　158

指導者に対し、事後法に強く処罰を行うたことについて大いなる不正が犯されたとの感想を抱くに至るかもしれない。

英国占領軍の厳格なる監視の下に審理された処刑を受けたオルレアンスの一少女ジャン・ダルクは、後にはフランス国民から殉教者、聖女と見做さるるようになった。これと均しく、征服者の治下において、被告人の一人に対し極刑が加えらるることがあるとすれば、それは平凡な一日本人をして、国民の殉教者、いなアジア解放の殉教者たらしむる危険を包蔵するものである。政治的又は宗教的指導者に科せられた死刑が、彼の罪科を浄めるだけでなく、さらに魔術的に、その平凡なる生涯に光輝を添えることとなった歴史的事例が多多存することは、裁判所の熟知される通りである。

かかる事後法的処罰は又、今や最高司令官の聡明な指導の下に、新憲法の厳格な遵守、従って又その不可分の一部をなす事後法による処罰禁止の規定の厳格な遵守を誓約している日本国民に対して、残酷な模範を示し、かれらの殊勝な熱意を冷却せしめることともなるであろう。かくしてそれはかれらに、勝利者の法と被征服者の法とは別物であるとの深い印象をあたえるであろう。かかる不正は、正しい法の支配なる「一つの世界」の建設に役立つことのない権力政治のあらわれに過ぎぬものとみられるであろう。

そればかりでなくさらに、この歴史的なそして又劇的な裁判において、かような前例が設けら

159　結　語

れることは、本裁判所に代表せられている戦勝諸国における刑事裁判の将来にも深刻な影響を与えることとなるかもしれない。そうした場合には、「血なまぐさい教訓は、必ずもとに戻って教訓者を苦しめる」という格言が妥当することもあるからである。それ故厳格に法を遵守することこそは、司法的勇猛心の表現であるばかりでなく、裁判所のとるべき正しく且つ賢明な道である。周知のそして確定した国際法の原理を固守することによってのみ、「文明」そのものの不可分の要因をなす法至上の灯光は、永遠に国際社会を照らし、揺く灯としてでなく、不動の灯明台として、嵐吹きすさむ世界に指標を与えることとなるのである。

dent in this historic and dramatic trial might, moreover, have far-reaching repercussions on the future administration of criminal justice within the territories of the victorious nations represented here, for in that case the maxim would be true that "we but teach bloody instructions which being taught return to plague the inventor." It would, therefore, be the part of right and discretion as well as an expression of judicial courage for the Honorable Tribunal to abide strictly by the law. By upholding the well-known and well-established principles of international law, and by that alone, can the Lamp of Legal Primacy, constituting an integral part of Civilization itself, be kept ever bright in the community of nations and shine as a fixed beacon, and not as a wavering light, for the guidance of a storm-tossed world.

ought to be subject. (Burlamaqui, *Principes de Droit Naturel*, Part II, Chapter 6, Section 6). This trial involves, on the one hand, the current Executive policy of the victorious nations ably represented by the Prosecution, and, on the other, the lives and liberties of the statesmen and leaders of a defeated but self-respecting nation — or may we not better say, the rights of man on an international level — for the safeguarding of which our American legal friends are here with us. We urge strongly upon the Tribunal that in rendering its epochal judgement in this unprecedented criminal trial, the sole guide should be the well-established law of nations. It will not be necessary to remind the wise and learned Tribunal that an injustice done by imposing severe punishment through *ex post facto* law for crimes unknown to the law would be calculated to leave such rancor in the hearts of generations to come as might check that permanent reconciliation otherwise so evident and certainly so necessary for amicable relations between the East and West and for the peace of the world. Future generations of Oriental peoples — indeed of the whole of mankind — who look back on this epochal judgement in a broad historical perspective might come to feel that a gross injustice had been done through *ex post facto* penalization of the leaders of an East Asian nation, remembering that Western statesmen and generals had never been penalized during the preceding three centuries for their aggressions on Eastern lands. Just as a simple daughter of Orleans, tried and executed under the vigilant eyes of the occupying English army, later became a martyr and saint in the eyes of the French people, capital punishment, if ever meted out to any of the accused under the auspices of the conquerors, would be fraught with the danger of converting a plain son of Yamato into a martyr in the eyes of his nation, or even a martyr to the cause of the freedom of Asia. The Tribunal is well aware that history is replete with instances where the death penalty imposed on a political or religious leader not only purges all his offences, but magically lends glory to an otherwise prosaic life. It would also be setting a cruel example to, and chill the enthusiasm of, the Japanese people now dedicated to the tenets of the new Constitution, the rule against *ex post facto* penalization forming an integral part thereof. It would create an enduring impression on their minds that there could be one law for the victors and another law for the vanquished. Such an injustice would be looked upon as a manifestastion of power-politics, which certainly does not conduce to the building of that one world in which just law reigns supreme. Such a prece-

be folly seriously to discuss international law, for it could be foreseen that it will be disregarded if in conflict with the policy of the Allied Government as expressed in the Charter."

These illusory notions, however, were largely dispelled by the solemn statement of the President of the Tribunal at the beginning of these sessions on 3 May 1946, that "Before assembling here today, members of the Tribunal signed a joint affirmation to administer justice according to law without fear, favor or affection," that "to our great task we bring our open mind in the facts and the law," and that "the onus will be on the prosecution to establish guilt beyond reasonable doubt" (Record, pp. 21-2). To persons who know the Anglo-American legal tradition which knows no other superior than the law — the implications of these statements by the President of the Tribunal were as clear as day. Doubting Thomases were certainly embarrassed, but they persisted in asserting that "according to law" was not employed synonymously with "according to international law," but only meant "according to the law laid down in the Charter." This modicum of doubt was removed by the Opening Address made by the Chief of Counsel who made it clear that the accused were to be judged not by the executive rulings on international law but by the law of nations actually in force, of which the Charter was intended to be but declaratory. The Chief of Counsel is himself an eminent lawyer bred in the common law and certainly imbued with that spirit of fair play characterizing Anglo-American trials in which the government enjoys no special privilege over private persons, and where executive interpretations on law may be rejected by an impartial Tribunal. The Defense, therefore, has constantly assumed that the guilt or innocence of the accused is to be decided by the Tribunal not by the *ipse dixit* of the Charter, under which few Japanese nationals might escape the charge of being "war criminals," but by that well-established law of nations which has been known to all, including the accused. The Defense has now taken up the gauntlet thrown down by the Prosecution, and has endeavored to show that by the canons of the law of nations in force the accused must be acquitted.

According to the belief both of the Prosecution and the Defense, therefore, the International Military Tribunal should symbolize the dignity of the law of nations to which all the governments of the world must bow. As Burlamaqui said two hundred years ago (1747), the Law of Nations is a law, obligatory in itself, to which the peoples or the sovereigns who govern them

CONCLUSION

Mr. President and members of the Tribunal: The International Military Tribunal for the Far East, though technically termed "Military," is not a rough and ready court military devoid of legal training and experience and of legal impartiality and patience instituted to deal summarily with war crimes in the heat of military conflict, with the fear of reprisals by the antagonist as the sole check on its arbitrary tendencies. On the contrary this Tribunal operates in the midst of a peaceful environment in which hostilities have long since terminated without the slightest prospect of their being revived. The Tribunal is, therefore, expected by all the world to combine the functions of a learned Bench of jurists wise in legal lore, and endowed with the qualifications of a Special Jury of statesmen, diplomats, military men and historians versed in the practical operations of world politics in general and of Far Eastern politics in particular. The accused are not ordinary felons, but were high ranking statesmen and soldiers who, divergent as they might have been in their philosophy of life and in their outlook on world politics, all endeavored according to their respective lights to steer the Ship of State through the stormy seas of Far Eastern politics — a sequel to political contact between the Far East and the Western Powers since the past century. Since Japan as a "stabilizing force" in the Far East has lapsed into past history, and the responsibility of securing peace and order in this part of the world has now fallen on the shoulders of other leading nations, the nature and character of the insistent difficulties which confronted the accused may he appraised in their true perspective. The eyes of the Far Eastern people, indeed of all mankind,are centered on its historic judgement.

Before these trials commenced, there were often heard whispers among legal circles in Japan: "the so-called Charter is but an arbitrary rule of thumb formulated in comprehensive terms irrespective of the current rules of international law, in order to empower and direct the Tribunal to punish the enemy political and military leaders; the so-called Tribunal was not a judicial but an administrative organ to apportion punishment accordingly; it would

A most notable admission is found in this paragraph which destroys the whole substratum of the Prosecution's case. It charges that the objectionable acts of the accused were breaches of law. Yet what do we find here? If the Lord Keeper, it is plainly said, was responsible by Japanese Law, that responsibility would be imposed by law: if not it would be one "in fact." Thus a responsibility imposed by fact is not in terms distinguished from a responsibility imposed by law. In other words, all these asserted individual responsibilities and obligations do not rest on Law at all.

Straws show which way the wind blows. The fact that the Prosecution when off their guard recognize that legal responsibility is a sharply distinguished thing from the responsibility that they are trying to assert that they unconsciously recognize the hollowness of their basic contention.

This paragraph makes the assumption unwarranted on the face of it, that the recommendation by the Lord Keeper of a Prime Minister was "fairly be said to be" part of the customary Law of Japan. That such a recommendation was to be made by somebody might be customary but was no more "customary law" than the conventions of the Constitution on the part of the United Kingdom and the United States. And that it should be made by the Lord Keeper was not even a convention; Marquis KIDO was the very first to be so consulted.

in the strongest terms the power of the High Command over foreign policy nevertheless persists asserting the responsibility of the Cabinet which could not control it. Were the Cabinet by resigning to leave the country without a government, or by refusing supplies to it to leave it without an adequate army? It is clear that a Cabinet cannot be condemned for deferring to its military advisers, nor is it or its members to be saddled with the responsibility for all their plans in which it did not participate. The Prosecution themselves say (K-21) that "responsibility for an act follow the power and duty to do the act." And the Cabinet had no power to control the Supreme Command.

(8) *The Privy Council (K-19)*. The Privy Council was not a Senate or House of Lords. It had only to give its opinion on certain important affairs of state. However, a claim is put forward to condemn those who *ex hypothesi* had no part in formulating the supposed "aggressive policy," namely, whose action on certain matters "*led to* the formulation of the aggressive policy." Where are such imputations to stop? It might be said that every communist publicist throughout the globe "*led to* the formulation of that policy."

(9) *The Lord Keeper (K-21)*. As to the Lord Keeper it is another hasty assumption to say "there is an ordinary presumption that responsibility for an act follows from the power and duty to do the act."

What alone can be meant by the so-called "presumption" is that a person who performs a duty of giving advice, free from any civil or criminal liability to A (the Japanese Emperor and public) is thereby placed under a liability to B (the prosecuting Powers). Unless everyone in each country, who is under a duty to give free and untrammelled advice, is to be bound to give it, not freely and unreservedly at all but subject to the possible repercussions it may have, such an "ordinary presumption," so far from being "ordinary" is seen to be extravagant and oppressive. The next step will be to assert that journalists are criminally responsible for the untrammelled statements they make in the performance of their duty to instruct and advise their public. Such a stifled press would be no free press at all.

The essential nature of the Lord Keeper's advice was that it was to be absolutely free from considerations of liability; that it was to be absolutely privileged. And now the Prosecution comes and arbitrarily denies the privilege, which it would concede to every legal adviser in Great Britain and the United States.

nothing to do with the impugned act or else must have opposed and advised against it, and that otherwise he is criminally responsible.

(6) *Responsibility of Cabinet Members (K-14).* This paragraph makes still another daring assumption. A Cabinet Minister might well consider himself personally incompetent to press his opinion on a matter on which his colleague in charge of such matters was presumably better informed than himself; at any rate to the point of resigning. A Cabinet Minister is not *ex officio* an expert on foreign relations and foreign policy. He may have his doubt about a proposal and push them to a division. But he is entitled to assume that his colleagues know better — particularly the Minister in charge of the mattes in question.

It is unfair to say that he goes on full cognizance and "conviction of the evil." He does not know that it is an evil. He is properly willing to accept the assurance of the rest of the Cabinet that it is not an evil, and that he is over-apprehensive. How can a Minister of Agriculture be liable for aggressive warfare, if the Ministers for War and Foreign Affairs assure him with their far superior knowledge that he is mistaken? Just as a bank director is not a criminal for concurring in putting out a mistaken report based on information regarding a property in New Guinea furnished by a codirector who has been there to inspect it.

It may be said that "aggressive war" is such an obvious thing that anyone ought to be able to recognize and repudiate it. On the contrary it depends on such subtleties as the nature of a state, the existence of "real" servitudes and their protection by force, the existence and formidable character of violent threats to national interests, and the whole intensely difficult and complicated question of self-defense, that the decision is extremely difficult. A Minister for Agriculture may be struck with a superficial aspect of a policy, and may even push his view to a division. But he is entitled to suppose that the question is after all a difficult one, and that he may well be mistaken. He need not hurriedly resign in a fit of self-importance, as the Prosecution would have him do.

Naturally, there are cases in which he should. But this is not one of those cases. It raises a question of the utmost complexity and uncertainty — that of self-defense, as to the definition of which no nation has as yet promulgated a satisfactory theory.

(7) *The High Command and the Cabinet (K-18).* This paragraph asserting

point will be treated fully in a later stage by another Defense Counsel.

(3) *Responsibility of Persons Invested with Ultimate Power (K-6)*. The paragraph is riddled with assumptions.

First, it represents the Cabinet, the Privy Council and the Lord Keeper as severally charged with the ultimate responsibility for the formulation of policy within their respective spheres of power. But the Privy Council was under no duty of formulating policy — only of criticizing it, while the Lord Keeper had even less initiative.

Secondly, it assumes a principle against which we have to protest vigorously, namely that if a person is invested with an ultimate power, he is liable for the misuse made of that power by his subordinates. Even in Anglo-American law, it is in most trivial cases that a person is subjected to penalty for the conduct of his servants and agents. If a barman sells his beer out of hours, the innkeeper can now be fined, and that is, we understand, about the extent of the principle in England and Scotland. It may be noted that the Prosecution itself does not seem certain of its proposition, for in one passage we find the remark that it is "particularly true" in a certain case. Either a proposition is true, or not. To say that it is sometimes "particularly true" is to admit that it cannot be admitted as simple truth.

Thirdly, it is stated that acquiescence in the decision of his associates or subordinates "may be" deemed a ratification of that decision and "tantamount" to a personal exercise of his power.

We repeat that such calm assumptions of a vicarious capital liability, without any warrant from anything but police court or *juge de paix* practice, are intolerable to any generous mind.

(4) *Responsibility of Superiors (K-8)*. This paragraph proceeds on the same theory of an assumed vicarious liability. It is not denied that the progress of events may make the corrective intervention of the superior official necessary, and for his failure, with full knowledge and opportunity to correct matters the superior may be constitutionally responsible. International responsibility, of course, we deny altogether.

(5) *Responsibility of Subordinates (K-13)*. This paragraph dealing with the responsibility of subordinate officials fails to take account of the fact that a subordinate has not necessarily the full information which would reveal to him the facts which would make the policy or conduct improper which he propounds. Yet the Prosecution urges that such official must either have

were made no faults could be found' ".

For the Prosecution to ignore such defense evidence is palpably unfair which is perhaps not unrelated to the basic theory of liability of the Prosecution. The learned President's supposed view that the Defense ought not to give evidence of good conditions but meet the charges of bad conditions is well enough as regards charges directly against the officials at those particular places. As regards higher officials, it is surely relevant to prove that in other places where they were in control the conditions were good. This raises an inference that the conditions were good in the challenged instance also. In the case of a defendant, charged with want of supervision, it is clearly relevant to that charge to show that his supervision was generally effective. If a man is charged with participation in an Anti-catholic riot, it is surely relevant to show that he is a Papal Chamberlain.

6. LIABILITY OF THE DEFENDANTS

(1) *Fallacious Analogy of Treason.* "No man has been charged with crimes against peace and conventional war crimes or crimes against humanity unless he is in some way responsible for the aggressive policy followed by Japan which gave rise to these crimes." (Para.K-3). This, however little such a person foresaw or expected that war was probable or that those crimes would happen!

This give us the master-key to the whole fallacious theory pervading the Indictment. It is an idea called up by the design of treasonable conspiracy or *complot* in municipal law. The Prosecution assures such a parallel with its usual assumption. But people on trial for their lives cannot be condemned in such an easy fashion.

Even so, the Prosecution cannot keep free from vagueness. Allowing themselves the sixteenth-century license to hold the least participation in the formation of a policy to involve liability for all its ramifications and consequences, they proceed where there exists no formulation of policy at all on the part of a given individual, to hold him responsible as if there were — because, forsooth, the "toleration of the situation" is "tantamount" to formulating it!

(2) *The Whole Principle of Embassies Nullified (K-4).* The argument on this

With regard to third degree methods employed by the *Kempeitai*, it is said in Para. J-156: "This uniformity cannot have arisen by chance; it must have been the result of a common training. But if such a common training had been given it must have been a matter of a Government policy."

The inference of "a common training" is unsupported by common sense, for the third degree methods may have been due to a common mentality of a certain profession. The further inference that the supposed "training" was a "matter of government policy" shows that by "training" is meant "military training" and is again unjustified. It is not the business of the government to supervise the details of military training.

(4) The use throughout this summation by the Prosecution of a comprehensive and undifferentiated phrase "the Japanese Government" may be in accord with the Prosecution's theory of liability. It is said to be used "in a wide sense as embracing not merely members of the Cabinet but officers of the Army and Navy, ambassadors and senior career public servants." It is so used in the following paragraphs that it amounts to covertly adding to the apparently simple definition, the words "or some or all of them." This is, it is submitted, unfair in a criminal trial against the individual accused — a technique which would not be tolerated in a domestic court of justice. For instance, when it is stated that certain alleged war crimes or other matters were known to the "Japanese Government," it is likely to lead to an inference that all of the persons comprised in the above definition were aware of them, while they were known, only to a few. When a certain policy is declared "governmental," it may only be a strategic policy of the Navy, of which other cabinet ministers or ambassadors or career public servants have nothing to do with. Yet it sounds as if all of them should be responsible for it.

The Defense respectfully submits that capital criminal responsibility must not be imposed on the accused even regarding this category of crimes on the basis of such misleading assumptions and express the desire that the Tribunal will not be misled by assumptions and surmises with which the entire summation is riddled.

(5) It is stated in J-6 "On the other hand this Part ignores defense evidence relating to camps or other places in respect of which no evidence has been given by the Prosecution. This has been done on the basis of his Honor, the learned President's remarks to the Defense, 'meet the charges made against you and do not try to prove that in other cases where no charges

varying methods detailed in these paragraphs. Even the Prosecution cannot see any pattern in them — for it hesitates to link them by any motive. It might, they guess, be to save trouble or it might be to terrorize. But there is no "pattern" alleged in it. All it amounts to if established would be that there were a certain limited number of "massacres" in the first three months of 1942, Does that not show that if such incidents took place they were immediately checked rather than their being "in accordance with the pattern of some" (undefined) "central authority?"

(b) Para. J-145. The massacres detailed were nearly all in Borneo, 1943, and appear to have been perpetrated, if at all, in the course of the suppression of local attempts at insurrection. Armed rebellion cannot be put down with rose-water. It is not the case that formal trials are a necessary preliminary to military executions in the face of force, of "war rebels" and "war traitors."

(c) Paras. J-146-7-8, evince no "pattern." They only show, if proved, that prisoners were sometimes killed when an invading enemy was at hand. The motive is only hazarded by the Prosecution that it might be to prevent the prisoners from giving assistance — avowedly a guess. How can a "guess" prove a "pattern"? The killing of prisoners in such circumstances may, indeed, sometimes be a proper and admissible military precaution. The inconsistency is manifest between professing to deal with events "in anticipation of" invasion, etc., and immediately citing a case (Tarawa) where the killing alleged "occurred *after* an air-raid." Very few cases of this "anticipatory" type are alleged. No "pattern" is discernible from them. Prisoners' stories of threats, and clerk's stories of secret orders are not a "strong corroboration" but very weak evidence.

Had such a "central" "over-all" Japanese policy existed, it would have been applied uniformly and always everywhere, and not merely in a few isolated places. It is not sufficient, in any event, to stigmatize such a supposed "over-all policy" as Japanese, without specifying *what* "*Japanese*" were responsible for its inculcation.

It may be that the Japanese military theory has been that the obligations to prisoners is not paramount to that of preserving the lives of the troops and in isolated instances commanders may have interpreted this principle with improper laxity. But that is not to say that they were instructed to do so. The principle itself is not contradicted by the Hague and the unratified Convention of Geneva of 1929.

mon pattern" as proof of "a common plan" or of an instruction emanating from the "central authority." (Pare. J-1. 30 seq.)

The Prosecution says:

"The fact that the crimes committed by the Japanese were found to be the same in nature, and in the manner of their commission, throughout Japan and *many* of the areas occupied by the Japanese would give rise to an almost irresistible inference that they had not been committed at the whim of the individual perpetrators but as a part of a common plan. It argues very strongly that they were committed as a result of special training towards that end, *or at the least* as a result from instructions emanating from *some* central authority."

This, it is submitted, is far too vague to be made the foundation of a highly criminal charge. It does not even say that the "pattern" was uniformly found everywhere. In some cases admittedly it was not. That does away with the inference of "special training towards that end," or at the least (note the hesitation of the Prosecution) of "instructions emanating from some" (note the uncertainty of the Prosecution) — "some (unidentified) central authority."

Moreover, a scrutiny of the alleged patterns will show that the alleged acts were sporadic and that no common plan or instruction from the central authority existed.

(i) The making of oaths or agreements not to escape. (Pares. J-31-9). The account in these paragraphs purports to show genuine cases of compulsion. It is significant that no such cases are cited regarding other places than Singapore (3 cases), Hongkong (2 cases), Borneo, Java, Batavia, Zentuji and Formosa. Nothing is said concerning India, Burma or the Philippines. So the pattern evinces unexpected gaps. In fact, there is little in common about the alleged acts of compulsion. Sometimes by threats, sometimes by confinement, sometimes by beating and sometimes by heat, sometimes a combination. Where is the common pattern? Of course the demand of an oath is a common feature, but that is admitted and justified as a fair offer of freedom from close guard. All these incidents took place in the first nine months of 1942. Is that not cogent evidence that there was no official policy of compulsion of unlawful coercion. If cruel events took place, they were the sporadic acts of local officers of inferior rank.

(ii) Massacres. (Pares. J-141-4).

(a) It is difficult to see any "pattern" in the alleged massacres in different

That such a declaration, followed by a provision that a delinquent state should pay compensation, and no word concerning Ministers, shall be distorted as implying personal liability on high Government officials will serve as a warning for future statesmen against the dangers of International Agreements unless drafted with the patient care of a Chancery barrister or a land title specialist. International Agreements have hitherto been drafted in the broad spirit of agreements between friends who have a common background of ideas.

Finally the Prosecution derives international duty of individuals from the word "Governments." When, however, the Hague Convention speaks of "Governments," it does not mean the individuals momentarily running the government in various capacities. The word is used as a synonym for States. Thus, treaties in the most recent practice expressed to be entered into between "governments" — yet none imagines that the gentlemen exercising the functions of Ministers are themselves parties in the treaty, still less that any of their subordinates are. No one supposes that German prisoners in Great Britain were or are in the personal custody of Mr. Atlee and Mr. Morrison and Miss Wilkinson. It is the State, the State alone that is intended. No one believes that Sir Stafford Cripps, Mr. Joseph Westwood and Lord Jowith are personally liable to pay their keep, yet according to Article 7 of the Hague Convention the Government into whose hands prisoners of war have fallen are charged with the cost of their maintenance.

The argument of the Prosecution is a transparent equivoque, based on a confusion between the two meanings of "Government," viz. (1) the persons carrying on the Government, (2) the impersonal incarnation of the sovereignty of the State. It is the State which is liable for the breach of the provisions of the Convention. There is no suggestion in the Convention from one end to another of there being any duty on the part of Ministers or other civil officials to supervise and control the conduct of warfare, not to speak of liability on their part to partake the guilt of the offender. The Convention *might* have introduced such duties and liabilities putting the whole machinery of government under the grip of military law, but its framers had more sense than to do so. What they refrained from doing expressly, it will not be wise to attempt by startling implication.

(3) "Common pattern." The Prosecution's dominant idea seems to be: *Dolus latet in generalibus*. It manifests itself most notably in the doctrine of "com-

of them. Japan's own counter-statements were no more binding. There was no agreement or "under-taking" (para. 160-B) — only note was taken of an intention, and a similar intention was expressed not in return for the prior intention but *ex gratia*. It is therefore inaccurate (Page j-24 line 11 up) to call the counter-proposal a "promise." It makes no difference whatever whether its issuance was beneficial to Japan, and it is immaterial what the reservation "mutatis mutandis" meant. Just as one tourist may tell another, "I am going to the *Kabuki* tomorrow — what about you?", and the other party may reply, "Yes, that's my idea too." There is no pretence of any agreement or undertaking, whether in morals or law. Or if this illustration be thought outside the sphere of law, suppose one member of the Bourse says to another, "I'm going to push Copper this week for all its worth — are you?" The other answers: "Yes, so am I." Both are perfectly at liberty to follow their own course and leave copper alone (Para. J-160B-161).

(2) The Hague and Geneva Convention. The Prosecution says: "In any event the Geneva POW Convention of 1929 merely makes explicit what was already implicit in the Hague Convention of 1907." But surely the Convention of 1929 was intended not only to codify but to improve the existing law of nations by securing improved conditions for prisoners of war.

The general statement of the Preamble to the Hague Convention, 1907, cannot be pressed to show more than that a State must be held liable in damages for the improper acts of its military commanders in dealing with unforeseen cases. It did not expect that States foresee those cases and issue instructions to their commanders accordingly. All that the Preamble declares is that the *Convention is not exhaustive* and that if unforeseen cases arise it will not suffice a State to say that the commander's judgment is final about the law to be applied. Preambles cannot enact anything. This preamble only declared that the enactments which followed were not exhaustive. In 1907 the main object of such Conventions was to secure the responsibility of the State. Little attention was paid to traditional liabilities, in occasional cases, of individuals, and certainly nothing was thought of any new liability of high Government officials. The question in the Preamble was not one of imputing responsibility to one set of officers or another set — the Commanders or to the Cabinet. It was a question of securing the responsibility of the State. Therefore it declared that a signatory State could not escape responsibility by sheltering itself behind the arbitrary judgment of its military commanders.

(4) That belligerency to be an excuse for homicide must be "lawful" is an unsustainable proposition since the whole argument defends on the absolute concurrence of all nations in treating homicide without just excuse as a capital crime. For it is not proved, or even probable, that all nations agree with the proposition that belligerency, if "unlawful" in the sense of being unlawful for the State, affords no defense to a charge of homicide. And their complete agreement in such a disputable proposition is the whole substratum of the Prosecution's argument.

(5) B-25 (Record, p. 39,033) advances the view that there is no distinction between illegal acts done in the course of hostilities and those which happen at its commencement. This misses the point, which does not reside in the relative, culpability of the acts, but simply in the scope of the Hague Conventions. A Convention framed to regulate the conduct of war cannot be supposed to have been intended to cover acts which have nothing to do with its conduct.

5. "CONVENTIONAL" WAR CRIMES

Conventional War crimes are discussed in the "Prisoners of War Summation" (J paras. 1-161). The latter is designed to be a summary of the facts only, the law being dealt with in "Liability of the Defendants" (K). However, the above summary is predicated on certain assumptions concerning the law. Here we shall comment only on a few aspects of those assumptions.

(1) Japan's so-called "agreement" to observe the Geneva Convention "*mutatis mutandis*" (Para. J-46).

The Prosecution assumes that there was an international agreement binding on Japan. In the submission of the Defense, this is an error. What the United State and Great Britain said in 1942 was that they "proposed to follow certain provisions" — not even "intended to follow" — and they hoped Japan would imitate them. The other declarations by those powers were *in pari materia*, and must be read in the same way. Evidently they were simply statements of present attitude and contained no binding promise. They were not contingent on any action of Japan, but were entirely independent and voluntary and were without "cause" or consideration. Nor did they become more binding on the United States and Great Britain when Japan took note

aggressive wars as no excuse. It is of no avail for it to show that such courts certainly regard the waging of aggressive wars as no excuse. So long as it cannot be shown affirmatively that they do, then there is no pretence for assuming that throughout the world aggressive war is treated as a capital crime. Of that there is no evidence whatever, and it is essential to the Prosecution's claim that all the rest of the world agree with them. Is it conceivable that a Swiss or a Persian court would condemn a Prime Minister to the penalties of unlawful slaying, because he had launched a war precipitately?

(2) That "the crime of murder" is "part of International Law" as stated in B-21 (Record, p. 39,030), is pure assumption. The broad statement by various authorities and in particular the great men who originally framed the Statute of the Court of International Justice was designed solely to indicate the sources of the law of nations as a law between nations and binding on nations. Those sources comprised (1) international conventions, (2) international custom, (3) the general principles of law recognized by civilized nations, (4) judicial decisions, (5) teachings of highly qualified publicists and (6) justice, equity and good faith.

But the original framers of this classification world have been astounded to find that anyone supposed that they were advancing the proposition that principles regarding the conduct of individuals were being made part of International law. "The general principles of law recognized by civilized nation," were evidently included merely by way of analogy as applicable to the conduct of States.It could mean nothing else.

(3) There is no justification whatsoever for the further statement that there is an international law of "murder" — and that with the ambiguous qualification for which no reason appears, that it must be "of an international character" — which can be dealt with (and apparently dealt with on its principles alone) by any court in the world. The qualification that the court must have jurisdiction leaves the violently debated question of jurisdiction unsettled. Besides, if the crime is "international," why should not every national jurisdiction be competent to deal with it? The whole argument is a tissue of assumptions and unrealities. The late Lord Phillimore and his colleagues of 1920 would have been considerably astonished to think that they were importing domestic law wholesale into the law of nations — and a singular sort of distilled domestic law at that!

civilized nations.

It may be noticed, moreover, that the Prosecution expressly admits, as if under the Hitlerite legislation, that its contention is based on *analogy* and analogy only. However, the analogy of treasonable conspiracy in municipal law would remain a fallacious one, unless and until a World State becomes a reality.

4. MURDER

(1) If the contention of the Prosecution is true (B-21, Record, p. 39,030) that the treatment by all nations of wilful killing without just cause or excuse constitutes it an international crime, then it necessarily follows that it is a crime everywhere without regard to the place or the persons concerned or to its "international character," whatever that may mean. The whole proposition always maintained by Great Britain and the United States and strongly asserted by France in the famous *Lotus* case, that "crime is territorial" would fall to the ground. That, in our submission, can never be admitted. Moreover, the excuses and justifications of homicide vary in every system. A state which abolishes the death penalty may not consider the order of a court a defense. One may concede wide powers to an injured husband, which another might refuse. How can such laws be represented as creating an international norm internationally enforceable? It would involve intolerable contradictions and anomalies. State A may consider X a murderer, while State B may consider it murder to execute X. The whole idea of an international crime called "murder" involving a capital penalty implies the existence of a World State and a World Law. No such World State exists, and no such World Law beyond the accepted laws of war prevailing as a *pis aller* in time of active conflict.

Murder is one thing in Persia and another thing in France. To take some kind of common element and erect it into an international law of murder is to put an abstraction in place of fact. But what can be said of the Prosecution's attempt to establish such an abstract international law of homicide and then to clothe it with all the incidents of particular systems?

The just excuses for homicide are quite various in different countries, and the Prosecution must show, before it can say that murder is the same everywhere, that in all nations the courts certainly regard the waging of

in the course of the execution of the design by anyone or more of them makes the rest guilty, not only of the designed offence but the crime so committed, irrespective of whether it was more or less serious than the designed offence. This may be called the principle of *Criminal Implied Agency*. This doctrine in all its comprehensiveness, it is submitted, is peculiar to the Anglo-American law based on historical grounds, and although the Prosecution refers to the notorious Supreme Court decision on Joint Crimes vehemently denounced by a majority of Japanese criminal jurists, the decision does not go so far as the Anglo-American doctrine of conspiracy, as the Prosecution seems to assert. Be that as it may, the Anglo-American doctrine of *Criminal Implied Agency* has not been proved by the Prosecution to be universal. The principle is, moreover, palpably contrary to our sentiment of justice. It cannot be deemed one of the "general principles of law recognized by civilized nations."

(d) The principle of *Civil Agency*, by which the employer is liable for the civil injuries committed by his servants or agents "in the course of employment" It is difficult for us to say to what extent this modern Anglo-American principle has now (1948) made its way into the civil laws of various nations. The majority, we presume, still adhere to the classical *culpa* principle. It certainly has no application in Criminal Law, even in Great Britain and the United States. Only in the most petty cases, are employers subjected to penalties for the offences of their subordinates. This principle is only mentioned here, because it seems to be laid hold of by the Prosecution (in K-7 seq.) to sustain the criminal liability of cabinet ministers.

(6) The very fact that the Prosecution has to fall back on the "general principles of law" clearly reveals that its contention is without any foundation in the established law of nations. For the said source of international law is designed to be draw upon, as is well known, only in cases where no positive international law can be found. It is intended to make provision for "a blind alley of *non-liquet*," to use Judge Huber's famous phrase, *i.e.* to prevent the Court to refuse to decide on the pretext that there is no applicable law. It may in some cases be a useful source of law to fall back upon in order to dispose of a dispute between States according to international law. That was the very object which the draftsmen of the Statute of the Permanent International Court of Justice had in view in 1920. It definitely has, and ought to have, no place in international *criminal* law. The resort to it would palpably contravene the principle of *nulla poena sine lege* recognized by

imputation of the deepest guilt upon everyone who touched treason with his little finger. But it must surely be rejected by the Law of Nature and of Nations, which, if it regards individual guilt at all must measure individual guilt by individual conduct.

(5) With regard to the arguments of the Prosecution on conspiracy, presented for the first time in its summation, we beg to add the following comments.

The argument that conspiracy is a "form of charge and of the proof of responsibility" is frivolous. To charge a person with and to make him responsible for a capital crime which is not proved to be an international crime under the guise of a procedural device is certainly preposterous.

In the submission of the Defense, the Prosecution's attempt to prove by drawing on comparative criminal jurisprudence that conspiracy is an international crime is a complete failure. The Prosecution cites municipal criminal codes with the view of showing that criminal conspiracy constitutes a rule of the law of nations under the head of the "general principles of law recognized by civilized nations," which is alleged to be a source of international criminal law. This thesis can easily be refuted, if we carefully distinguish four things in Anglo-American law.

(a) *Treasonable Conspiracy.* This is really treason. Treason, the gravest of crimes, may indeed involve everyone who takes the smallest part in this crime, who may be punished capitally. However, the fact that the security of the State or its basic institutions are protected in all states under the severest criminal penalty proves nothing in this case. For clearly there does not exist a World State on which alone the Crime of Treason including treasonable conspiracy can be predicated.

(b) *The substantive crime of Conspiracy.* This consists in a concerted design to commit any unlawful act (or even an immoral act). This is the crime which has so vehemently been criticized by judges and jurists as already mentioned.

The broad Anglo-American doctrine of misdemeanor of conspiracy is not, so far as we are aware, recognized in the civil law countries. Some may punish a plot to commit a *felony*, others may not, as is admitted by the Prosecution. Here, therefore, there are no "general principles of law recognized by civilized nations."

(c) *Criminal Implied Agency.* The odd principle according to which, if several people are engaged in a common unlawful design, any crime committed

and perhaps in most countries have not only made such plots a most terrible crime, but should, in their fierce recoil from it, have made equally responsible and equally guilty, everyone who had the least part in the plot, even those who had not any knowledge of it. There could be no degree of guilt, nor did it matter how far the plot was put in execution. All was treason, and all were equally guilty.

But how different is the case here. There is no World State. There is no World Government which can restrict or punish a nation imposing tariffs on the exports of other nations without any regard for their convenience, or a nation which provides for rational armaments which might someday be employed against other nations. It is certainly salutary for educators throughout the world to bend their efforts for cultivating a sense of a World Community in the minds of youth. But a sense of a World Community is still weak, and world politics still operate on the hypothesis of a society of sovereign states. You might lament over the fact but it is a fact and a reality, on which alone the rules of international law must be predicated. Statesmen and soldiers of the world still perform their duties on that hypothesis, and it would be a height of injustice to judge of and penalize their conduct by the assumed rules of a game under a World State which does not exist.

International War is a terrible evil, and a growing evil. Everyone hates and fears it. Agreements have been made by states to refrain from it. Everyone attaches value to the engagements and hopes they will be kept. But where in the world is the parallel between a person who conspires to wage war even an "aggressive" war against another State with a person who is a traitor to his country? The traitor is breaking down the whole fabric of society and touching a vital nerve. The planner of war is disappointing a pious hope of a world community in which the lion lies down with the lamb.

Far be it from us to ridicule such a pious hope. We only desire to point out that there is no parallel whatever between the planning of a war on the one hand and traitorous conspiracy on the other — no parallel which would in the remotest degree justify the sweeping fury of the municipal law of treasonable conspiracy or *complot* in a novel and startling application to the acts of independent statesmen and soldiers.

(4) The introduction of treason under the name of conspiracy is an attempt to foist upon International Law the sweeping vindictiveness of the hoary feudal English Law based on allegiance — with its indiscriminate

3. CONSPIRACY

(1) It is a striking illustration, which the learned members of the Tribunal will readily appreciate, of the danger of attempting to create new international crimes, by drawing on fancied analogies of municipal law, that the term "conspiracy" is highly ambiguous. In Anglo-American law, upon which the Chief of Council relied in his opening statement by citing a federal decision, it is the specific name of a certain minor crime, namely a concerted attempt to accomplish any unlawful act. That is a so-called "misdemeanor," carrying in England only a maximum of two years' imprisonment. We have already stated in that specific sense it is probably peculiar to Anglo-American law. But in popular language, the word is used to denote what is everywhere regarded as one of the most flagrant crimes, namely a concerted plot to subvert the Government by violent means: in plain English, treason. The Prosecution refrains from giving its charge that name — and why? Because it would then be evident to the merest child that it is a crime of which these accused could not possibly be guilty. For there is no world State which they were trying to subvert.

(2) The tradition of criminal process has always been such that the Prosecution should prove its case in the clearest and plainest manner, refraining from everything that bears the appearance of straining a case. The Prosecution must, therefore, be called upon to show some reason why the Crime of Treason should be applied internationally beyond its imagination and hope that it should be so applied. Although the Defense is convinced that the point is clear, it will endeavor to show affirmatively the essential difference between a State and International Society which makes the crime of treason inapplicable to the latter.

(3) In the case of treason, we have men who are members of a well-established community which is constantly present to them at every point of their lives, and on which they depend for every step they take and every mouthful they eat — the Nation to which they belong. In treason we have an attempt by them to destroy the organization which keeps that nation together, and to replace it by force with one of their fancy. No wonder, perhaps, that the easily startled apprehensions of mankind should in some

nation must be the judge of what constitutes its own self-defense, that it is not to be referred to any tribunal by the United States or by any other nation and that public opinion would regard a state's alleged action in self-defense with approval or the reverse. These statesmen meant exactly what they said. They meant that the act of alleged self-defense incurs the only sanction of the law of nations — general disapproval. They did not mean and could not have meant anything more. How would it have satisfied a James G. Blaine, insisting on the right of the United States to go to war in defense of the Monroe Doctrine in Central America, to be told that her leaders might be liable to be tried for their lives, if they fell into the power of the enemy.

A personal view of a text-writer like Oppenheim possibly based on his own theoretical preference, or of a group of Japanese jurists possibly advanced to wield a restraining influence of their government cannot alter the well-established rule of international law that in the interpretation of a treaty the prime principle is to ascertain the real intention of the contracting parties which can and must be gathered not solely by the wording of the text of the treaty but in the light of diplomatic correspondence and declarations of leading statesmen made before or at the time of its making. No evidence has been adduced to prove that basic principle of International Law has changed. International law may certainly grow by the common consent of the nations, but internal treaties cannot be extended or modified without the consent of all the signatories. This is true of multilateral treaties relative to the general rules of international law like the Declaration of Paris or the Geneva Convention of 1929 or the Pact of Paris as well as bilateral treaties.

(3) In relation to the contention of the Prosecution in B-16, (Record, p. 39,025) that self-defense can only apply in the case of a reasonably anticipated armed attack and cannot be extended to cover "encirclement" either military or still less economic, the Tribunal is respectfully reminded of the express statement denying such contention made by Secretary Kellogg to the Senate Committee on Foreign Relations, (*General Pact for the Renunciation of War*. Committee on Foreign Relations. U. S. Senate December 7, 1928). But this matter will be treated elsewhere by another Defense Counsel.

The Tribunal may also be reminded of the express statement by the Chairman of the Senate Committee on Foreign Relations, already cited, that each nation is entitled to decide for itself what constitutes an attack to itself.

the belligerent who desires to punish an aggressor beyond his own sentiment. This alone sharply differentiates the two things which the Prosecution represents as indistinguishable.

(7) In para. B-15, (Record, p. 39,025) it is advanced as an essential element that there should be reasonable grounds for an honest belief on the part of an accused. It is submitted that as a general doctrine of criminal jurisprudence this is going much too far. It would make a man criminally and capitally responsible for his honest but stupid or over-anxious mistakes. It would make a man a criminal for being "unreasonable."

2. THE PACT OF PARIS AND SELF-DEFENSE

The Pact of Paris in its relation to national self-defense has been fully dealt with in our previous argument. However, a few remarks should be made in view of certain new arguments offered by the Prosecution on that topic.

(1) The Prosecution assumes in B-10 and B-12 (Record, p. 39,019-21) that permissible self-defense is restricted to self-defense against invasion. But that is contradicted in express terms by what Secretary Kellogg formally told the Senate Committee and by the statements of Mr. Borah, Chairman of that Committee, made to the Senate, and also by what is implied by Sir A. Chamberlain's Note on accepting the Kellogg-Briand Treaty — all of which have already been referred to. It certainly extends to the protection of Japanese forces legitimately stationed in China and Manchuria, as it extends to the protection of American forces legitimately stationed in the Panama Canal Zone.

It may also he added that the Franco-Soviet Mutual Assistance Treaty of May 2, 1932, stipulating that should either country be subjected, in certain circumstances, to unprovoked aggression by any European State, the other should immediately come to its assistance, limited the aggression thereby envisaged to aggression involving violation of French or Soviet territory, clearly demonstrating that self-defense against aggression is not necessarily limited to defense against invasion.

(2) The assertion that self-defense is a matter to be decided by a tribunal implied in B-14 (Record, p. 39,025) is contrary to the repeated declarations of leading American statesmen of the highest rank when they stated that each

Although such evidence would by no means be conclusive it might serve as forcible evidence in the Prosecution's favor. That the Prosecution failed even to take this step which was peculiarly within its power places the contention of the Prosecution in an extremely dubious light.

Moreover, it would not only be frivolous but quite unfair in a historic case like this to leave this momentous issue to the technical procedural rule of the burden of proof. The point should, in the interests of truth and justice, be clarified by the Tribunal, if necessary, on its own motion.

(4) The argument based on the Agreement and Charter published on August 8 regarding the trial of German accused has no application here, for the Japanese making a conditional surrender naturally expected those terms to embody different treatment. Nor is the argument in para. B-7 (Record, p. 39,014) of any greater validity. It is not a question of what the opinion of the Nuremberg tribunal was as to the comparative heinousness of waging aggressive war and breaking a Hague Convention. It is a question of what the accused were entitled to consider the meaning of the current term "war criminals." Our submission is that to these accused it meant the criminal breach of the accepted rules governing the conduct of armed forces in the field and analogous acts during the progress of hostilities, and that it is oppressive to extend it beyond that previously universal understanding.

(5) In para. B-7 (Record, p. 39,015) it is observed that the German Emperor was an absolute monarch. This is quite inadmissible. The federal constitution of the Empire was by itself sufficient to prevent such a thing. Yet no German King or Minister was arraigned. And the extraordinary statement must be repudiated which alleges that a single unconsummated attempt to try an Emperor (which failed largely because it was startling to the conscience) "established a right." (Para. B-8, Record, p. 39,017).

(6) The assimilation (para. B-9, Record, p. 39,017) of persons responsible for the war to conventional war criminals is hasty and unfounded. The latter classes fall under Long-established principles, so do their penalties. Above all their treatment is controlled by the constant possibility of reprisals: which the former are not. At one time in the XVIth century so instructs us Dr. T. A. Walker in his "Science of International Law," the experiment was made in the course of the wars of Religion of abolishing the laws of war altogether. But the crescendo of reprisals was such that "these things made them admire antiquity," and the laws of Arms were restored. But there is no check upon

of war can be found in that demand made by the German Government at the close of World War I which was certainly known to the Japanese statesmen. In that historic instance the persons who were to be tried were not "persons responsible for war" but "persons responsible in the course of war."

The accused TOGO's statement in answer to the question put by the Bench confirms the latter interpretation (Record, p. 36, 131).

At any rate KIDO's entry regarding the proposed conditions is merely hearsay.

Even assuming for argument that "senso sekinin sha" meant "persons responsible for war," which is denied by the Defense, there is no reason why the Japanese authorities should not have mooted the possibility of themselves going further. In a serious case like the present such trivial and ambiguous utterances recorded by hearsay ought surely to receive the most favorable interpretation.

(2) The Prosecution says: "if there was any doubt it could have been cleared up by a question." The answer is that the natural meaning of the wording of Clause 10 was, as has been shown, so clear that no doubt could be entertained on this point.

(3) The Prosecution says: "it would be necessary for the Defense to show, as a matter of construction, that the phrase in the Potsdam Declaration could not include those responsible for the war, before they could have any hope of attacking with success the basis of the Charter of this Tribunal or the Counts in the Indictment founded upon it, even if it were now open to them to do so."

The answer is that the Defense has shown that in view of the natural and universally accepted meaning of the term "war criminals" as well as of the circumstances attending the emitting of the Potsdam Declaration on July 26 that the term used in the Potsdam Declaration can but bear one meaning.

It is then for the Prosecution to show that the natural and universally accepted meaning was not the meaning of the term as employed in the Potsdam Declaration. The only evidence it adduces is (1) the Cairo Declaration which does not throw the slightest light on the point at issue and (2) the vague entries in the KIDO Diary.

The Prosecution which represents the Allied Governments might easily have produced affidavits of the Allied statesmen who were actually at Potsdam so as to clarify what they intended by the use of that term.

PART II

We have heretofore answered the arguments of the Prosecution in its opening statement at the commencement of this trial. In its summation the Prosecution has presented some new arguments and amplified those referred to previously. We shall answer these in the following order:
1. War Criminals.
2. The Pact of Paris and Self-Defense.
3. Conspiracy.
4. Murder.
5. "Conventional" War Crimes.
6. Liability of the Defendants.

1. "WAR CRIMINALS"

We have already shown that the term "war criminals" employed in the Potsdam Declaration as embodied and accepted by the Instrument of Surrender should, for the reasons already stated, be interpreted as referring to conventional crimes.

(1) The Prosecution cited two entries in Kido's Diary to prove that the Japanese Government understood the term to mean persons responsible for war (B-3, Record, p. 39,001).

"Senso sekinin sha" (literally "war responsible persons") in the Japanese language did not prior to the armistice necessarily mean "persons responsible for war" but equally meant "persons responsible in the course of war." And we understand that the accused KIDO himself used the word in that latter sense. The latter interpretation is entirely compatible with the Emperor's remarks, for they might comprise generals or admirals in whom His Majesty placed his trust and confidence.

A well-known precedent for a proposal by way of conditions for leaving to the Japanese Government the trial of persons charged with violations of laws

defeated, they are unlikely to be penalized. The risks of defeat are terrible enough in themselves to be a most potent deterrent; and in the anticipated event of victory, penal consequences are no deterrent at all, for the victor will impose them, instead of suffering them. Would Bismark have been deterred from war in 1870 by the fear that if France were victorious he might be tried and condemned by a military court? Indeed such a doctrine of individual crimes of leaders may have the most deplorable effect of making future wars more cruel and inhuman. For political and military leaders in belligerent countries will be all the more intensely bent on quick victory by fair means or foul, not only to save the lives of their compatriots but to save their own necks. In the process of such wars the laws and customs of war such as were recognized by the Hague and Geneva Conventions will be disregarded by both belligerents as "legal trivialities." The doctrine of military necessity of *kriegsraison* will be in the ascendant. Moreover, an international lid placed on a national boiling pot by threats of punishing the leaders of an exasperated nation will never secure peace, so long as there is a strong national feeling of injustice. Resentment will breed conflict unless adequate machinery is provided for peaceful and just change. The road to world peace must be sought elsewhere, viz., in international cooperation, in the economic and social amelioration of mankind and the conciliation of differences between nations, if they occur, in the spirit of amity and justice.

igencies of a temporary executive policy any fundamental principle of that body of law which has been developed by civilized nations through centuries of arduous travail. Was it not very wise and far-sighted of the Judicial Committee of the British Privy Council to have advised the Crown in the leading case of *The Zamora* (Law Reports [1916] 2 Appeal Cases 77):

> "The idea that the King in Council, and indeed any branch of the Executive has power to prescribe or alter the law to be administered by courts of law in this country is out of harmony with the Principles of our Constitution."

It is well known that Karl Schmidt and others in Germany attempted to build up a new international law to suit the political exigencies of the Third Reich. That attempt has been looked down upon as unworthy of the glorious traditions of the legal profession for it meant the subservice of law to politics. Such an attempt, however well-intentioned, is especially to be avoided at a time when war's hates and prejudices remain undiminished. It has been said that it is the duty of every generation to consider its conduct under a deep sense of responsibility to future generations and uninfluenced by that emotional hypocrisy which facilitates a reversion to evil practices under righteous pretences. For the sake of our posterity, may we not here stop and ponder not only that well-known Johnsonian aphorism, "Hell is paved with good intentions," but Walter Bagehot's not ineptly expressed paradox, "The work of the wise in this world is to undo the mischief done by the good."

The Chief of Counsel vigorously denies the "small meaner objects of vengeance and retaliation" (Record, p. 387). However, persons who have studied the history of World War I may be permitted to recollect that the public passion caused by German *schrecklichkeit* created a popular clamor in the Allied countries for the punishment of the authors of the war, and that their leading statesmen could but respond at least for a time to that popular sentiment. May it not be surmised that history is repeating itself in this respect in World War II, and that the Prosecution is doing its very best to give effect to the policy of their respective Governments, acting knowingly or not in consonance with the supposed similar popular sentiment.

The Chief of Counsel asserts that the establishment of this principle is necessary for deterring future aggressors (Record, p. 387). But it is not necessary for that desirable end. For statesmen will never be disposed to make aggressive war in the face of probable defeat. And if their country is not

oblivion, amnesty and pardon which used to characterize the termination of war in the East as well as in the West. It will be to introduce a disturbing element in the peaceful intercourse of nations. If nations are to continue as a unit they would not like to be eternally reminded of the stigma of crime set on their forehead by other nations whom they may not deem to be above reproach or wholly disinterested and unprejudiced. If war is outlawed altogether, and persons who prepare for war, either defensive or aggressive, are made punishable by law domestic and international, the proposal may be more just, reasonable and calculated to promote world peace than the qualified and equivocal undertaking of the Kellogg-Briand Treaty. But to add to the "war" to be outlawed the adjective "aggressive" or "in breach of international law or treaties," though sounding reasonable enough in the abstract, is practically fraught with the serious danger of functioning as "a trap for the innocent and a signpost for the guilty."

We must also realize that such a basic change will have far-reaching effects on international and domestic law. In an address by Dean Roscoe Pound on "*The Future of Law*," delivered at Tokyo University on February 20, 1937, he sounded a weighty warning to ardent but rash law reformers that a change in a body of norms may have effects at many other points, and that the stability of the economic order may be greatly disturbed thereby. He showed how a novel doctrine such as that of a sit-down strike, asserting a vested interest of the employee in the *locus* of performing the job, undermines the foundations on which are based the common-law doctrines regarding the employer's criminal and civil liability, by which the general security has been maintained — since the owner of the locus has no longer the control or choice of the persons who work there. The doyen of American jurists here referred only to the effects of a comparatively minor change in domestic law. But the criminal responsibility of the authors of a war comprising all persons plotting, preparing, initiating and executing it, and made still more comprehensive by the use of the Anglo-American doctrine of conspiracy, if introduced into the law of nations, will have far-reaching effects on other portions of international law and may have unexpected repercussions on domestic law. For it is an innovation which undermines the very foundations on which all doctrines of the law of nations have been built and will engender confusion and chaos in the conduct of state affairs, whether political, economic or military.

It is a dangerous undertaking to attempt to alter to conform to the ex-

8. THE NEW DOCTRINE OF INTERNATIONAL LAW PROPOSED BY THE PROSECUTION

The Chief of Counsel strongly urges the Tribunal to create by an unprecedented and historic decision a novel and, in his opinion, salutary principle in the law of nations that aggressive wars and wars in breach of international law and treaties are international crimes for which persons who acted on behalf of such a State are punishable with all the ignominy of common felons (Record, p. 389).

Before importing a proposition so far reaching in effect into the law of nations, we must examine it not merely as an expression of a glowing and irreflective moral sentiment but as a legal principle as it actually functions, not in the texture of a state or super-state, but in that of a complicated society of sovereign states. It is conceivable that at a time of revolutionary excitement, when the public passions aroused by war have not yet subsided, an international body might unanimously adopt the proposal. It is, however, greatly to be doubted whether it can ever be technically elaborated in the form of a treaty which can be accepted by all nations, great and small, as soon as they are fully conscious of its practical implications.

It is a notorious fact that in time of war "aggressor" is the epithet which each of the belligerents in self-righteousness and for purposes of soliciting public sympathy hurls at the other. When one of the parties is defeated, will the victor ever admit that it was the aggressor and punish its responsible statesmen and officers? Unless human nature is fundamentally altered, it will always be the defeated nation that will be declared the aggressor and the violator of international law and treaties. A defeated nation has from time immemorial been penalized by the loss of its territory and by the payment of indemnities. Its statesmen and military officers were penalized through the loss of their prestige and their fortunes and by the pain of seeing their beloved country reduced to ruins. To add criminal penalty to all this would only signify a long step farther away from that elevated spirit of perpetual

the East as well as in the West. We beg to reiterate here that except in the case of "conventional" war crimes the criminal law laid down in the Charter is clearly and entirely *ex post facto* and therefore excluded by the Potsdam Declaration as not being "stern justice" but the Hitlerite "justice" of vague "popular feeling": the anti-thesis of justice according to law.

common sense to suppose that such a peculiar and unfair doctrine, based on purely historical grounds, is accepted as law by all the nations of the world.

The Chief of Counsel asserts that excepting one point, namely, the doctrine that their official position does not protect the accused, the law laid down in the Charter represented the rules and principles of the law of nations not only at the time the Charter was penned, but at the time of the acts alleged to have been committed by the accused. The question regarding *ex post facto* law is not, according to the Chief of Counsel, involved in this case and the accused can justly be punished (Record, p. 474). We beg squarely to join issue with the Chief of Counsel on this question of *ex post facto* law. Allow us to take a concrete example. Suppose that one of the accused in this trial were to be sent to the United States and were to be charged with the crime of conspiracy or the crime of aggressive war by a military tribunal created by the President of the United States with or without the cooperation of other nations. Suppose also that having been sentenced to prison, he were to seek a writ of *habeas corpus* from a Federal Court. Would the Chief of Counsel seriously contend that the prisoner would not be entitled to be released on the ground he was held in violation of the *ex post facto* clause of Article I, section 9, of the Federal Constitution? Will not the case clearly fall under the said clause according to the classical interpretation of Justice Chase in *Calder* v. *Bull* which is as follows:

> "1st. Every law that makes an action done before the passing of the law, and which was innocent when done, criminal; and punishes such action."

> "2nd. Every law that aggravates a crime, or makes it greater than it was when committed."

> "3rd. Every law that changes the punishment, and inflicts a greater punishment than the law annexed to the crime, when committed."

> "4th. Every law that alters the legal rules of evidence, and receives less or different testimony than the law required at the time of the commission of the offence in order to convict the offender." (3 Dallas 386, 390 (1798)).

It may be noted that the rule against *ex post facto* penalization is not a technical rule of American jurisprudence. It is a rule based on natural and universal justice. As fire burns and water flows alike in Washington and Tokyo, so a violation of that rule will be felt to be unjust and oppressive in

good and preservation of the whole. But these two, under favour, are not to be confounded in Judgement. We must not piece up want of legality with matter of conscience, nor the defaillance [sic] of prudential fitness with a pretence of Legal Justice."

It may be "high time" that the principle of individual responsibility in these exalted circles of government was introduced. But let it not be done in a manner which will inevitably cast suspicion and discredit on it, by making it appear as the unilateral opinion of a conqueror; that will set back its acceptance for centuries.

After urging the Tribunal to take this opportunity to effect a fundamental change in the system of international law, the Chief of Counsel closes his discussion of the criminal law of the Charter by again invoking the notorious doctrine of criminal conspiracy, as if it already constituted an institute of the law of nations.

Thus totally disregarding the eminently sound principle that guilt is personal, he declares that "these men, who held positions of power and influence in the Japanese Government and by virtue of their position conspired to, and planned, prepared, initiated, and waged illegal war, are *responsible for every single criminal act resulting therefrom*" (Record, pp. 433-4).

He also endeavors to invigorate his thesis by referring to another theory of domestic criminal law (Record, p. 434) — apparently recognized in some jurisdictions — that all who participated in the formulation or execution of a criminal plan, in the execution of which crimes happen to be committed by some of their number, are liable for each of the offences committed and for the acts of each other, without regard to whether they knew of them and whether they had forbidden them.

On this cognate topic we also urge that this Tribunal will reject, as forming any part of the law of nations, the illogical Anglo-Saxon doctrine that if several persons are engaged in the accomplishment of an unlawful design, however insignificant, they are all equally liable for the penalties of a crime, however atrocious, committed in its furtherance by one of their number, although without their knowledge or against their express instructions. For instance, if a party of hunters is taking game unlawfully and one of them deliberately kills a warden who interferes, all the rest by this doctrine are held guilty of murder, although they know nothing of his act and would have done their utmost to prevent it if they had known. It is an offence to

opinion widely differs, and the principle proposed is contrary to all well-established principles and startling to all previous conceptions and practice. Scholars throughout the world are declaring that the novelty of the process is a bar to its reception, that it is an attempt to penalize men for their opinions and to conclude questions of statesmanship and politics by *ex parte* pronouncements of law. These declarations of great jurists may be right or wrong. The point is that they are made and cannot be ignored, and with their existence the alleged parallel vanishes into thin air.

A revolutionary legal change can properly be made only after prolonged discussions as to the pros and cons of the proposal by all concerned, which can not be undertaken by a tribunal, where the evidence for or against such change in law is extremely limited, depending as it does in large measure upon the facilities and learning which happen to be available for the counsel of the contending parties. If any fundamental change in the law of nations is necessary, an international body like the United Nations might be a proper organ, if it develops into a world legislature. But it is certainly not a task for an International Court of Justice or for a Military Court, national or international. The Chief of Counsel says that the development of the art of destruction has proceeded to such a stage that the world cannot wait upon the debating of legal trivialities (Record, p. 461). But law is not a triviality. The rules and principles of the law of nations built up by centuries of experience, tested by reason, should not brusquely be set aside as "legal trivialities." Perhaps the Chief of Counsel has here been seized with that zeal for a new order of things which has characterized every generation which has become conscious after a great war of its own pivotal position in history. But we must bear in mind that "a new order of things" and "emergency" are the well-known technique for disregarding due process of law by the powers that be. If it were really the universal sense of the nations of the world that new principles governing their intercourse be set up to avert disaster to mankind, as alleged by the Chief of Counsel, the method well settled for such purposes, i. e. multilateral treaty-making, might easily be resorted to. It may not be inappropriate here to remind the Tribunal of Lord Digby's famous dictum made in 1641 regarding the Strafford Bill of Attainder:

> "There is in Parliament Double Power of Life and Death by Bill, a Judicial Power, and a Legislative, the measure of the one is what is legally Justice, of the other what is Prudentially and Politically fit for the

but to interpret existing law. If a tribunal attempts to revolutionize the law, it arrogates to itself the function of a legislature.

It is true that sometime the courts virtually legislate in the guise of rendering legal interpretation. But such judicial legislation proceeds by the slow process of tentative and meticulous inclusion here and exclusion there, not by the overhauling of any fundamental principle of the particular legal system it administers. In *Southern Pacific Co.* v. *Jensen* (224 U. S. 205, 221 (1917)), Justice Homes says:

> "I recognize without hesitation that judges do legislate, but they can do so only interstitially; they are confined from molar to molecular motions. A common law judge could not say I think the doctrine of consideration a bit of historical nonsense and shall not enforce it in my court. No more could a judge exercising the limited jurisdiction of admiralty say I think well of the common law rule of master and servant and propose to introduce it here *en bloc*."

A parallel has sometimes been drawn between the present attempt to import new crimes into the law of nations and the introduction of new crimes into medieval English law. The parallel is superficial and the justification based on such analogy is certainly fallacious. The English criminal law in medieval times was designed to regulate a small community held together by a single faith — that of Rome — which pervaded all affairs of life and conduct. The society which international law is intended to regulate today is a world-wide community of sovereign nations with manifold cultures and divergent social and political outlooks. In medieval England the judges were mostly Catholic ecclesiastics and their judgments in criminal matters reflected the medieval conception of justice. Here the eminent judges represent nations with different religions, social and political outlooks, and different legal traditions. The new crimes introduced by the Court of King's Bench in medieval England were all flagitious conduct according to the Christian code of morals, and the process of introducing them was a gradual extension of an admitted legal system already judicially administered. No one could be surprised or complain if the Court treated them as crimes imposing appropriate penalties. No protesting voice impugning the novelty of a crime was to be heard. Not even the accused complained that they were being tried and condemned for something novel. They felt, like the rest of the world, that they were criminals. Here the proposed new crimes are political acts on which

jeopardizing relations between the countries immediately concerned *and other states*. Also, the securing of evidence from independent sovereign states must always be precarious or often impossible, because of the dislike or refusal of the latter to reveal compromising or secret matter of importance to themselves. Such considerations seldom, if ever, hamper the defense in municipal prosecutions.

These matters sharply differentiate the responsibility of those who conduct the affairs of state from that of persons who have nothing to do with them. It is obvious that the Law of Nations and the signatories of International Conventions have been well aware of this all important fact. Justice cannot be done to statesmen without the production of evidence which might set the world in a blaze. It is not any undemocratic discrimination in favor of statesmen as such. Nor is it derived from an outmoded doctrine of corporate fiction as applied to the state. It is the just recognition of a truth that statesmanship cannot properly be defended without that enormous danger. And as nations will not incur that dangerous risk, statesmanship cannot properly be defended in courts of law. That is one of the reasons why impeachments, bills of attainder and bills of pains and penalties turning on foreign policy have been so uniformly discredited and disliked. The hands of the accused are tied by the impossibility of obtaining the evidence of foreign chanceries and the danger of disturbing foreign relations. The Panama Scandals, the Dreyfus case, Caillaux case, are only pale reflections of the difficulties of doing anything like real justice when an international governmental element is indirectly concerned. The immunity of statesmen is not a mere tradition: it is a necessity.

We heartily agree with the Chief of Counsel that law, international and national, can grow by judicial decision as well as by legislation. But, we submit, the development of law by judicial decision proceeds and ought to proceed within the bounds of the spirit and fundamental principles of a legal system.

A reference to the history of the law in Europe or America will show how exceedingly careful and moderate the courts have been in their development of the law they administer. They have worked like the processes of Nature, gradually and imperceptibly, not suddenly nor violently. Therefore, their work has been permanent. The court exists to administer the established law. The court is expected by its decision not to effect a revolutionary chance in law,

Briand Pact was designed to establish any exception to the general principle, by introducing individual responsibility for acts of State, as the Chief of Counsel contends. If that was really the intention of the contracting parties, they would have expressly said so.

The above system of responsibility is grounded on the realities of our community of states, and is the only system which can practically function with justice in view of those realities. It would surely be an act of folly to criticise the system with a mind permeated with notions derived from municipal law, or on the erroneous assumption that the world state is a present reality or can he established in the immediate future. Persons both wise in municipal law and with sincere aspirations for the welfare of mankind have participated in the building up of the present system. If acts of State loom large in that system it is but a reflection of the realities of the society of nations, in which peace and order is primarily maintained by means of the fullest recognition of state sovereignty, which the nations of the world seem not yet prepared to replace by the sovereignty of a world state and the reign of the universal governmental law. Would it not be to be blind to the realities of the community of nations to think that the business of government, whether political, economic, or military, can possibly be conducted, if an officer of state has to decide for himself in every case as to whether the command of his government is in violation of international law, treaties, agreements and assurances, lest he should some day be declared a war criminal by an alien judge?

That at least might be one of the potent reasons why many a state would ponder long before signing a treaty by which the conspiring for, preparing, initiating and executing of a war liable to be some day declared by the victors aggressive or in breach of an international agreement is a criminal act, involving the personal responsibility of its statesmen and military officers. At any rate it is quite clear that there exists in the law of nations no crime against peace involving personal responsibility unless and until express provision is made for such criminal responsibility by an international agreement.

May we not here state another reason why it cannot be supposed that the treaties like the Kellogg-Briand Treaty and the Hague and the Geneva Conventions intended to impose individual penalties upon statesmen. It is to be found in the fact that international relations are so intimately interwoven that the true situation cannot be revealed by evidence in court without gravely

stated:

> "The inability of a court to exercise jurisdiction in regard to a sovereign act of a foreign government...... should apply where the defendant is sued personally for acts done by him in his capacity as a public official...... though he no longer retains that capacity at the time of the proceedings...... or under powers conferred upon him by a sovereign State." (Publications of the League of Nations, Legal, 1927, Vol. 9 in *A. J. I. L.* 1928, Vol. 22, Supp. p. 125).

Woerterbuch des Voelkerrecht und Diplomatie, herausgegeben von Karl Strupp (1925), Vol. 2, p. 2, also says:

> "The State is responsible for the acts of all its organs, but the organs are not responsible at all insofar as they act in their capacity as organs of the State."

This fundamental rule of the law of nations is not, however, without a few well-known exceptions, as is clearly the case in espionage and war treason which, even if committed by command of the government of the enemy State, can be punished as "war crimes." But such exceptions to the general rule of the immunity of individuals must clearly be established by special rules of the customary or conventional law of nations.

Individual responsibility either for acts of State or for non-official acts can be provided for by international treaties. This is true of slave-trading, cable-cutting and pelagic sealing. A more recent (but abortive) attempt at establishing such an exception to the general principle of immunity was the treaty relative to the use of submarines concluded at Washington February 6, 1922. Article 3 of the treaty provides that:

> "Any person in the service of any State who shall violate any rule of this treaty relative to the attack, capture, or destruction of commercial ships whether or not he is under order of a government superior, shall be deemed to have violated the laws of war and shall be liable to trial and punishment as if for an act of piracy and may be brought to trial before the civil or military authorities of any power within the jurisdiction of which he may be found."

In view of the extreme reluctance of the nations to recognize exceptions to this basic principle of the law of nations and the meticulous care which is exercised in establishing such exceptions by international agreement, it must be said to be amply clear that neither Hague Convention III nor the Kellogg-

cannot invoke the principle of the freedom of the open seas to protect him, and other States are not authorized to resort to reprisals or war against the State whose subject or vessels have committed acts of piracy. Another well-known group of exceptional instances is breach of blockade and carriage of contraband of war. International law provides for specific sanctions against blockade-runners and contrabandists in the shape of confiscation of the cargo, which can be enforced by the prize courts of the capturing State. A third group of exceptions is violations of the law of warfare, or so-called "war crimes", in which persons even though not belonging to the armed forces of a State can be summarily punished by its military tribunals.

A State assumes collective responsibility for its own act, that is to say, for an act of State performed by individuals at the government's command or with its authorization. To say that an act is an act of State means that the act in question is imputed to the State and not to those individuals who have performed the act. It is a well-established principle in the law of nations that the State injured by such an act can hold the State alone responsible for an international delinquency. It cannot, without violating the law of nations, hold the individuals responsible without the consent of the State. In the famous MacLeod case, MacLeod, a member of the British forces dispatched in 1837 into the territory of the United States in order to capture the *Caroline*, was arrested in 1840 in the State of New York and indicted for the killing of an American citizen on that occasion. Mr. Webster, Secretary of State, wrote to Mr. Crittenden, Attorney General, on March 15, 1841:

> "All that is intended to be said at present is, that, since the attack on the Caroline is avowed as a national act, which may justify reprisals, or general war, if the Government of the United States in the judgement which it shall form of the transactions and of its own duty, shall see fit so to decide, yet that it raises a question entirely public and political, a question between independent nations: and that individuals connected in it cannot be arrested and tried before the ordinary tribunals as for the violation of municipal law. If the attack on the Caroline was unjustifiable, as this Government has asserted, the law which has been violated is to be sought in the redress authorized by the provisions of that code." (Moore, *Digest of International Law*, Vol. 2 Sec. 179).

In the Report adopted by the Committee of Experts for the Progressive Codification of International Law at its third session, March-April, 1927, it is

personal responsibility. As the Tribunal is well aware, international law is a delicate and unaggressive body of law governing the community of sovereign states. If the family of independent nations should evolve a world government, international law as we know it would *ipso facto* disappear and be replaced by the universal law. Those essential characteristics of the law of nations, which arose from the conditions obtaining in European society since the Renaissance, still remain today after centuries of its development and despite the extension of its orbit to other contingents. The law of nations is, therefore, enforced not by a universal government but by organized states capable of exercising an effective control over their respective territories and of assuming a certain measure of responsibility for acts of all persons subject to their sovereignty as well as for their own conduct.

The principles of international responsibility can be understood in their true perspective only when this basic fact in this particular legal system of ours is fully realized.

It is the general principle of the law of nations that duties and responsibilities are placed on states and nations and not on individuals. The breach of an international duty gives rise to the collective responsibility of the delinquent state. The specific sanctions of international law, such as reprisals and war, are directed net against the individuals through whose conduct international law has been violated but against the state itself, *i. e.* against all the individuals composing such state. In a regime of the world state with its universal law, justice would require that criminal or civil sanctions be directed against the guilty alone and not against innocent citizens, just as the punishment for treasonable acts committed by certain citizens of the State of New York is meted out to guilty persons alone and not to the entire population of that State. Such, however, is not the system prevailing in the Community of Nations.

Through the practical experience of intercourse between nations both in war and peace, however, there came to be recognized a few well-known exceptional cases, real or apparent, in which individual responsibility might be imposed. The oldest exception is that of piracy. According to custom antedating the rise of modern international law, a pirate was regarded as an outlaw, a "*hostis humanis generis.*" Under the law of nations a pirate loses the protection of his home State and all nations are entitled to seize and punish him. By this exceptional rule the State of which the pirate is a national

7. PERSONAL RESPONSIBILITY

The Chief of Counsel then proceeds to the question of personal responsibility on the part of the accused. He cites a decision of the Supreme Court of the United States, *Ex parte Quirin*, the saboteurs' case, in support of his thesis that the planning, preparation, initiation, and execution of war in breach of international law or of treaties involves individual responsibility (Record, pp. 431 *et seq.*). But *Ex parte Quirin* is a case concerning the question whether an American act of Congress can, instead of crystallizing in permanent form and in minute detail every offense against the law of war, adopt the system of common law, applied by military tribunals so far as it should be recognized and deemed applicable by the courts. This is simply a question of the interpretation of an Act of Congress, which might enact in constitutional terms whatever it pleased. The interpretation put by the Court on the will of the Congress cannot bind other nations.

It is, moreover, a far cry from adopting by reference the well-established common law of warfare in which individuals have by established custom been tried by military tribunals, to the adoption of a perfectly revolutionary doctrine that the planning, preparation, initiation, and execution of war in violation of international law and of treaty involves not alone responsibility of the state concerned, but criminal responsibility on the part of individuals acting on its behalf. Such a criminal responsibility has been expressly denied by the consensus of international jurists as well as by the custom of nations, and was assuredly never thought of by responsible statesmen of any country when they negotiated international treaties. If such an interpretation had been proposed at the time of the negotiation, those treaties would never have been concluded. Can it for a moment be supposed that the parties to the Kellogg-Briand Treaty intended that if they went to war in contravention thereof, they should be guilty of murder? The Charter of the United Nations does not contain such a doctrine, and if such a provision had been made, the Charter might never have been adopted.

Let us now cast a glance at the principles of the law of nations affecting

concludes:

> "These murders followed such a wide range of territory and covered such a long period of time, and so many were committed after protests had been registered by neutral nations, that we must assume only positive orders from above; those accused here in this prisoners' dock made them possible." (Record, p. 429).

But it must surely be shown at what exact level the assumed command issued; an indiscriminate assumption of guilt at all levels or at all above a certain level would be essentially contrary to justice and would be revolting to the conscience of the world.

Even if the alleged atrocities or other contraventions assume a similar singular pattern of acts it cannot justify such an assumption. Such a pattern may have been a sheer reflection of national or racial traits. Crimes no less than masterpieces of art may express certain characteristics reflecting the *mores* of a race. Similarities in the geographic, economic, or strategic state of affairs may in part account for the "similar pattern" assumed. The existence of a command from above, and from whom it issued, has certainly to be proved beyond any reasonable doubt in a case of this grave character. The impression prevails after listening to the testimony of the witnesses alleging atrocities, that they follow not a uniform pattern but manifold patterns according to the nationality of the witnesses, not only negating "orders from above" but telling an entirely different story.

6. "CONVENTIONAL" WAR CRIMES

As for the "conventional" war crimes, and the "crimes against humanity" in so far as they are part of the "conventional war crimes," we admit that they may and should be punished, if guilt is proved according to the established rules of international law before a duly constituted tribunal.

War is a brutal affair. Stripped of all human justifications and excuses, and judged by the highest of human standards indicated by the Prince of Peace, war, defensive or aggressive, may be regarded as an institution necessarily involving murderous action. It is a notorious fact, amply shown by the history of war, that war has a tendency to make the participants brutal, giving rise to many cruelties to opposing combatants and to civilian populations, especially where the latter are suspected of hostile actions. These are the deplorable accompaniments of the bloody operations.

However natural and inevitable this may be in the war, the dictates of the established law of nations require that punishment be imposed upon the guilty, and indeed that "stern justice be meted out" to the perpetrator of such crimps is clearly within the purview of the terms of the Instrument of Surrender to which the Japanese Government plighted its honor.

Persons who may be actually guilty of atrocious acts in contravention of the laws and customs of war may properly be punished by a duly constituted court. But we call the attention of the Tribunal to the fact that the American members of the Commission of Fifteen at the Versailles Conference altogether denied assent to the doctrine of "negative criminality," *i. e.* responsibility for failure to prevent "conventional" war crimes, and that negligence in preventing death is only non-capital manslaughter in England.

Perhaps on the facile assumption that the German and Japanese situations were the same, the Chief of Counsel imagines that there were orders from the accused officers for every offense against the law of war which might have been committed by delinquents on various battlefields. But such "orders from above" can not be proved. The Chief of Counsel, therefore, bases his charges of "orders from above" on assumption and on assumption only. For he

provided for in Convention III.

The parable of the "rabbit trick" seems to be the fashion of the day. In criticizing the Government plans for the nationalization of inland transport before the British Parliament, Lord Reading said that the Government in a relatively short time had shown themselves extremely adept at bringing "socialized rabbits out of a nationalization hat." At the All-India Congress, Mr. Acharya Kripaland, criticizing the proposed Constitution introduced by the British, said in Hindustani that like magicians, they produced rabbits or eggs from the hat whenever it suited them. May we be pardoned for following this world-wide fashion with a view of dissipating once for all the cobwebs of fine-spun casuistry which, it is respectfully submitted, characterizes the argument of the Prosecution. You see the conjurer borrow an ordinary hat. He plants it on the table, and mutters some incantations over it. Then he lifts it up — and the table is swarming with little rabbits. There were no rabbits in the hat. He put them there.

The argument of the Prosecution, we venture to say, is exactly like that. It takes an ordinary hat, the nice well-known, respectable hat of International Law, covering states and nations. It places the hat on the table and intones over it some weird incantations among which we can catch the words, in a crescendo, "unlawful," "criminal," "murder." And then the hat is lifted, and immediately the Tribunal swarms with new-born little doctrines drawn from odds and ends of municipal law, to the extreme amazement of us all. Where the Prosecution got them is immaterial. They were surely not in our silk hat. The Prosecution put them there.

the law of war." (Lawrence, *Principles of International Law*, 7th edition (1925), revised by Percy Winfield, p. 323).

It is true that pirates are punishable as criminals against all mankind. But pirates act without any authorization from any government, and it is strange learning to treat members of the regular forces acting with the authorization of the government or persons politically responsible for the commencement of war as murderers simply because the war was allegedly commenced in an illegal manner.

It may be noted that within a State, a well-organized community, persons who plan, prepare and initiate civil war are clearly acting illegally. Municipal law naturally treats them as guilty of high treason. But it normally treats them as political offenders, not as common "felons" or as murderers, and the law of nations excludes them from extradition.

The Chief of Counsel further cites various provisions of Hague Convention IV (Record, pp. 425-7) of which Article XXIII runs as follows:

"In addition to the prohibitions provided by special Conventions it is especially forbidden:

(2) To kill or wound treacherously individuals belonging to the hostile nation or army."

The Chief of Counsel draws this conclusion from the foregoing provision:

"therefore, an attack without warning upon another nation with which Japan was at peace constituted treachery of the worst type, and *under the provisions of the Hague Convention the killing of any human being during such attack became murder.*" (Record, p. 427).

It may seriously be doubted in view of the opinions of such eminent authorities as Westlake and Bellot, quoted above, whether a sudden and strategic attack made by one nation after grave provocations and after prolonged efforts through diplomatic negotiation, and when the other nation knew that the situation had become so tense that it expected and was prepared for the opening of hostilities at any moment, can be illegal under Hague Convention III or can be dubbed "treachery of the worst type." But even if this be admitted for purposes of argument, the conclusion of the Chief of Counsel does not follow from the foregoing provision for the phrase to "kill or wound treacherously" clearly means "in the course of war already in progress"; otherwise there could be no "hostile cation or army." The provision cited by the Chief of Counsel does not envisage any act relating to measures

5. MURDER

Next, we are confronted with an explanation by the Chief of Counsel of the strange charge in the Indictment that the accused are guilty of murder.

The Chief of Counsel argues that in civilized countries the intentional killing of a human being without legal justification is murder, citing the Japanese Criminal Code (Record, p. 425). This may be admitted, with the grave qualification that an illegal killing is not necessarily the capital crime of murder even in Great Britain or the U. S. A. It may be a mere manslaughter and entail only a month's imprisonment or a fine. And in some jurisdictions homicide is never capital at all. Then he says, "In the case before us, the deaths all occurred as a result of belligerency of war, and since the war was illegal, all the natural and normal results flowing from the original act are also illegal. This is even true under Japanese law." (Record, p. 425).

With respect, we cannot follow the logic of the Chief of Counsel. He begins by using the ambiguous epithet "illegal," meaning "illegal by the Law of Nations," and then erroneously uses the same word to mean, "illegal with all the consequences and accompaniments of acts illegal by municipal law."

As a matter of fact every student of the law of nations is aware that this is not so in international law.

It is the consensus of international lawyers that even if war is commenced in breach of international law or treaties, nevertheless a state of war comes into being and both belligerents have a right to be protected by the rules of war.

Professor Lawrence cites an extreme case of an attack made without provocation and without any previous diplomatic negotiation, and says:

> "To attack another state in a period of profound peace, without having previously formulated claims and endeavored to obtain satisfaction by diplomatic means, would amount to an act of international brigandage, and would probably be treated accordingly. But the state of things set up by such abominable means would nevertheless be war, and both sides would be expected to carry on their operations according to

individuals responsible for initiating war in breach of such treaties.

punishment for the other.

The Chief of Counsel particularly cites Hague Convention III as an example (Record, p. 421). We shall not repeat here what has been said before. Even allowing for the moment that its violation is illegal in all cases, it does not constitute a crime on the part of individuals responsible. The *punishment* of "crimes against peace" in violation of treaties has never been known to the law of nations. The thesis was, as stated before, rejected as untenable at the Versailles Conference. The law is settled in a direction contrary to what the Chief of Counsel asserts it to be. Of course the accused did not "know" that their acts were "criminal" as the Chief of Counsel alleges (Record, p. 421), for everyone "knew" that they were not criminal at all in the law of nations.

It may be noted that the above-mentioned Draft Convention of 1939 on Rights and Duties of States in Case of Aggression, contains the following passage in one of its comments on the text:

"(1) The United States is a party to the Third Hague Convention of 1907, which, in Article I provided that hostilities must not commence without a previous and explicit warning, in the form either of a reasoned declaration of war or of an ultimatum with conditional declaration of war. The United States goes to war without issuing an ultimatum or declaration of war; the United States has not committed an 'aggression' within the meaning of this Convention."

"(2) Japan is a party to the Washington Nine-Power Treaty of 1922, which in Article I provides that, the parties will 'respect the sovereignty, the independence, and territorial and administrative integrity of China.' Japan, without justification, conquers and annexes Chinese territory; Japan has not committed an "aggression" within the meaning of this Convention." (p. 896).

This means that the authors of the Draft Convention who proposed *de lege ferenda* to clothe "aggression" with certain legal consequences unfavorable to the aggressor determined as such by procedure to which such state has given its previous assent, did not regard war merely on account of being in breach of treaties such as the Third Hague Convention or the Nine-Power Treaty as constituting such "aggression." It also implies that even jurists of the sanctionist [sic] school certainly do not go so far as to hold the broad proposition alleged by the Chief of Counsel to be the settled law, nor do they propose under the suggested regime to impose criminal punishments on

4. WAR IN VIOLATION OF INTERNATIONAL LAW, TREATIES, ETC.

Next, the Chief of Counsel deals with the so-called "Crimes against Peace" relative to the planning, preparation, initiation, or waging of war in violation of international law, treaties, agreements and assurances.

We are told that "here the law is well settled and has been enforced for generations" (Record, p. 420).

When it was stated by the American Secretary of State at the time of the making of the Kellogg Pact that the limits of self-defense have been clearly defined by countless precedents, students of international law remarked that it would be interesting to know what these countless precedents were but their curiosity has never been gratified. So when we are told this part of the so-called "Crimes against Peace" is well-settled and has been enforced for generations, every student of international law will rub his eyes and lament his profound ignorance.

International law and treaties ought to be observed. No sensible persons, including all the accused, will doubt that. The Chief of Counsel asks, "Do these accused contend that these (*i. e.*, treaty stipulations) are empty words?" (Record, p. 422) Of course not. It is most unfair to attribute to the accused moral depravity of such a low level as to think that a nation may disregard international law and treaties. True, nations may in a particular case have a different interpretation of international law and treaties, and sometimes one nation may attribute to the other party a breach of the law or of the plighted word. But that is a matter which ought to and could be decided by an impartial tribunal. If a rule of general international law or any provision of a treaty is violated, nobody doubts that it is *illegal.* But it is a long way from pronouncing a national action to be illegal to the condemning as criminal, and capitally so, of the individual leaders of a nation that initiated such an action. Every civilized nation does not treat every breach of a contract or every tort as a crime. Compensation is the usual remedy for the one, and

charge of *ipse dixit*, if not of subserviency to popular prejudices or of a wilful travesty of history. Aggression is, after all, a matter of opinion. To hold a man a "Murderer" because you differ from him is to kill him with a word. And it would certainly be the height of injustice to brand a statesman as a criminal and a felon for the mistakes he might make in his political decisions of the most delicate kind.

Equity — and natural law — is a roguish thing, if not in civil justice, at least in that category of criminal justice which is closely related to politics, national or international. If we give up the definition of aggression and leave the matter entirely to a tribunal to decide in each case whether a particular war was aggressive or defensive, its decision, without any measure to abide by, is likely to be swayed by contemporary political prejudices. For the term "aggressor" like "American Imperialism" or "Red Imperialism" — is a vituperative epithet, often employed in international politics merely with a view to stigmatizing a political opponent as a pariah in the eyes of the world.

In view of the preceding considerations, we not only contend that the Chief of Counsel's thesis is not the law as it is but humbly submit that the proposition ought not to be the law. It may at first sight appeal to uninformed and unreflective minds, but when carefully considered it is seen to be a juridical principle which will not work without doing injustice. Its practical application could not but be such that the general public gets the impression, not that wrong has been conquered but that Bulwer's dictum "Earth's law: the conquered is wrong" remains ever true. Its application would be a most dangerous precedent for future victorious aggressors to exploit against their victims. We submit that it is a pseudo-juristic doctrine which should be excluded from the holy precincts of the law of nations.

"As experience has conclusively shown that the attempt to decide the question of the aggressor on first appearance is reckless of justice, we must, unless our purposes are unholy, rely on an impartial investigation of the facts. But this takes time. The Assembly of the League of Nations assumed jurisdiction of the Sino-Japanese conflict on September 18, 1931, the report of the Lytton Commission was signed at Peiping, China on September 4, 1932; the assembly adopted the report of its own committee on February 17, 1933. The actual time covered by the proceedings was seventeen months and even then a final conclusion was not reached." (Moore, *Appeal to Reason*, pp. 568-9).

And the Report of the Lytton Commission itself says in the concluding Chapter:

"It must be apparent to every reader of the preceding Chapters that the issues involved in this conflict are not as simple as they are often represented to be. They are, on the contrary, exceedingly complicated and only an intimate knowledge of all the facts, as well of their historical background, should entitle anyone to express a definite opinion upon them. This is not a case in which one country has declared war on another country without previously exhausting the opportunities for conciliation provided in the Covenant of the League of Nations. Neither is it a simple case of the violation of the frontier of one country by the armed forces of a neighboring country, because in Manchuria there are many features without an exact parallel in other parts of the world."

It may also be noted that under the actual state of international world organization in the first half of the twentieth century, serious problems confronted all conscientious statesmen regarding the scope of national authority to act in what they conceived to be necessary self-defense. Was that not the reason why the statesmen of America, Great Britain, France and Japan made comprehensive reservations in signing the Kellogg-Briand Treaty? It may be that the Hitlerite wars presented little difficulty to the Nuremberg Tribunal regarding their "aggressive" character, for the reason that they were commenced by those who did not themselves believe that they were in immediate danger of being attacked by others. But does not the Record of this trial clearly show that the cases of Germany and Japan are quite different in this and other respects, and that an "aggressive" or "defensive" character of Japanese war cannot so readily be pronounced without being subjected to the

territory not their own" caused Major General Fuller to declare that whoever thought it out must have been a lunatic or a humorist. They all failed, because they were attempting to define the undefinable. Did not Sir Austen Chamberlain say: "I, therefore, remain opposed to this attempt to define the aggressor because I believe that it will be a trap for the innocent and a signpost for the guilty." And did not Secretary Kellogg, at the time the Kellogg-Briand Treaty was being discussed, object on that very ground, to the French proposal limiting the scope of an anti-war treaty to wars of aggression? (Kellogg, "The War Prevention Policy of the United States," in *A.J.I.L.*, Vol. 22 No. 2, p. 259)

The authors of the Draft Convention on Rights and Duties of States in Case of Aggression, mentioned above, are, of course, wise enough to abstain from defining "aggression" except in a formal way. The Draft Says:

"(As The term is used in this Convention) "Aggression" is a resort to armed force by a State when such resort has been duly determined by a means which that State is bound to accept, to constitute a violation of an obligation."

The Draft Convention, as stated above, speaks de *lege ferenda* only. It will be remembered that under the Pact of Paris, the signatories implicitly reserved a wide margin of self-defense, of which the State resorting to self-defense was to be the sole judge. They were not then minded to allow any other State or any group of other States or any international body to determine whether the employment of armed force was made "as an instrument of national policy" or in self-defense. It was one of the objects of the Draft Convention to ameliorate this state of the law. By the Charter of the United Nations the Security Council was invested with the power of deciding on questions of aggression. However, the interminable discussion in that august body concerning the unanimity principle as governing its decisions, indicates that any decision on aggression would be likely, in the present state of international affairs, to be motivated solely by a political alignment against a particular state or states. It indicates also the inherent limitations of that penal conception of world peace which envisages the abolition of armed conflict by making every war a world war.

At any rate, the provision in that Charter brings us no nearer to a definite knowledge of what "aggression" is.

Judge Moore says:

"...... the taking of a forcible initiative may be the only means of safety; and the importance of this principle is necessarily enhanced by the insistence of nations or groups of nations on maintaining preponderance of military power. Portugal acted on this principle when, in 1762, the combined forces of France and Spain were hovering on her frontiers." (p. 568)

Take, in the second place, the definition also cited by the Chief of Counsel:

"The aggressor being that state which goes to war in violation of its pledges to submit the matter of dispute to peaceful settlement, having already agreed to do so." (Record, p. 419)

An obviously imperfect definition, since there are infinite possibilities of aggressive war where no treaty of arbitration exists. And it ignores also the possibility that a nation, which has agreed to arbitral processes, may find it necessary to exert warlike efforts in self-defense; and further ignores the possibility that there may exist no dispute, but simply a serious menace.

Would or would not the definition justify the landing of troops to *preserve order in a disintegrated state* as has often been done in Mexico, South American republics and also in China? (Herbert Arthur Smith, *Great Britain and the Law of Nations, a selection of Documents illustrating the Views of the Government in the United Kingdom upon matters of International Law*, Vol. I (1932), section 2 (Disorganized States), pp. 18-30).

Was or was not the United States an aggressor when American forces suddenly seizes and occupied Vera Cruz in April, 1914, in disregard of the Treaty with Mexico of 1848, which expressly provided that neither party should resort to force before trying peaceful negotiation, and if that should fail arbitration? Or was the dispatch of British troops to China in 1925 without recourse to the methods of settlement provided by the League Covenant an aggression? (For the defense of its legal position by the British Government on this point, see Note of 8th February 1927 addressed by Sir Austen Chamberlain to the Secretary-General of the League of Nations cited in Smith, *Great Britain and the Law of Nations*, pp. 25-29).

We need not dwell on the many attempts at definition, short or long, which have not been cited by the Chief of Counsel. The longest, as elaborated by the Soviet Government has been characterized as lexicographic rather than lucid. The shortest, like the French proposal, "the presence of troops on

as a war of aggression but the only step taken was expulsion from membership. There was no thought of criminally punishing the Soviet Union or its political or military leaders.

Lastly it must emphatically be stated that in this trial the guilt or innocence of the individual accused and not that of the State of Japan is the issue. The two are entirely distinct legal questions. The Chief of Counsel failed to prove either that treaties have been entered into or that a custom of nations has been established, by virtue of which individual authors of an aggressive war art made punishable; which, it is confidently submitted, is fatal to the Prosecution's case.

B. AGGRESSIVE WAR AS A JURIDICAL CONCEPT

Another serious difficulty with the thesis presented by the Prosecution, that aggressive war is an international crime, is that the terms "aggression" and "aggressor" are too vague to be defined.

Take, in the first place, the simplist lexicographic definition in *Webster's Dictionary* cited by the Chief of Counsel:

"A first attack." (Record, p. 419) The aggressor is one who fires the first shot. "A cannon shot is a cannon shot," says Briand, and "you hear it and it often leaves its traces." So you can. That is, however, a physical test; it has no necessary moral or juridical connotation, and you would be required further to distinguish just from unjust aggression. Says Judge Moore: "Although nations when they go to war always profess to repel overt acts yet they frequently do not go to war on account of them; but an assurance of associate force would necessarily increase their propensity to do so. Moreover it is notorious that overt acts are sometimes craftily provoked for the purpose of justifying aggression" (Moore, Appeal to Reason, *Foreign Affairs*, Vol. II No. 4 p. 568). And that is perhaps the reason for Webster's alternative definition, "an unprovoked attack." But what modern nations go to war without any provocation? Would the opening of hostilities by Japan on December 8, 1941 fall under the definition? It appears that some high public officials outside Japan thought even prior to the armistice that there was considerable provocation and that to deny it would be a travesty of history.

Judge Moore continues:

respect. But he is not a world legislator. In this article he is, we suppose, speaking not as a judge, but as an advocate, avowedly writing *ex parte*, as he is perfectly entitled to do, in support of his government's thesis. His very positive contention certainly does not represent the consensus of jurists versed in the law of nations, which alone — not the policy of governments nor the views of their avowed advocates — can be relied upon by a tribunal, national or international, regarding the question whether an international custom exists concerning this matter. "One swallow does not make a summer."

Even if Lord Wright's thesis were to be endorsed by all contemporary students of international law in the year of grace 1948, which is assuredly not the case, and if international law had rapidly and bewilderingly transformed itself during the War, of which we were unaware, it is palpably *ex post facto* action and unjust to apply those novel rules to the accused at the bar.

In order to prove the thesis that aggressive war is an international crime, the Chief of Counsel relies not so much on international agreements as such, which are obviously insufficient, as on the custom of nations. it may, however, be noticed that international jurists speak of a custom, when a clear and continuous *habit of doing certain actions* has grown up under the aegis of the conviction that these actions are, according to international law, obligatory or right (Oppenheim, *International law*, Vol. 2, p. 24). Article 38 of the Statute of the Permanent Court of International Justice mentions as a source of the law of nations "international custom, as evidence of a general practice adopted as law." The drafting of the phrase may be inelegant and open to criticism, but it is amply clear that in order to show that an international custom binding on all states has grown up, a *general practice* as well as the *opinio necessitatis* must be proved.

Vague and often rhetorical declarations made at international assemblies and in treaty preambles are surely not enough. We must look not only to the *animus* but to the *corpus*, a general practice of nations. The practice of nations, however, contradicts the thesis that an aggressive war involves criminality either on the part of a responsible State or on the part of responsible individual members of a State. The invasion of Ethiopia by Italy was regarded as an "aggressive war" by the League of Nations, but the only sanction imposed by that body was economic severance. And no one suggested the criminal punishment of Italy, to say nothing of Mussolini and his cabinet. The invasion of Finland by Soviet Russia in 1939 was stigmatized by the League

among scholars throughout the world with a view to the further clarification of the subject." (p. 827)

Whether or not one agrees with the contents of the Draft Convention, great respect is certainly due to Professor Phillip C. Jessup and members of the Advisory Committee for having pursued dispassionately the study of "a subject embroiled in political controversy and emotion," and "not affected by momentary currents of diplomacy, enthusiasms and prejudices."

It may be noted particularly that neither the Budapest Interpretations nor the Draft Convention — both certainly products of the school of collective sanctions — suggests that a breach of the Pact of Paris or "aggression" constitutes an international crime. Indeed the latter makes apologies for the choice of the word "aggression" which has acquired a "psychological fringe." (p. 847) It also says that the purpose of the Draft Convention is to define legal relationships between States in cases where a resort to armed force has been in violation of a legal obligation not to resort to such means and *where such violation has been duly determined by a procedure to which the lawbreaking state has previously agreed*. It is not designed to indicate any opinion for or against a system of "collective security," nor to "implement" any specific treaty such as the League Covenant or the Pact of Paris, nor to enter into the field of "Just" and "unjust" war. (p. 825)

It may also be noticed that in considering the legal consequences of war in breach of the Pact of Paris or war of aggression, no idea of punishing the individuals responsible for such war was expressed by those jurists favoring collective sanctions who participated in the preparation of the Budapest Articles and the Draft Convention. This, we submit, is practically conclusive on the question of the attitude of contemporary thought. It repudiated the criminal liability of individuals altogether: it never even discussed such a thing.

From the foregoing it is clear that the argument which the Chief of Counsel presents fails to substantiate his conclusion that an aggressive war has become a crime in international law by custom recognized by civilized nations.

The Chief of Counsel quotes from Lord Wright's article on "*War Crimes and International Law*" as evidence that his conclusion meets with the approval of students of international law (Record, pp. 418-419). Lord Wright is certainly a very distinguished jurist and his ideas are entitled to great

not have provided appropriate and graduated penalties and procedures to suit so novel a case as the infliction of penalties on public officials?

It is true that since the first World War certain international lawyers and publicists found the road to world peace in the administration of collective sanctions to an "aggressor" state. They have vigorously combated the views of the orthodox school which found the road to peace in the strict observance of the rules of neutrality and the consequent localization of force and anarchy. The former endeavored to enforce the sanctions provided in the League Covenant and implement the Kellogg-Briand Treaty by modifying the prevailing rules of neutrality. The latter attempt was made at the meeting of the International Law Association in Budapest, September 1934, at which the well-known "Budapest Articles of Interpretation" were drawn up after a discussion of the legal consequences of a breach of the Pact of Paris (International Law Association, Report of the 38th Conference, p. 66). Again since 1936 a similar, though not exactly the same, attempt had been made by a group of American jurists and the result of their studies was embodied in the "Draft Convention on Rights and Duties of States in Case of Aggression," published in October 1939 by the American Society, of International Law, as part of the Harvard Research in International Law (33 *A. J. I. L.*, No. 4, supplement section). The Budapest Articles of Interpretation were intended to be a statement of the existing state of the law, although the soundness of that interpretation was a subject of heated discussions (*e. g.*, the discussion of the Budapest Articles in the British Parliament on February 20, 1935, Vol. 95, H. L. Deb., 5th Series, Col. 1007 ff.), although such an interpretation is of course not binding on the signatories of the Pact of Paris. The Draft Convention on Rights and Duties of States in Case of Aggression, on the contrary, speaks *de lege ferenda* (p. 828). It was avowedly an academic attempt "to suggest a possible future development of the law rather than the law now in force" (p. 826). It is also stated:

> "The considerations of the Draft Convention on Right and Duties of States in Case of Aggression revealed fundamental differences of opinion regarding the general organization of the Draft, its underlying theories, and a number of the specific rules and principles set forth therein. The Research nevertheless presents it, without any implication that the Draft as published reflects even a consensus of the members of the Advisory Committee, hoping that its debates upon the problem may be continued

is shown clearly by the record (70 *Congressional Record* 1730).

By the Kellogg Pact the parties renounced war as an instrument of national policy and pledged themselves to settle all differences by peaceful negotiation. In the light of these interpretations, however, this was not done without a clear and definite prior agreement that each party should interpret the engagement for itself.

It may finally be noted that the United States was particularly concerned with Central and South Americas and with her Monroe Doctrine, Great Britain with certain unspecified regions, possibly including Belgium and the borderland of her far-flung Empire, France with the Rhineland and the Locarno treaties, and Japan with her neighbor China, particularly the regions of Manchuria and Mongolia. Their common understanding was that all forcible measures which might be necessary to be taken by them were covered by national self-defense, of which they were the sole judges which was never intended by the signatories to be referred to any Tribunal.

The Chief of Counsel admits that the text of the Pact does not use the word "crime" (Record, p. 417), and indeed not only the text but the entire deliberations fail to reveal any such idea. The League conception of "sanction" was, as was well known, anathema to the American Secretary of State. The Chief of Counsel, however, asserts that the signatories made an aggressive war "illegal" (Record, p. 417). The dulcet term "aggressive war" as will be shown later, is amorphous, elusive and indefinable. But it may be granted that a non-defensive war admitted as such by the belligerent who wages it is illegal under the Pact. The Chief of Counsel then declares that it is an international "crime". The learned Counsel's logic is beyond our comprehension. To us the fact that the Contracting Parties to a treaty have agreed to make illegal a war not considered as self-defense by the belligerent does not make violation of the treaty a crime. It may be a breach of contract or a tort, but it is not a crime. How can an agreement to make a thing illegal convey of itself that the thing is a crime?

We desire to draw particular attention to the well-known principle in the interpretation of contracts, that the paramount rule is to ascertain the *intention* of the parties. Can it be supposed that it was the intention of the parties to any of the contractual instruments referred to in this case that a breach of their terms would involve the liability of individuals to arbitrary penalties? If they had meant so would they not have said so, and would they

Locarno treaties which guarantee general peace. In its reply to the American Government, therefore, the Imperial Government added its understanding that the Pact did not deny to any independent nation the right of self-defense, and that it was not in any way in conflict with the obligations to guarantee general peace under the League Covenant and Locarno treaties."

Thus it may be emphasized that the Foreign Minister's explanations in the Japanese Privy Council regarding the nature of self-defense were substantially the same as those made by Secretary of State Kellogg to the United States Senate.

Governments, of course, do not make these declarations and reservations as idle gestures not to be taken seriously. On the contrary, they constitute the frank and honest avowals of the governments' understanding of the obligations contracted. They constitute an inherent and essential part of the treaty obligations as if they had been written into Article I of the Pact.

In view of the declarations made by leading statesmen and especially those of Secretary Kellogg and Senator Borah to the American Senate, it was apparent that the intention of the Contracting Parties was;

(1) that self-defense was not precluded by the Treaty,

(2) that self-defense was not confined to the defense of territory,

(3) that self-defense comprised the right of any nation to take such measures as it believed necessary for the defense of the country or to prevent occurrences that might endanger the country,

(4) that the nation resorting to measures of self-defense was to be the sole judge on the question of self-defense,

(5) that the question of self-defense was not to be submitted to any tribunal,

(6) that no nation should have anything to do with deciding the question of self-defense regarding the action of any other nation unless such action constituted an attack on itself.

It is true that in the United States Mr. Kellogg and others denied that there were "amendments" or "reservations". But it is beyond any doubt in the light of the Record that what they meant was that the prior declarations of the signatories could not be called "amendments" or "reservations" for they were "interpretations" of what was meant by the Pact itself, taking nothing out of it. That the U. S. Senate ratified the Pact on the same explicit understanding

(d) Japan

In a note handed by Baron Tanaka, Giichi to Mr. Edwin L. Neville, American Chargé d'affaires in Tokyo, on July 20, 1928, the Japanese Foreign Minister refers to the aforesaid speech of Mr. Kellogg made on April 28, stating: "You proceed to reinforce in detail the explanations made by the Secretary of State in his speech of the 28th of April," and says:

> "In reply, I have the honor to inform you that the Japanese Government are happy to be able to give their full concurrence to the alterations now proposed, their understanding of the original draft submitted to them in April last being, as I intimated in my Note to His Excellency Mr. MacVeagh dated the 26th of May, 1928, *substantially the same as that entertained by the Government of the United States*. They are therefore ready to give instructions for the signature on that footing of the treaty in the form in which it is now proposed."

When, on June 17, and 26, 1929, Councillors Tomii and Kubota asked the Government at the Privy Council whether self-defense is confined to the defense of territory, suggesting the applicability of the Pact to forcible measures which might become necessary in China and especially in Manchuria and Mongolia, and whether it would not be more prudent to be as explicit in those matters as Great Britain, the Government's answer was that self-defense was not limited to the defense of territory, but extended outside of the territory. The protection of rights and interests in Manchuria and elsewhere by forcible means was sufficiently covered by the fact that self-defence was not precluded by the Pact. And that fact is clearly stated in the Report of the Privy Council concerning the General Pact, adopted on June 26, 1929. It states:

> "Upon receipt of the proposal made by the American Government, the Imperial Government adopted the broader interpretation that the operations of national self-defense were not confined to actions to be taken for defending the territory of our own country, but extended to actions which might be adopted by the Empire in order to safeguard its vital rights and interests in China, especially in the regions of Manchuria and Mongolia, but regarded it as more opportune to refrain from making such a declaration on this occasion. It also adopted the view that it was not in conflict with the Covenant of the League of Nations and

(b) Great Britain

On May 19, 1928, the British Government issued a circular which, after quoting the renunciation of war as an instrument of national policy, declared that there were certain regions of the world the welfare and integrity of which constituted a special and vital interest for that government's peace and safety, and that as their protection against attack was a measure of self-defense no interference with them could be suffered. It may be noted that the regions were not named and complete liberty of action as to their future designation was reserved. The note was an interpretation by the British Government in more or less concrete terms of that doctrine of "self-defence" which was expounded by Secretary Kellogg's speech. And in order effectually to forestall any subsequent challenge or quibble, Sir Austen Chamberlain in a note of July 18 attached the unequivocal condition which follows:

> "As regards the passage in my note of the 19th May relating to certain regions of which the welfare and integrity constitute a special and vital interest for our peace and safety, I need only repeat that His Majesty's Government in Great Britain accept the new treaty upon the understanding that it does not prejudice their freedom of action in this respect."

It is true that the Soviet and Persian Governments refused to recognize the British reservations, but it was thought unimaginable that the British Government, if accused of any violation of the Kellogg fact, would not invoke its own interpretation of self-defense drawn up with such meticulous care and duly deposited with the League of Nations, together with the text of the Treaty.

(c) France

M. Brand in his note of July 14 declared:

> "The Government of the Republic is happy, moreover, to take note of the interpretations which the Government of the United States gives to the new treaty with a view to satisfying the various observations which have been formulated from the French point of view.......In this situation and under these conditions, the Government of the Republic is happy to be able to declare to the Government of the United State that it is now entirely disposed to sign the treaty......"

"The Committee reports the above treaty with the understanding that the right of self-defense is in no way curtailed or impaired by the terms or conditions of the treaty. Each nation is free at all times and regardless of the treaty provisions to defend itself, and is the sole judge of what constitutes the right of self-defense and the necessity and extent of the same."

"The United States regards the Monroe Doctrine as a part of its national security and defense. Under the right of self-defense allowed by the treaty must necessarily be included the right to maintain the Monroe Doctrine which is a part of our system of national defense."

"The committee further understands that the treaty does not provide sanctions, express or implied...... In other words, the treaty does not, either expressly or impliedly, contemplate the use of force or coercive measures for its enforcement as against any nation violating it......"

Senator Robinson expressed his skepticism in the meeting of the Foreign Relations Committee of the U. S. Senate:

"If you recognize the right of every nation to construe for itself what it aggressive war and what is defensive war, you have not accomplished much by agreeing to renounce war......"

Secretary Kellogg replied:

"Senator, if I had started out to define what aggression was and what self-defuse was I would not have been able to negotiate a treaty during my life-time or that of anybody present here." (*General Pact for the Renunciation of War*. Committee on Foreign Relations. U. S. Senate December 7, 1928-p. 16).

And we are told by Judge Moore that:

"I have always surmised that Senator Borah, as an advocate of the 'outlawry of war', played in this transaction a larger part than is generally known, especially as I observed that in the national campaign of 1928 he did not abate his appeals for the maintenance of an effective navy — not, of course, for the purpose of providing the renunciation of war with 'teeth', but for the purpose of enabling the United States to exercise the right of self-defense that had been so amply safeguarded." (Moore, *Appeal to Reason, Foreign Affairs*, Vol. II, No. 4 p. 553).

"There is nothing in the American draft of an anti-war treaty which restricts or impairs in any way the right of self-defense. That right is inherent in every sovereign state and is implicit in every treaty. Every nation is free at all times and regardless of treaty provisions to defend its territory from attack or invasion and it alone is competent to decide whether circumstances require recourse to war in self-defense. If it has a good cause, the world will applaud and not condemn its action."

Then Secretary Kellogg in his note of June 23, 1928, addressed to the governments invited to sign the treaty, after embodying his own "constructions" of the treaty with reference to the six major "considerations" emphasized by France and the British note mentioned below, states:

"In these circumstances I have the honor to transmit herewith for the consideration of your excellency's government a draft of the multilateral treaty for the renunciation of war containing the changes outlined above."

In the United States, as is well known, there was much concern about the effect of the General Pact on the Monroe Doctrine, but Mr. Kellogg assured the Committee on Foreign Relations of the U.S. Senate on December 7, 1928 that the safeguarding of the Monroe Doctrine was covered by the fact that self-defense was not precluded, of which the United States is solely entitled to judge for itself. He further states that "the American Government had a right to take such measures as it believed necessary to the defense of the country or to prevent things that might endanger the country," and admitted that "the whole of that rule would apply equally to every other country." The American Secretary of State also said that "the American Government would never agree to submit to any tribunal the question of self-defense and that no other Government would."

Senator Borah stated during his speech and debates in the Senate on January 3, 1929 that "no nation would surrender the right to determine for itself what constitutes an attack or what is justification for defense," and that "the United States would have nothing to do with deciding the question of self-defense with reference to the action of any other nation unless the action of that nation were in the nature of an attack upon the United States itself" (Congressional Record, 2nd Session, pp. 1268 & 1271).

The Executive Report of the 70th Session U.S. Senate, January 15, 1929, states:

negotiators. That intent naturally is assumed to be stated in the text of the treaty itself, but it also may be sought elsewhere, either in specific reservations attached to treaties at the time of signature or ratification, or in interpretation, clarifications, understandings, constructions, qualifications or actual conditions set forth during the negotiations prior to the ratification. Hence, it is to be expected that in any future divergence of opinions concerning the nature of the obligations assumed under the General Pact for the Renunciation of War recourse must necessarily be had, not only to the official correspondence of the negotiations, but to various official utterances of such government spokesmen as Sir Austen Chamberlain, M. Briand, Secretary Kellogg and Senator Borah. Their interpretations of this instrument will be entitled to the closest scrutiny and respect. So far as the commitments of the United States are concerned, the Report of the Senate Committee on Foreign Relations giving its understanding of the "true interpretation" of the Pact conditioning the American ratification must also be taken into account, whether by a judicial tribunal or by international public opinion...... To make certain of the intent of every signatory to the Pact; to hold every signatory to the strict fulfilment of its commitments under that Pact, it would appear good sense and good ethics as well as good law, to give due weight and credit to the interpretations placed on this momentous declaration by every signatory prior to ratification." (p. 379)

The following words of Professor Charles C. Hyde may also be kept in mind:

"It remains...... to take special note of the effort of judicial tribunals, whether international or domestic, to rid themselves of the influence of any formula purporting to regard the form of an instrument which regards accord as decisive of the character of the obligations of the parties thereunder, in the face of extrinsic evidence establishing an opposite design." (Hyde, *International Law*, 2nd edition (1945), Vol. 2, Section 531, p. 1472).

With that accepted canon of interpretation as a guide, we shall now turn to statements made by responsible statesmen in those days.

(a) The United States

In a speech made on April 28, 1928, Secretary Kellogg said:

contrary effect of affirming the legality of a defensive war.

With this well-known historical background in mind, we shall proceed to analyze the exact legal obligations undertaken by the signatories, especially Japan,which the Prosecution alleges were broken by Japan.

It is admitted by all international lawyers that in interpreting international treaties we must get at the real intention of the parties. And it is also admitted that the real intention must be ascertained not only by the text of a treaty itself, but also by the preliminary material as well. And courts, arbitrators and diplomats have given great importance to preliminary material in the interpretation of treaties.

Ralston states in his authoritative work, *The law and Procedure of International Tribunals:*

> "The events leading up to the signing of a treaty are often referred to as explanatory of the intentions of the parties entering into the treaty and so of prime importance in determining their intention". (Sec. 26, p. 18)

When, in 1912, the proposed arbitration treaties between the United States, Great Britain and France were before the Senate, Mr. Root stated clearly the settled law when he declared that if the treaties were ratified the prior recorded understandings would at all times be competent in determining their true interpretation; that the rules in international intercourse were much more liberal than were the rules of municipal law relating to the construction of statutes and contracts; that, in interpreting treaties, it was and always, had been universally accepted than every declaration made before or at the signing, and all correspondence and expressions of opinion by the representatives of both countries were to be considered, and that there never could arise a situation when the declarations in question would not be laid by the side of the text to determine...... the scope and effect of the stipulations contained in the instrument (45 Congressional Record 2935 (1912)).

With special reference to the Pact of Paris Phillip Marshal Brown says in his well known essay on "The interpretation of the General Pact for the Renunciation of War" published in the *American Journal of International Law*, April, 1929:

> "No rule of international law would seem more firmly established than this rule of interpretation of treaties in the light of intent of the

phrases "the neglect to use the toothbrush is a hygienic crime!", or "The Albert Memorial is an aesthetic *crime*!" The Chief of Counsel himself employed the words "unpardonable crime" in his opening statement (Record, p. 393) where it was employed in that emphatic sense. The same can be said of the resolution of the Sixth Pan-American Conference of February 18, 192, cited by the Chief of Counsel, which declares that "war of aggression constitutes an international *crime* against the whole human species" (Record, p. 417). Such condemnation, motivated as it may be by political or moral considerations, is without any legal connotation whatsoever.

5. Lastly, the Chief of Counsel mentions the Pact of Paris of 1928.

The vague stipulation of that multilateral treaty, which developed out of the proposal of an American-French bilateral treaty by M. Briand, made on June 20, 1927 with a definite political purpose, has, as is well known, caused an abundance of speculation as to its true import, political as well as legal.

The text of the Pact consists of very simple and abstract formulae, a general renunciation of war as an instrument of national policy and a general pledge to settle all differences by pacific means.

It may be recollected that some saw in it the advent of a *novus ordo seclorum*, an epoch in history, a revolution in human psychology which would make all rules of the traditional law of nations out of date. Skeptics with an analytical eye, however, saw in it nothing but a pious expression of the will to peace, just like declarations contained in treaties of amity and commerce expressing a more categorical will to peace, viz., that there shall be "perpetual peace" or "a perfect and inviolable peace" between the contracting parties.

Astute European statesmen, like M. Briand, saw in it a gesture of the United States evincing its willingness to be drawn into the League, and into European politics. Did not M. Boncour, M. Briand's friend, authoritatively tell us that for M. Briand, before all else, it was a means to draw the United States into the League of Nations? (*The New York Times*, April 10, 1932, cited in "An Appeal to Reason" by John Bassett Moore, *Foreign Affairs*, Vol. 11, No. 4 (July, 1933) at p. 554).

Many of the leading publicists who carefully analyzed not only, the text of the Pact but prior correspondence between the powers have come to the conclusion that the Pact merely had the effect of changing the vocabulary of international law, the classical "just war" having been replaced by "defensive war". Some contended that the Pact, instead of outlawing war, had the

that the above Article does not regard an aggressive war or a war in breach of a treaty as an "international crime," or any legal offence, it being only an offence against morality and good faith. The Government of the Netherlands acted perfectly within its right when it refused to surrender the Squire of Doorn for an "offence" which was not among those listed in its extradition treaties. Indeed James Brown Scott, legal adviser to President Wilson at the Versailles Conference, was of the opinion that "Holland has made the world its debtor by refusing to surrender the Kaiser for the commission of an offence admittedly political" (Scott, "The Trial of the Kaiser" in House and Seymour, *What Really Happened at Paris* (1921.), p. 231). It is too well known to require mentioning that both the American and Japanese members of the Committee of Fifteen opposed the trial of the Heads of State. It may be worthy of note, however, that the Commission refused to recognize "those acts which provoked the World War and accompanied its inception" such as the invasions of Luxemburg and Belgium, constituting a violation of treaty obligations, as a sufficient ground for making any criminal charge against the responsible authorities and individuals. The wording of Article 227 must certainly be read against this background.

4. The Chief of Counsel then takes up the Preamble to the Geneva Protocol of 1924, and the Declaration of the eighth Assembly of the League of Nations of September 27, 1927, in which the expression, "a war of aggression is an international crime" appears. (Tr. p. 416)

It may be noted that these statements reflected the Geneva sentiment with its supra-state ideologies then dominant. The Soviet Union, however, was then outside the "anti-communistic" League and so was the United States, which feared to be entangled in European affairs. Indeed the letter's foremost international jurist, John Bassett Moore, denounced Genevan international law and the Protocol inspired by it — proceeding as they did on the facile assumption that there was a close analogy between the law within a State and the international system governing a society of sovereign nations — as a "bedlam theory," destructive of sound international law. Great Britain herself refused to ratify the Geneva Protocol, because she was not prepared for compulsory arbitration and was not sure as to how such a Pact could work in practice. The Protocol never came into effect, nor can that Conference bind the world. The term "*international crime*" in treaty preambles, moreover, is employed as merely expressive of emphatic condemnation, just as in the

mainly a question of strategy. And the passage here cited stands unaltered in the 1937 edition of the same work, edited by another scholar.

There are, however, other authors who assume that a legal duty was undertaken by the signatories of the Convention III. Oppenheim, for instance, states:

> "There is no doubt that, in consequence of the Convention III recourse to hostilities without previous declaration of war, or a qualified ultimatum is prohibited." (Oppenheim, *International Law*, 5th Ed. Vol. II Section 96, p. 249)

And he further intimates that the states which deliberately order the commencement of hostilities without a previous declaration of war or a qualified ultimatum commit an international delinquency. Is Oppenheim's "international delinquency" synonymous with "international crime"? The author himself gives the warning that international delinquencies must not be confused either with so-called Crimes against the Law of Nations or with so-called International Crimes (Oppenheim, *International Law*, Vol. I, 5th Ed., Sec.151, p. 275).

Even assuming, therefore, that the latter view is correct, and that a breach of such a technical rule of international law is an international delinquency, the illegal act would even in Oppenheim's view be in the nature of a breach of contract or possibly a tort but certainly not of an "international crime," as the Chief of Counsel asserts. Indeed no international lawyer ever imagined that the signatories to Hague Convention III thereby agreed that statesmen who participated in a breach of this technical rule should be criminally punishable — not to speak of being executed.

3. The Chief of Counsel proceeds to say, "In 1919 the victorious nations of the last war, including Japan, agreed that the violation of international treaties was a justifiable offence." (Record, p. 416).

Perhaps the Chief of Counsel is referring not to Articles 228-30, but to article 227 of the Treaty of Versailles. For the former deal with the trials which were to be conducted by the military tribunals of the Allied and Associated Powers of persons accused of having committed acts in violation of the laws and customs of war, *i.e.* "conventional" war crimes. Article 227 provides for the public arraignment of William II of Hohenzollern "for a supreme offence against international morality and sanctity of treaties and for his trial before a specially constituted tribunal." It must be noted, however,

Stationery Office, 1883) examining the commencement of various wars that had taken place from 1700 to 1870, wrote in April 1904, in "The Nineteenth Century and After" as follows:

"Numerically, within the time I more particularly examined, Britain struck thirty of these blows, France thirty-six, Russia seven (not reckoning her habitual practice towards Turkey and other bordering Asiatic states, including China), Prussia seven, Austria twelve, the United States five at least."

Would it not be chimerical to assert that the leading powers such as Great Britain, France, Russia, Prussia, Austria and the United States were habitual delinquents in treachery and perfidy in war for the breach of this technical recommendation of international law?

Whether or not Hague Convention III imposed any legal duty on the signatories is a matter of controversy, whatever views various governments, including the Japanese, American and British, may have entertained about the matter. Eminent international jurists in England such as Lawrence, Westlake, and Bellot are of opinion that the wording of the original French text ("Les Puissances contractantes *reconnaissent* que les hostilités entre elles *ne doivent pas* commencer sans un avertissement préalable et non équivoque, qui aura soit la forme d'une déclaration de guerre motivée, soit celle d'un ultimatum avec déclaration de guerre conditionnelle") indicates that this did not impose any legal duty on the signatories. Westlake thinks that the Convention did not seriously affect the previous law on the subject. Pitt-Cobbett's classic *Leading Cases on International Law*, (1924 edition by Hugh H. L. Bellot) says on p. 18 of Vol. II:

"At the same time, the signatories do not pledge themselves absolutely to refrain from hostilities without a prior declaration, but merely *recognized* that as between the belligerents hostilities '*ought* not to commence without previous and unequivocal warning.' The object, no doubt, was to exclude *cases in which it might be necessary to use instant force in order to repel some hostile preparation or movements occurring* either at a place where communication with the war declaring authority would be difficult, or *under circumstances where the other party would obviously have no cause for complaint on the ground of surprise.*"

And Bellot concludes his discussion by saying that despite the limits imposed by custom and convention, the opening of hostilities appears to be

contracting parties of such a duty, as illustrated in the case of The Netherlands, in Appendix A, Section 10 of the present Indictment, where it is said:

"Consequently, the Netherlands Government immediately after the last mentioned attacks, declared war on Japan in self-defence."

2. The next convention he cites is Hague Convention III (Record, p. 416). The Chief of Counsel asserts that by that agreement undeclared wars were branded as *international crimes*, which, it is submitted, is sheer *ipse dixit*.

This convention recognizing that hostilities should not commence without previous and explicit warning is a technical rule which is considered desirable mainly for purposes of clarifying the time at which a state of war comes into being. The fact that even the 24-hour interval proposed by the Netherlands delegation was rejected at the Conference goes to prove that it was not designed to place the stigma of crime, or any ban at all, on a "surprise attack" conducted for strategic purposes. Treachery is largely a matter in the forum of conscience and a war can be treacherous with or without a declaration. In ancient and medieval societies east and west the declaration of war was connected with gallantry. That idea still lingers in the popular imagination which, as is well known, is fully utilized for purposes of war propaganda by denouncing the enemy as "treacherous." Grotius, however, says in his *Jus Belli ac Pacis*:

"The cause for which nations have required a declaration for a lawful war was not, as some allege, that they might do nothing secretly or by a clever trick, for that consideration belongs rather to the perfection of gallantry than to law, as we read some peoples even appointed the day and place of combat, but that it might appear with certainty that the war was not waged by private audacity but by the will of the people on either side, or their heads; for that is the source of its peculiar effect which have no place in a contest with brigands or in one between the king and his subject" (3. 3. 71)

The main purpose in regarding declarations of war as desirable in the modern society of nations is no more gallantry — a matter of subjective conscience — but technical legal expediency in determining the consequence of a state of war. Since the days of Grotius, however, many a Great Power despite Grotius' injunction opened hostilities without any declaration of war. Brevet-Lt.-Col. J. F. Maurice of England, who published in 1883 his laborious work, entitled *Hostilities Without Declarations of War*, (London, His Majesty's

action of many civilized nations on a matter of general welfare *ipso facto* establishes a general principle of international law. The authorities he cites do not propose to lay down that sort of doctrine. Take, for example, the famous Declaration of Paris.

"Privateering is and remains abolished" formed part of the Declaration adopted at the Conference of Paris in 1856 with reference to Maritime Law, and all civilized states have since become signatories of the declaration except the United States, Spain and Mexico. Did this declaration in 1856 by many civilized nations elevate the prohibition of privateering to a principle of international law? Is it not a well known fact that the Declaration was regarded by all international jurists as banding as between the signatories only, and that privateering might be used by and against the three countries mentioned above?

In 1898, the United States Government announced its intention not to resort to privateering, but to adhere to the rules of the Declaration. Does this not show that she was not otherwise bound to refrain from resorting to privateering? Was not Spain regarded as perfectly justified and as not violating any principle of law of nations in having maintained her right to issue letter of marque?

Again, the Geneva Convention of July 27, 1929 Relative to the Treatment of Prisoners of War has been signed by many civilized nations. Does the Soviet Union, for instance, which has not signed it, consider itself bound by the provisions of the Convention, as embodying a general principle of the Law of Nations?

However, the Chief of Counsel seems to assume that the thesis holds not alone as a matter of historical process but as a juridical principle. On that assumption he cites a number of international conventions which, he alleges, prove that aggressive war has long been an international crime. But it is respectfully submitted that the evidence adduced palpably fails to prove the proposition.

1. The first convention he cites is the first Hague Convention (Record, p. 416). The phrases "as far as possible" and "as far as circumstances allow" mentioned in the provisions the Chief of Counsel has in mind prove, on the contrary, that the signatories were not prepared to be legally bound to settle all their difference by pacific means. Apart from "vital interests" and "national honor" self-defence may not indeed have allowed the assumption by the

3. WAR OF AGGRESSION

A. Is Aggressive War an International Crime?

The Chief of Counsel next deals with "War of Aggression." He asks: "Is this a crime under international law and has it been so understood during all the period of this Indictment......?" He claims that it is and proposes to establish two things: "first that there is international law covering the subject, and second that it is a crime under that law." (Record, p. 405).

He first cites some general statements on the growth of international law by custom made by such respectable authorities as Justice Cardozo, Lord Wright, Sir Frederick Pollock, the Judicial Committee of the Privy Council, the Statute of the Permanent Court of International Justice and the decision of the Mixed Claims Commission, United States and Germany. The views there expounded on this head of growth of international custom are, of course, for the most part commonplaces well known to every student of international law.

Then the Chief of Counsel concludes:

"Having...... shown that when many civilized nations have acted on a matter of general welfare it becomes recognized as a principle of international law, we shall now attempt to show that the question of aggressive war has been considered by so many nations and deliberately outlawed by them that their unanimous verdict arises to the dignity of a general principle of international law" (Record, p. 415).

By citing the high authorities mentioned above, the Chief of Counsel may have shown that as a historical process concerted action of many civilized nations tends to the establishment of a principle of international law, and that international tribunals should not exercise their functions relying on the creations of their unrestricted fancy but must strictly abide by certain sources of the law of nations, among which international custom is comprised. But he has *not shown* and *cannot* show any juridical principle that the concerted

The Tribunal at Nuremberg ruled that under its Charter it had no jurisdiction to try persons participating in a common plan to commit War Crimes or Crimes Against Humanity (Trans. p. 16,884). Moreover, it denied that any and every significant participation in the affairs of the Nazi Party or government is evidence of a conspiracy that is in itself criminal. It says that "conspiracy must be clearly outlined in its criminal purpose. It must not be too far removed from the time of decision and of action" (Trans. p. 16,882). This has in a certain measure disarmed the doctrines of conspiracy of those most oppressive features which, convenient as they may be for enmeshing the innocent, shock the juridical conscience. But the judgement did not reject the doctrine itself. It should be remembered, however, that the law of the Charter was regarded, like an English act of parliament, as absolutely binding on the Tribunal in Europe, while here the Charter is like an American act of the legislature, subject to a higher law, viz., the express terms laid down in the Potsdam Declaration and solemnly accepted by the Instrument of Surrender.

And it is our contention that even in the attenuated form of the Nuremberg decision as applied to the alleged "Crimes against Peace," it was not an institute of the law of nations at the time the alleged "crimes" were committed, and no international lawyer ever dreamed of it.

"Under such a principle every one who acts in cooperation with another may some day find his liberty dependent upon the innate prejudices or social bias of an unknown judge. It is the very antithesis of justice according to law" (Sayre, p. 413, *supra*).

"It is a doctrine which has proved itself the evil genius of our law wherever it has touched it. May the time not be long delayed in coming when it will be nothing more than a shadow stalking through past cases" (Sayre, p. 424, *supra*).

What would pre-eminent jurists like the late Lord Russell of Killowen and the late Justice Oliver Wendell Homes, Jr. say to a proposal to import this oppressive doctrine into the international arena, not to mention its induction by *ex post facto* methods? The apt warnings of Judge Hudson may also be cited:

"It would indeed be dangerous practice for judges of an international court to conceive of themselves as permitted to introduce into international law principles of the particular system of national law with which they happen to be familiar......" (Manley O. Hudson, The Law Applicable to the Permanent Court of International Justice, in *Harvard Legal Essays Written in Honor of and Presented to Joseph Henry Beale and Samuel Williston* (1934), p. 133, 137).

Especially strange is the Chief of Counsel's application of the doctrine in the form of what he terms "progressive conspiracy". Unlike in the case of the Third Reich he cannot, of course, prove that the accused were a "united band who were in agreement with one another" and admits that "there appear to have been sharp differences of opinion between them and fierce rivalries" (Record, p. 471). Nevertheless, the Chief of Counsel, like a true prosecutor, endeavors to read, if not sermons in every stone, a conspiracy, a constructive conspiracy, into every progressive turn of events in a nation's international career in a world in which national armaments, use of armed force for safeguarding national interests and the institution of wars are not yet relics of bygone days. If his logic is correct, you could equally read "progressive conspiracies" in the expansion of England, France and Holland, the growth of the Russian Empire, and the gradual expansion of the original thirteen American states into the great American Republic, for which their foremost statesmen and generals must be held criminally responsible, whether they were imperialistic or anti-imperialistic in their personal convictions.

unfair and shocking to the juridical conscience:

> "All of the conspirators need not join in the commission of an overt act, for if one of the conspirators commits an overt act, it becomes the act of all the conspirators". (Record, p. 404)

We must confess this is going back to the collective responsibility which prevailed in the tribal age of mankind. It is all the more reprehensible as it is designed, as the Prosecution contends, to extend to all alleged crimes against peace, war crimes and crimes against humanity. For this means that once a war is somehow declared to be aggressive or in breach of international law or treaties, any person who rendered war service to his own country, whatever his motives, is held responsible for murder and for all shocking crimes committed by others, even if he is totally unaware when, where, and by whom these crimes were committed.

Followers of the civil law are frankly told by their Anglo-Saxon confreres that the doctrine of conspiracy is a convenient legal weapon for prosecutors and judges bent on punishing groups in disfavor with the powers that be. They might also be told that it was used in England with effect in order to punish members of the trade unions — a social group highly obnoxious to the dominant class in the eighteenth century — as we read in Adam Smith (*An Inquiry into the Wealth of Nations*, Bk. l, c. 10, pt. 2, p. 221) and also so employed in the nineteenth century as is pointed out by the late Lord Passfield (Sidney Webb, *History of Trade Unionism*, 2nd edition (1920), p. 73). And they might further be told that enlightened judges and jurists in the English-speaking countries do not look upon this particular doctrine as an ornament calculated to lend luster to the common law.

In a dissenting opinion in *Commonwealth* v. *Donoghue*, (250 Ky. 343, 63 S. W. (2nd-3) it was said:

> "...... its chief danger lies in the fact that for all time to come, it will be the basis for the creation of new crimes never dreamt of by the people."

Did not Professor Sayre after making a careful study of the subject in his article in the Harvard Law Review mentioned heretofore say:

> "A doctrine so vague in its outlines and uncertain in its fundamental nature as conspiracy lends no strength or glory to law, it is a veritable quicksand of shifting opinion and ill-considered thought" (Sayre, p. 395, *supra*).

2. CONSPIRACY

The Chief of Counsel does not state in so many words that the doctrine of conspiracy as a crime is an institute of the law of nations. But he assumes it, for he states, "this section of the Charter creates no new law" (Record, p. 396). And by "law" the Chief of Counsel must mean the law of nations. In this particular case, however, the Chief of Counsel does not as he did in the case of aggressive war cite any assembly participated in by large groups of nations which recognized conspiracy as an international crime. He does not cite any treaty, declaration, or resolution by which it was designated as an international crime. Instead he merely cites the opinion of the United States Circuit Court of Appeals in *Marino v. United States* and says:

> "This offence is known to and well recognized by most civilized nations, and the gist of it is so similar in all countries that the definition of it by a high Federal Court of the United States may well be accepted as an adequate expression of the common conception of this offence".
> (Record p. 402)

This is certainly astonishing! Are not all comparative jurists aware that the doctrine of criminal conspiracy is a peculiar product of English legal history? (Stephen, *History of Criminal Law of England,* Vol. 3 pp. 202-227; Winfield, *The History of Conspiracy and Abuse of Legal Procedure*, 1921.; R. S. Wright, *The Law of Criminal Conspiracies* (1873); Francis B. Sayre, *Criminal Conspiracy,* 35 *Harvard Law Review* 393-424). It is a theory of criminal jurisprudence unknown, we believe, in other legal systems and certainly not known to all — as it must be in order to possess international validity. Says Professor Sayre of the Harvard Law School: "It is a doctrine as anomalous and provincial as it is unhappy in its results. It is unknown to the Roman law; it is not found in modern continental codes; few continental lawyers ever heard of it" (Sayre, p. 427, supra). Unlike what is observed in the instances of parliamentary government, the rule of law, the criminal jury, *habeas corpus* or the trust, civilians do not entertain any high regard for this particular Anglo-Saxon institute. Especially that part of the doctrine which is stated below is palpably

time of the commission of the alleged acts, and it is clearly *ex post facto* law— regarded as unjust, whenever and wherever the question of Justice has been reflected upon. To apply such law to the accused at the bar is not civilized justice, not "justice" as envisaged in the Potsdam Declaration.

In view of the natural interpretation of the term "war criminals" in the Potsdam Declaration on the one hand, and of the universal concepts of civilized justice, on the other, it is our submission that that part of the Charter providing punishment for "Conspiracy," "Crimes against Peace," and "Crimes against Humanity," insofar as they are not comprised in the category of "war crimes," is not the law for this Tribunal. Just as that part of an act of the American Congress which is in contravention of the Constitution of the United States, and that portion of a statutory order-in-Council which goes beyond the authority delegated by a British Act of Parliament is null and void, so that part of the Charter which is contrary to the fundamental document — the Instrument of Surrender, in which the terms of the Potsdam Declaration have formally and expressly been incorporated — must be declared void. It is a universally-recognized general principle of law that the obligations undertaken by one party can not arbitrarily be increased by the other party or parties.

"Any person who commits an act which the law declares to be punishable or which is deserving of penalty according to the fundamental conceptions of a penal law and sound popular feeling, shall be punished. If there is no penal law directly covering an act it shall be punished under the law of which the fundamental conception applies most nearly to the said act."

The Permanent Court of International Justice declared in an advisory opinion on December 4, 1935 that the application of this Hitlerite legislation to Danzig was in violation of the requirement that the government of the city be by rule of law(Rechtsstaat). The Germans, as is well known, authorized the beheading of Van der Lubbe for burning the Reichstag, when the penalty for arson at the time of the fire was a term of imprisonment only. And this shocked the juridical conscience of the whole world, including that of the Far Eastern islanders. The principle which the Chief of Counsel invokes, viz: "a principle that follows the needs of civilization and is a clear expression of the public conscience" (Record, p. 435) may appear to untutored minds as sound as "deserving of penalty according to the fundamental conceptions of a penal law and sound popular feeling." As a matter of fact, such a vague principle when it actually operates in the administration of criminal justice is just as cruel and as oppressive as the penal doctrine which characterized the Third Reich. It is to the honor and credit of the Siamese judiciary that, if the report be true, on March 24, 1946, it released Marshal Pibul and eleven major "war-criminals" who had collaborated with Japan during this war, on the grounds that a new law punishing war criminals is *ex post facto* and cannot he applied retroactively. The sentiment that punishment by *ex post facto* legislation is sheer lynch law in the guise of justice is not a product of the so-called Era of Enlightenment in Europe, but represents the universal conception of justice, ancient and modern, East and West, though the principle was frequently violated by despots down through the ages. If a code of international criminal law is to be made by civilized nations providing for the punishment of individuals for a breach of international duties, the *nulla poena* principle will and must certainly constitute one of its basic principles.

It is our submission that criminal conspiracy, the so-called crimes against peace and crimes against humanity (apart from cases which form part of the "war crimes") were crimes unknown to the law of nations. And if that has ever become law binding on nations during the war, it was not law at the

attests to the fact that the Allied nations themselves intend to administer this "justice" according to law.

In the administration of criminal justice especially, the wisdom of the canon that justice ought to be administered in conformity with established rules has long been tested by past experience, political and otherwise. The history of the Star Chamber in England amply shows that the machinery of criminal law can easily be utilized by the powers that be for suppressing, eliminating or "liquidating," through the most nauseating travesty of trial, political groups or persons of whom they disapprove. The rule against *ex post facto* law has been accepted by all civilized nations as a canon of criminal justice. And this canon should assuredly be respected in a case involving political offences, national or international.

The omnipotent English Parliament has since 1688 never resorted to *ex post facto* legislation to punish political offenders. *Ex post facto* laws, state or federal, are banned by the Constitution of the United States. And it seems that retroactive laws relative to political offenses have been extremely rare in the whale history of American legislation. It is true that there were such attempts after the Civil War, and two cases were brought to the Supreme Court of the United States involving laws, state and federal, penalizing those persons who had rendered assistance to the Confederacy. It is, however, the permanent glory of that Tribunal, that in the midst of intense popular passions it declared, through Justice Field, that both laws were unconstitutional and void. (Cummings v. Missouri, 4 Wallace 277 (1866); *Ex parte* Garland, 4 Wallace 333 (1860)). A "Report on Essential Human Rights," received by the American Law Institute, February 24, 1944, says in Article 9:

> "No one shall be convicted of crime except for violation of law in effect at the time of the commission of the act charged as an offence nor be subjected to a penalty greater than that applicable at the time of the commission of the offence" (cited in Quincy Wright, War Criminals, 38 *American Journal of International Law* 257, N. 3)

And it is said that this principle is in substance comprised in the constitutions of thirty countries. Indeed, whether constitutionally guaranteed or not, *nulla poena sine lege* constitutes one of the basic principles of criminal justice in civil law countries. It is true that in Nazi Germany the principle was mercilessly destroyed by an act of June 28, 1935 authorizing judges to decide cases according to the "sound popular feeling." It reads:

sense — that it was not their intention at all to have the phrase understood by the political and military leaders of Japan as comprising so-called "crimes against peace."

5. If, notwithstanding all this, any shade of doubt still remains and the Tribunal deems the term ambiguous and susceptible of two meanings, we beg to draw the attention of the Tribunal to that well-known rule of interpretation that a document which is ambiguous must be construed against the party who made it. *Verba fortius accipiuntur contra proferentem.* That this maxim is a general principle of law applicable in the interpretation of an agreement of an international character is shown by a decision of the Permanent Court of International Justice. In the *Brazilian Loans Case,* it was said to be a familiar principle for the construction of instruments that where they are ambiguous, they should be taken *contra proferentem* (Publications of the Court, Series A, No. 20/21, p. 214).

We also beg leave to draw the attention of the Tribunal to the advisory opinion concerning the interpretation of the treaty of Lausanne where it was said to be a sound principle that if the wording of a treaty provision is not clear, in choosing between several admissible interpretations, the one which involves the minimum of obligations for the parties should be adopted. (Series B, No. 12, p. 25). We also call the attention of the Tribunal to another equally well-known canon of legal interpretation. The expression of one thing is the exclusion of another. *Expressio unius est exclusio alterius,* This maxim has also been applied in the Permanent Court of International Justice (Series A/B, No. 42, p. 121).

EX-POST FACTO LAWS — "JUSTICE"?

The Potsdam Declaration says, "stern justice shall be meted out." It is "justice," however stern and unmitigated by mercy, that is to be meted out.

Justice means in civilized communities justice according to law. It means that justice is to be administered by established legal rules and principles, not according to the sense of right and justice of the judge, however good or wise he may be.

The fact that the present Tribunal is composed not of professional military men but includes eminent lawyers and jurists from among the Allied nations

an unnecessary and dangerous complication to resort to prosecution for the "crime" of aggressive war, involving a doctrine open to debate and one which might require long and historical inquiries not suited to judicial proceedings. Further reflection upon the problem has led the writer to the conclusion that for the purpose of conceiving aggressive war to be an international crime, the Pact of Paris may, together with other treaties and resolutions, be regarded as evidence of a sufficiently developed *custom* to be acceptable as international law.

In "The Backstage at Nuremberg" by Ernest D. Hauser (*Saturday Evening Post, Overseas Edition* for February, 1946) we are told that Jackson's novel idea met with opposition on the part of Allied representatives in the six weeks' London negotiations, and that it was not until August 8 that they finally agreed upon the policy embodied in the London Agreement. That decision was made with reference to the trial at Nuremberg and it may be presumed that it was at a later date that the Allied governments agreed to adopt the same policy at the trial in Tokyo.

The Potsdam Declaration was issued on July 26, 1945. In 1944 Professor Glueck in America was deeply concerned whether his anxiety to punish the makers of an aggressive war could legitimately be satisfied by such an extension of the well-known words "war crimes," and Justice Jackson was representing that extension as a novelty in 1945. The allied policy for the extension of the term was, after prolonged negotiations, decided upon as late as August 8, 1945, in London. How can such an extension be read into the Potsdam Declaration of July 26, 1945?

4. Moreover, it would be a gross insult to the political intelligence of the Allied statesmen assembled at Potsdam to contend that in their laudable endeavor to make the Japanese statesmen and military men lay down their arms they imposed as one of the conditions that there should be severe punishment meted out to those Japanese leaders as "war criminals," apart from the recognized crimes of belligerent barbarity. In view of the war situation then prevailing, it must have been amply clear to the allied leaders that such a condition would naturally involve the danger of forcing the Japanese leaders to carry on the war to the very last extremity. Moreover, if the Allied statesmen had desired to insert that term in the Potsdam Declaration, prudence would certainly have made them refrain from doing so. It must, therefore, be concluded — and such conclusion is only a matter of horse

of them, so far as we are aware, refers to the so-called crimes against peace. Even the reference in the Moscow Declaration of November 1, 1943, to "major criminals whose crimes have no geographic location" is shown by its context simply to mean persons in authority whose orders were executed "not only in one area or one battlefield but affected the conduct of operations against several of the Allied armies," clearly referring to the violations of the law of war, not to the so-called "crimes against peace." It seems that the said Declaration was taken as the basis of the London Agreement of August 8, 1945, by an extensive construction which, it is submitted, deviated from the natural interpretation of the Declaration in view of its historic context. At any rate it was a declaration addressed solely to Germany and not to Japan, and the express term of the Potsdam Declaration of a later date makes it clear that the Moscow Declaration cannot justify an interpretation unilaterally modifying the natural meaning of the phrase "war crimes."

This is corroborated by a statement made by Professor Sheldon Glueck in his article on "The Nuremberg Trial and Aggressive War." (Glueck, 59 *Harvard Law Review* 397) He says:

"Judging from available published data, this idea of including the launching of an aggressive war — a 'crime against peace' — among the offences for which the Axis Powers were to be held liable had its origin, so far as American policy is concerned, in a report to the President made on June 7, 1945, by the American Chief of Counsel for the prosecution of major war criminals."

"Justice Robert Jackson there said:

'It is high time that we act on the judicial principle that aggressive war-making is illegal and criminal.'"

In a note on the same page Professor Glueck confesses:

"During the preparation of the author's book, *War Criminals: Their Prosecution and Punishment* (1944) he was not at all certain that the acts of launching and conducting an aggressive war could be regarded as international crimes. He finally decided against such a view, largely on the basis of a strict interpretation of the Treaty for the Renunciation of War (Briand-Kellogg Pact) signed in Paris in 1928. He was influenced, also by the practical question of policy. Since, liability of the leading Nazi malefactors under familiar principles of the laws and customs of war and the Hague and Geneva Conventions was clear, it seemed to be

by Lauterpacht, pp. 452-3). Here "war crime" is not used in the moral sense of the term but only in a technical legal sense. It comprises violations of certain recognized rules regarding warfare committed by members of the armed forces and other persons, including the ill-treatment of prisoners of war, all hostilities in arms committed by individuals who are not members of the armed forces, espionage and war treason, and marauding acts. War crimes are acts committed during the war, especially in the field of operations, and usually dealt with summarily by military courts. Minor divergence of juristic opinion may exist regarding categories to be comprised in the term "war crimes." They certainly do not comprise any act committed prior to the outbreak of a war, though they may be connected historically with a war. When this technical term appears in diplomatic correspondence, it must, unless the contrary be shown, be construed in the technical sense, according to the well-known canon of legal interpretation.

2. This construction is further justified by the ensuing phrase, "including those who have visited cruelties upon our prisoners of war." The maltreatment of prisoners of war is but a type of the "war crimes" in the technical sense of the term.

That this, the ordinary and accepted meaning of "war crimes", is the meaning intended by the Potsdam Declaration, is supported by the fact that when that instrument means to include such a special category of those crimes as the treatment (possibly also by civilians) of prisoners of war, it carefully says so, and specifies them as within its scope. If it was really intended that the terms be used as comprising the so-called "crimes against peace" and "crimes against humanity," that fact, not merely the maltreatment of prisoners of war, would have been particularized in the qualifying phrase.

3. This construction is further justified in the light of the so-called "warnings" addressed to each of the Axis nations by Allied governments and their leading statesmen. (Cf. Glueck, the Nuremberg Trial and Aggressive War, 59 *Harvard Law Review* 392, 418, 419, note 75).

A careful study of the declarations and statements made by various governments and their leaders, keeping in mind the background of the occasions on which they were made, would reveal that when they speak of crimes alleged to have been committed by the Axis nations they are speaking of acts committed during the progress of war, such as atrocities to the civilian population in occupied areas and the maltreatment of prisoners of war. None

Instrument of Surrender, it naturally follows that, unlike the situation in Germany, there are certain limits to the demands which the Allied Governments can make of her. Japan is in duty bound to perform all the demands made by the Allies within those limits but, at the same time, it has a right to insist that those limits shall not be overridden. If so, there are corresponding duties involved which the Allied Powers too must observe. For no legal relation can be unilateral. And the criteria for those reciprocal rights and obligations are set forth in the terms of Potsdam Declaration constituting part and parcel of the Instrument of Surrender.

Do not the noble words of the Supreme Commander for the Allied Powers at the time of the surrender proceedings in Tokyo Bay stress the high importance of the strict observance by the victor and the vanquished alike of the understanding embodied in the Instrument of Surrender:

> "It is not for us here to meet, representing as we do a majority of the people of the earth, in a spirit of distrust, malice or hatred. But rather it is for us, both victor and vanquished, to rise to that higher integrity which alone benefits the sacred purpose we are about to serve, *committing all our people unreservedly to the faithful compliance with the understanding they are here to assume.*"

The juridical basis on which this trial in the International Military Tribunal for the Far East is conducted lies in that term of the Potsdam Declaration, embodied by reference in the Instrument of Surrender, which says: "...... stern justice shall be meted out to all war criminals, including those who have visited cruelties upon our prisoners of war."

"WAR CRIMES"

Now, we respectfully request the Tribunal to consider the interpretation of the term, "war criminals" in above passage — not at this stage of the proceedings from the point of view of Jurisdiction, but from the entirely different one presented by the interpretation of the law of the Charter.

1. "War Crimes" and "war criminals" are well-established terms in the law of nations. War crimes, according to Oppenheim, are such hostile or other acts of soldiers or other individuals as may be punishable by the enemy on capture of the offenders (Oppenheim, *International Law*, Vol. II, 5th Ed. (1935) edited

for the judgment itself. That, at least, is the doctrine on which the Nuremberg decision is based. We respectfully direct the attention of this Honorable Tribunal to the undoubted fact that the legal relation between the Government of Japan and the Allied Governments is altogether on a different footing from that subsisting between Germany and the Allies.

The powers of the Allied Governments are indeed comprehensive, yet those powers are not unlimited. General MacArthur is invested with the supreme power only in so far as its exercise is deemed proper and necessary for the effectuation of the terms of the Instrument of Surrender. The Allies as represented by him are not, therefore, in a position similar to that of Louis XIV, but one resembling that of modern constitutional monarchs like William and Mary.

This basic legal distinction between the position of Germany and that of Japan is, of course, owing to the circumstances upon which the armistice was predicated. Unlike Germany, Japan was not at the time of its surrender overrun by the Allied forces. The Japanese mainland was still unoccupied and Japan was then in a position to offer strenuous armed resistance for some time to come, necessarily involving losses to the Allied forces. The Japanese Government consented in such circumstances to accept the peace offer of the Allies, the "terms" of which are laid down in the Potsdam Declaration. The Instrument of Surrender formally and expressly referred to the terms of that Declaration. That document states:

> "We hereby undertake for the Emperor, the Japanese Government and their successors to carry out the provisions of the Potsdam Declaration in good faith, and to issue whatever orders and take whatever action as may be required by the Supreme Commander *for the purpose of giving effect to that Declaration.*"
>
> "The authority of the Emperor and the Japanese Government to rule the State shall be subject to the Supreme Commander for the Allied Powers *who will take such steps as he deems proper to effectuate these terms of surrender.*"

The document styled the Instrument of Surrender is in the nature of an international agreement by which not alone the unconditional surrender of the Japanese Armed forces but several other terms are provided which are binding on the contracting parties. If Japan's obligations to the Allied Powers under that Instrument are not unlimited, but confined to the terms of the

PART I

1. THE INSTRUMENT OF SURRENDER AND THE CHARTER

The judgment in the Nuremberg Trial concerning the law of its Charter states as follows:

"The making of the Charter was the exercise of the sovereign legislative power by the countries to which the German Reich unconditionally surrendered: and the undoubted right of these countries to legislate for the occupied territories has been recognized by the civilized world."
(Trans. p. 16,871)

The German Government ceased to exist in May 1945 through conquest by the Allies, or by what is commonly known as *debellatio* in the language of the law of nations. The Allied Powers could, therefore, exercise rights of sovereignty in the territories over which they had complete control. They could govern the country in whatever way they pleased. They could, if they liked, behave as an absolute monarch like Louis XIV. They could, if they were so minded, set up a Tribunal to punish those persons they disfavored by laying down an *ex-post-facto* law, the rule of abstention from such legislation being a principle of justice not absolutely binding on their sovereign authority. (Trans. p. 16,871). Or perhaps they might have gone further and disposed of them by executive action without any trial at all. At least such an exercise wound not contravene the tenets of the law of nations. It was therefore:

"not strictly necessary for the Tribunal to consider whether or not the planning, preparation or initiation of an aggressive war was an international crime involving personal responsibility before the conclusion of the London Agreement" (Trans. p. 16,871).

The discussion of international law in the Nuremberg decision is, therefore, a Sort of *obiter dictum*, a display of learning which was not strictly necessary

mainly in their relation to international law, with a view to refuting *seriatim* and as a whole the interpretations placed upon them by the Chief of Counsel in his Opening Statement made on June 4, 1946 (Record, pp. 383-475, esp. pp. 394-435). As far as possible we shall here follow the order in which the Chief of Counsel developed the thesis of the Prosecution, and divide our discussion into the following eight sections:

1. The Instrument of Surrender and the Charter.
2. Conspiracy.
3. War of Aggression.
4. War in violation of International Law, Treaties, etc.
5. Murder.
6. "Conventional" War Crimes.
7. Personal Responsibility.
8. The new doctrine of international law proposed by the Prosecution.

prived of territory as the case may be. In such cases the political responsibility of her leaders to the nation for their mistakes in policy would indeed be serious. However, whether their acts constitute criminal offences on the part of such leaders by the canons of international law is entirely a separate and distinct question. If they do constitute such offenses, American, British and Soviet leaders in similar situations should also be subjected to penalties provided by international law. If they do not constitute such offences by that law these accused should be pronounced "not guilty." The accused must, in our submission, be declared innocent, unless it is proved beyond a reasonable doubt that they committed some criminal offense known to the established law of nations.

If the law of crimes provided in the Charter had been designed as an act of force, a fiat issued irrespective of the terms of the Instrument of Surrender and of the well-recognized rules of international law, it would be futile for the Defense to discuss the law of the Charter in the light of that law. Judging from the Opening Statement of the Chief of Counsel, however, that is not the position taken by the Prosecution. Its contention is that the accused should be declared "criminals" not because their acts fall under the formula of crimes unilaterally decided upon by the policy of the Allied Governments, but because they constitute criminal offenses under the law of nations. The Prosecution, therefore, endeavors with an ingenious display of learning and much logical acumen to prove that the law of crimes laid down in the Charter is declaratory of the current rules of international law. The Defense readily agrees with the Prosecution that the law of the Charter ought to be interpreted in the light of international law. They flatly deny, however, that the said law of crimes is declaratory of the law of nations.

It is a source of encouragement to the Defense that the Nuremberg Tribunal rejected some of the interpretations placed thereon by the Prosecution. It is respectfully submitted that inasmuch as the factual and the consequent legal situations in Germany and Japan are entirely different, the Tribunal here has the broader task of deciding on the relations between the Instrument of Surrender and the law of the Charter, and that the Charter, contrary to what was the case at Nuremberg, should serve only as a convenient guide for ascertaining the real rules and principles of international law, under which latter alone the guilt or innocence of the accused should be decided.

We propose, therefore, to discuss the criminal provisions of the Charter

FORWORD

Law is a common consciousness of obligation.

Criminal Law is a common consciousness of obligation coupled with an obligation to suffer penalties if it is disregarded.

Statesmen perform their transcendently important functions under a common consciousness of obligation under International Law.

But statesmen have not hitherto performed their functions under any common consciousness of obligation to suffer the arbitrary penalties of military law in case the obligations of International Law are broken.

The absence, *as a patent fact*, of any such common penal consciousness, prevents the existence of such a penal law. Whether there ought or ought not to be such a consciousness of penal liability is irrelevant. In the absence of such a Law, the imposition of such penalties would be nothing but lawless violence.

If any of the accused conceived, like Professor Spykman and Mr. Walter Lippmann, world politics and diplomacy in terms of military strategy, and ever conspired with others to promote the Triple Military Alliance (which to Spykman lay in the logical sequence of world events), or to establish a Greater East Asian Sphere of Common Prosperity in those terms of military strategy alone, such behavior might most certainly be offensive to the Soviet Union or the United States or Great Britain. Such an attitude towards world politics is indeed incompatible with the tenor and spirit of the New Constitution of Japan which provides for her total disarmament and is inspired by the ideal of abolition of the institution of war itself. But such political behavior, however unpalatable to enlightened minds, falls, in our submission, within the sphere of freedom of opinion and of combination which has not been banned nor declared a criminal offence by the law of nations. If any act done by the Government of Japan was illegal under international law or was declared so by an international body to whose determination she had agreed to submit, or, if Japan was defeated in her war, the entire nation would have to bear the consequences. She must pay reparations or indemnities or be de-

FORWORD 3

PART I
1. THE INSTRUMENT OF SURRENDER AND THE CHARTER 6
    "WAR CRIMES"   8
    EX-POST FACTO LAWS — "JUSTICE"?   12
2. CONSPIRACY 16
3. WAR OF AGGRESSION 20
    A. Is Aggressive War an International Crime?   20
        (a) The United States   28
        (b) Great Britain   31
        (c) France   31
        (d) Japan   32
    B. AGGRESSIVE WAR AS A JURIDICAL CONCEPT   38
4. WAR IN VIOLATION OF INTERNATIONAL IAW,
    TREATIES, ETC. 43
5. MURDER 46
6. "CONVENTIONAL" WAR CRIMES 49
7. PERSONAL RESPONSIBILITY 51
8. THE NEW DOCTRINE OF INTERNATIONAL LAW PROPOSED BY
    THE PROSECUTION 62

PART II
1. "WAR CRIMINALS" 66
2. THE PACT OF PARIS AND SELF-DEFENSE 69
3. CONSPIRACY 71
4. MURDER 75
5. "CONVENTIONAL" WAR CRIMES 77
6. LIABILITY OF THE DEFENDANTS 83

CONCLUSION 88

THE TOKIO TRIALS
AND
INTERNATIONAL LAW

Answer to the Prosecution's Arguments on International Law
Delivered at the International Military Tribunal for the Far East
on 3 & 4 March 1948.

BY
KENZO TAKAYANAGI

高柳賢三（たかやなぎ・けんぞう）

英米法学者、法学博士。1887年生、1967歿。東京帝国大学法科大学卒業。同大学助教授を経て、1921年東京帝国大学法学部教授、1948年退官（名誉教授）。のち成蹊大学学長（名誉教授）。東京裁判で弁護人を務め、貴族院議員として新憲法案の審議に参加。憲法調査会会長、学士院会員、米国学士院会員、国際比較法学会正会員、国際仲裁裁判所裁判官。主要著訳書『英米法講義』（第1巻『英米法源理論』第2巻『英国公法の理論』第3巻『司法権の優位』第4巻『英米法の基礎』）、『天皇・憲法第九条』、ロスコー・パウンド『法と道徳』（共訳）、ロスコー・パウンド『法律史観』ほか。

極東裁判と国際法　極東国際軍事裁判所における弁論

刊　行　2019年10月
著　者　髙柳　賢三
刊行者　清藤　洋
刊行所　書肆心水

135-0016 東京都江東区東陽 6-2-27-1308
www.shoshi-shinsui.com
電話 03-6677-0101
ISBN978-4-906917-96-9 C0032

乱丁落丁本は恐縮ですが刊行所宛ご送付下さい
送料刊行所負担にて早急にお取り替え致します

―既刊書―

自由・相対主義・自然法
現代法哲学における人権思想と国際民主主義

尾高朝雄著

**民主主義に対する倦怠感が兆し、
リベラリズムが空洞化する時代への警鐘と指針**

戦後の国際秩序を支えてきた理念を無視する力による世界の再編が進行し、リベラルな国際秩序がグローバルな特権層の活動の場とみなされ、格差が再び拡大する現在、共産主義理念が国政の現実的選択肢としてはもはや存在せず、リベラルの空洞化が有害なレベルにまで達した社会にいかなる道がありうるか。近代から現代への思想史的理路を法哲学の立場から確認し「現代」の基盤を示す、ノモス主権論の構築と並行して練り上げられた自由論を集成。

6900円+税

不戦条約論

信夫淳平著

**国際関係が不安定期に移行する現在、
不戦の国際合意が実現した経緯を振り返る**

国家間の不戦の約束は、いかなる事情で構想され、いかにして現実のものとなってきたのか。不戦の約束に伴って必要となる制度と解決すべき問題を、具体的な経緯と政治的技術に即して詳説する、パリ不戦条約前夜に著作された歴史的基本文献。

6300円+税

―既刊書―

ノモス主権への法哲学

法の窮極に在るもの
法の窮極にあるものについての再論
数の政治と理の政治

尾高朝雄著

民主主義はなぜ選挙が終点であってはならないのか――
ポピュリズム時代の法哲学の核心、ノモス主権論

ポピュリズムが広まり、行政国家化が深まり、象徴天皇制が再定義されつつある今、ノモス主権論があるべき道を指し示す。ノモス主権論へと至る尾高法哲学理解のための主著三冊を合冊集成。安倍政権時代におけるノモス主権論のアクチュアリティを示し、ハンス・ケルゼン、カール・シュミットとノモス主権論の関係を論じる寄稿論文「ノモスとアジール」（藤崎剛人著）を附録。　　　　7200円＋税

軍隊と自由

シビリアン・コントロールへの法制史

藤田嗣雄著

軍事に詳しい法制史学者のユニークな業績

具体的な法制化の歴史をたどり、文民統制の歴史的厚みを示す。近世・近代・現代において、軍隊の制御はいかに進展してきたのか。主要各国（英米仏独日）ごとに歴史をたどり、その違いの意味を説く。「政治憲法と軍事憲法が対立する明治憲法の本質が、今次の敗戦を決定したところの、唯一の原因では、もちろんなかったとしても、憲法的見地からは、最も重要視されなければならない。」　6900円＋税

―既刊書―

天皇・憲法第九条

高柳賢三著

九条の異常性を直視する第三の道

日本国憲法に対してなされるべきは、大陸法的解釈か、英米法的解釈か。改憲論議における不可欠かつ第一級の知見でありながら、長くかえりみられてこなかった「日本国憲法と大陸法／英米法問題」の原点の書。九条幣原首相発案説の論拠として広く知られる本書の議論は、近代日本法学の主流である大陸法型の解釈と英米法型の解釈の対立の問題を経て、そもそも憲法という法文はいかに解釈されるべきものかという問いに及ぶ。　　　　　　6300円＋税

制定の立場で省みる日本国憲法入門

（第一集）芦田均著
（第二集）金森徳次郎著

制定現場の空気と論理と駆け引きと

当事者の生の声により日本国憲法をリアルに歴史の問題として捉え直す。制定過程の経験談と、制定者としての立場による逐条的解説の二部構成。なぜそう変わったのか、変わらなかったことは何か、議論が紛糾したことは何か。制定の事情と機微を理解することによって、今なら変えてもよいところ、今でも変えてはいけないところを見定める。

各3800円＋税